The Jewish Family
in Antiquity

Program in Judaic Studies
Brown University
BROWN JUDAIC STUDIES

Edited by
Ernest S. Frerichs
Shaye J. D. Cohen, Calvin Goldscheider

Number 289
The Jewish Family in Antiquity

edited by
Shaye J.D. Cohen

The Jewish Family
in Antiquity

edited by
Shaye J.D. Cohen

Scholars Press
Atlanta, Georgia

The Jewish Family
in Antiquity

edited by
Shaye J.D. Cohen

© 1993
Brown University

Library of Congress Cataloging-in-Publication Data

The Jewish family in antiquity / edited by Shaye J.D. Cohen.
    p. cm. — (Brown Judaic studies ; no. 289)
    Includes bibliographical references and index.
    ISBN 1-55540-919-9
    1. Jewish families—History. 2. Parent and child (Jewish law)
    3. Jews—Social life and customs—To 70 A.D. I. Cohen, Shaye J. D.
    II. Series.
    HQ507.J49 1993
    306.85'089924—dc20   93-36509
                                       CIP

Printed in the United States of America
on acid-free paper

Table of Contents

Introduction

The family in classical antiquity has been the subject of intense study in recent years. Several dozen books and dozens of articles (many of them cited in the essays below) have appeared on fathers, mothers, sons, daughters, women, marriage, slaves, private life, demography, the household, the domestic economy, etc. etc. in classical antiquity. But this scholarship has not yet had an impact on the study of Jewish antiquity.[1] I know of no monograph-length study of the subject. Even the number of relevant articles is small.[2] The explanation for this scholarly reticence is not lack of evidence, because the evidence is relatively abundant. There is literary evidence (most obviously the rabbinic corpora, which frequently treat family matters and family law), papyrological evidence, epigraphical evidence (hundreds of epitaphs from Israel, notably Beth Shearim, and the diaspora, notably Rome), and archaeological evidence (the excavated remains of numerous ancient Jewish towns and houses). Of these bodies of evidence, perhaps the epigraphic has been studied the most frequently for information about Jewish demography and family life, but even here the evidence has not yet been exhausted; when confronted by new questions it will yield new data.[3] The most important body of evidence concerning the ancient Jewish family, the Babata archive, has recently been published (in part); the publication of the remainder of the archive is promised for the near future (see Kraemer's essay for a brief discussion). I repeat: the explanation for the scholarly

---

[1]Modern Jewish historians have realized the importance of the history of the Jewish family (witness the recent works of Paula Hyman, Marion Kaplan, and others), as have medieval Jewish historians (see especially S.D. Goitein, *A Mediterranean Society III: The Family*), but ancient Jewish historians have not.

[2]Only two of the twelve essays in *The Jewish Family: Metaphor and Memory*, ed. David Kraemer (New York: Oxford University Press, 1989) are devoted to Jewish antiquity. Some additional articles and essays are cited below by Yarbrough.

[3]See for example Pieter van der Horst, *Ancient Jewish Epitaphs* (Kampen: Kok Pharos, 1991), and the forthcoming work of Leonard Rutgers, cited below by Martin.

reticence about the Jewish family in antiquity is not the lack of evidence. The explanation, rather, is the lack of interest, and the purpose of this volume is to stimulate interest in this underexplored field.

This volume consists of papers (or the offspring of the papers) that were delivered at the Hellenistic Judaism section of the 1990 and 1991 annual meetings of the Society of Biblical Literature. I and my co-chairs of the section, William Adler of North Carolina State University in 1990 and Benjamin Wright of Lehigh University in 1991, solicited papers on the general topic "The Ancient Jewish Family." In recognition of the fact that so little work had been done on the subject, we did not ask the presenters to answer a single set of questions, focus on a single body of evidence, or utilize a single methodology. Rather we wanted to get some sense of the range of possibilities suggested by the topic. The variety in this collection mirrors the variety of our evidence and the variety of questions that can be asked of it. The singular noun and the definite article in the title of the volume *The Jewish Family* should not be taken to imply that any of the contributors believes that there was a single model of what *the* (Jewish) family was or should have been in antiquity (see the opening remarks of Pomeroy, and the discussion of this point by Peskowitz). We are all aware of the elusiveness and variety of the subject; "The Jewish Family" is a convenient way of referring to "Varieties of Jewish Families" (just as the singular noun "Judaism" does not necessarily imply a the existence of a single undifferentiated system).

Our anthology opens with the wide-ranging paper of Miriam Peskowitz (Duke University), "'Family/ies' in Antiquity: Evidence from Tannaitic Literature and Roman Galilean Architecture." Peskowitz argues that "family" is a plural (that is, varied, multiple) concept; that the construction of, and the meanings imputed to, "the family" were varied as well, because they were (and are!) determined by the perspective of the observer and interpreter; that the distinction between "private" and "public" space is often misleading in the context of discussions of the family in antiquity; and that the family was in large degree an economic unit, a locus of production (on this point see Pomeroy's essay). These conclusions are supported not only by contemporary theoretical literature but also by the evidence of rabbinic literature and Galilean archaeology.

The central portion of our anthology concerns "Parents, Children, and Slaves." The striking conclusion that emerges from all four papers in this section is that the Jewish family in antiquity seems not to have been distinctive by the power of its Jewishness; rather, its structure, ideals, and dynamics seem to have been virtually identical with those of its ambient culture(s). Each paper in its own way confirms this point. In his essay "Parents and Children in the Jewish Family of Antiquity," O. Larry

Yarbrough (Middlebury College) discusses the theoretical framework of the relationships between parents and children. Jewish moralists and jurists spelled out the obligations of parents to their children, and of children to their parents. Much of the evidence derives from Wisdom literature (Proverbs, Ben Sira), Philo, and rabbinic literature; all of the evidence is prescriptive. How Jewish parents and their children related to each other in reality, is another question entirely. The Jewish values and expectations governing parent-child relationships were entirely consonant with, and almost indistinguishable from, those of Greco-Roman society.

The Philonic perspective on the relations of parents and children, discussed in passing by Yarbrough, is the subject of sustained analysis by Adele Reinhartz (McMaster University) in her "Parents and Children: A Philonic Perspective." Philo conceived of the relationship between parents and children in hierarchical terms: parents create, hence are superior to, their children. But parents also have a string of obligations towards their children, just as children have a string of obligations towards their parents. Like Yarbrough, Reinhartz, too, concludes that Philo's fundamental conception of the parent-child relationship is consonant with, and almost indistinguishable from, that of Greco-Roman society. It is precisely this pedestrian and unexceptional nature of Philo's conception that leads Reinhartz to suggest that perhaps Jewish families in Alexandria actually lived, or were expected to live, in accordance with the ideals delineated by Philo, and that the various threats or challenges to family life excoriated by Philo were social ills that were real and present dangers (dangers from Philo's perspective) to Alexandrian Jews.

Like most writers of paraenetic literature in antiquity, Philo is more interested in fathers and sons than in mothers and daughters. Ross S. Kraemer (University of Pennsylvania) in her essay "Jewish Mothers and Daughters in the Greco-Roman World" attempts to redress this imbalance. The proverb "Like mother, like daughter" is at least as old as the prophet Ezekiel (Ezekiel 16:44), and was still current in rabbinic times (Y. Sanhedrin 9 end (20d)). The Babylonian Talmud assumes that a daughter would learn from her mother how to observe the rituals of purification after menstruation (*serekh bitah*, Niddah 67b). In contrast, however, Kraemer argues that the bonds between Jewish mothers and their daughters could not have been strong in antiquity, since family structure, marriage law, and the high mortality of both parturients and infants, militated against intimate bonding. In this respect, too, Jewish families will have been virtually indistinguishable from those of general Greco-Roman society.

In "Slavery and the Ancient Jewish Family," Dale B. Martin (Duke University) treats the slave members of the household. In antiquity there were Jewish slaves and Jewish slave owners. The rabbinic prescriptions regarding slaves apparently had no bearing on real slaves and slave owners (it is not clear that the rabbinic prescriptions were even intended to have a bearing on real society); the status and fortunes of Jewish and Jewish owned slaves were determined, rather, by the norms of Greco-Roman society. The bulk of the evidence surveyed by Martin is epigraphical; clearly a major body of evidence on this topic yet to be explored properly is the rabbinic literature beyond the Mishnah.

Our last two essays treat other questions and other approaches. "Reconsidering the Rabbinic *ketubah* Payment," by Michael Satlow (Jewish Theological Seminary), is a study of rabbinic law. Satlow argues that the rabbis of the second century introduced the *ketubah* payment, the obligation incumbent upon the husband or his estate to pay a stipulated amount of money to the wife should the marriage be dissolved either by divorce or by the death of the husband. Satlow distinguishes the *ketubah* payment from the biblical *mohar*, bride price, and from the Greek *proïx*, dowry. Other cultures of the ancient near east imposed financial penalties upon the husband in the event of divorce, but these penalties are neither identical with, nor the source of, the rabbinic *ketubah* payment. When and why Israelite (or Jewish) society shifted from the bride price to the dowry, and why the rabbis, in turn, introduced the *ketubah* payment, are questions that await investigation.

The 1991 session of the Hellenistic Judaism Section was greatly enhanced by the participation of Sarah B. Pomeroy (Hunter College and City University of New York), a prominent classicist and authority on women and the family in antiquity. In her "Some Greek Families: Production and Reproduction," Pomeroy argues that in some professions, notably medicine, sculpture, and the theatrical arts, the family was not so much an agglomeration of relatives but a training ground and a business center. Children inherited not only their parents' talent but also their trade. We may presume that this phenomenon will have been true also in the case of some Jewish families in antiquity, but the matter requires investigation. In his "The Sons of the Sages," Gedalyahu Alon argued that to some degree rabbinic society was dynastic in character, with the sons of sages inheriting their fathers' status and prerogatives, but whether we may call "rabbinic status" a profession is not clear.[4]

---

[4]Gedalyahu Alon, *Jews, Judaism, and the Classical World*, trans. I. Abrahams (Jerusalem: Magnes, 1977) 436-457.

In conclusion, I would like to thank the contributors to this volume and express the hope that their work will encourage others to investigate the Jewish family in antiquity.

Shaye J.D. Cohen
Brown University

Part One

ASSUMPTIONS AND PROBLEMS

1

'Family/ies' in Antiquity: Evidence from Tannaitic Literature and Roman Galilean Architecture[1]

Miriam Peskowitz

In Fredric Jameson's now-famous turn of phrase, the family is considered to be an always-already component of Jewish life.[2] Common generalizations about "the synagogue and the family" envision these institutions as paired stations of Jewish religious life, and at times even construct "the family" as the most crucial and central element of a singularly defined, "Judaism". The pairing often implies the gender associated with each institution. The synagogue and study house –the domain of masculine leadership– are to complement the feminine realm

---

[1] I would like to thank these people for their critical help in formulating and revising this essay at various stages: Eric Meyers, Tolly Boatwright, Maxine Grossman, Laura Levitt and Susan Shapiro, Cynthia Baker, and especially, David Gutterman. I want to thank Shaye Cohen for spurring this topic of study, and the Hellenistic Judaism section of the SBL for responses to the initial oral presentation of this paper.

[2] F. Jameson, *The Political Unconscious: Narrative as a Socially Symbolic Act* (Ithaca: Cornell University Press, 1981), 9. The "always-already-read" text is one apprehended "through sedimented layers of previous interpretation" or "through the sedimented reading habits and categories developed by those inherited interpretive traditions." The term 'text' of course is not limited to a written document but would refer to any interpretable cultural object, document, or artifact.

9

of the home.[3] These gender coded realms, synagogue and family, public and private, would synthesize Jewish life into a neat and harmonious whole.[4] The family would fulfill a role as an essential foundation of everyday religious and social life and Jewish identity.[5] In Victorian tinged perceptions, the family is the haven from the cruel social world outside its walls; in mid-to-late twentieth century criticism, the family would be the last bastion of Jewish identity against encroaching cultural assimilation.

These popular generalizations and unexamined conceptions inform, to a large degree, the scholarly presuppositions that have undergirded and guided the reconstruction and interpretation of the past. Generalizations about "the family" as a concept, and as a cultural construction, remain unproblematized; "the family" is spoken of as nearly timeless, historical, and as already understood. Furthermore, the kind of totalizing language that most often characterizes discussions of "the Jewish family" incorporates similarly ahistorical and unproblematized beliefs about the universal and unchanging roles of women in families; unexamined conceptions of "family" contain within them an array of unexamined conceptions of women and gender.

Scholars of late antique Judaism have written a good deal about the development of the synagogue and other communal structures during the Roman period; considerably less attention has been accorded studies of families.[6] In part this may result from the historiographical notion that

---

[3]As in M. Meiselman, *Jewish Woman in Jewish Law* (New York: Yeshiva University Press and Ktav, 1978), 16: "The family has always been the unit of Jewish existence, and while the man has always been the family's public representative, the woman has been its soul."

[4]As in J.R. Wegner, "The Image and Status of Women in Classical Rabbinic Judaism," in *Jewish Women in Historical Perspective*, ed. J. Baskin (Detroit: Wayne State University Press, 1991), 83.

[5]As in the conceptualization of family in relation to constructed notions of identity and ethnic/religious survival by sociologists A. Dashefsky and I.M. Levine, "The Jewish Family: Continuity and Change," in *Families and Religions: Conflict and Change in Modern Society*, ed. W.V. D'Antonio and J. Aldous (Beverly Hills, CA: Sage Publications, 1983), 163-190, who note "the persistence of Jewish identity to which the family has been linked as the central institution" and cite the description of Jewish family given by the *Encyclopedia Judaica*: "The constant insistence upon the valuing of the family as a social unit for the propagation of domestic and religious virtues and the significant fact that the accepted Hebrew word for marriage is *kiddushin* (sanctification) had the result of making the Jewish home the most vital factor in the survival of Judaism and the preservation of the Jewish way of life, much more than the synagogue or school."

[6]For example, L. Levine, ed., *The Synagogue in Late Antiquity* (Philadelphia, PA: ASOR, 1987); J. Guttmann, *Ancient Synagogues: the State of Research* (Chico, CA: Scholars' Press, 1981); L. Levine, ed., *Ancient Synagogues Revealed* (Jerusalem:

social change happens only in the public realm: "family," in the Roman context of Jewish religious history, is perceived as timeless, as not subject to change, as a sturdy structure around which other aspects of life are built. Alternately, the particular stereotypes of the social relations of gender that characterize contemporary Euro-American societies find their way into reconstructions of Jewish family life in the first few centuries. Such is the case in a recent text on social history and daily life in first century Palestine in which the reconstruction of the family was construed as centered around a male breadwinner and producer, and a wife and children as unproductive consumers.[7] Reconstructions such as these do little more than redeploy contemporary gender relations onto the ancient Jewish family. The family is less widely perceived as a social institution in itself, and less commonly studied as a site or focus of specific and historically changing religious and ideological attention. As a rule, research into "the family" in this period assumes that we know, for the most part, what that family was and what that family meant. In fact, putting untested assumptions aside, we know very little.[8]

In the face of these popular notions and their scholarly consequences, it becomes the task of critical historians of Jewish religious life to pose and pursue questions about the cultural creation and perpetuation of "the Jewish family." To begin such an inquiry, the Jewish family, in all its forms in Greco-Roman antiquity, should not be construed as an essential, timeless, unchanging or biologically determined entity, just as we no longer construe Greco-Roman Judaism as a singular, unified, unchanging

---

Israel Exploration Society, 1981); R. Hachlili, *Ancient Synagogue Art and Archaeology in the Land of Israel* (Leiden: Brill, 1988). These sources list the relevant excavation reports.

[7]D. Fiensy, *The Social History of Palestine in the Herodian Period: The Land is Mine* (Lewiston: Edwin Mellen Press, 1991), 95. Masculinist assumptions about social arrangements and organization predominate in the scholarly literature on Hellenistic and Roman period Judaism; my citation of Fiensy is not meant to single out one scholar in particular but to note a trend.

[8]The introduction to D. Kertzer and R. Saller, *The Family in Italy from Antiquity to the Present* (New Haven: Yale University Press, 1991) is a good example of the inclusion of these concerns in the most recent volume on the family in Rome/Italy. Other recent studies on family and marriage in Roman society include B. Rawson, *The Family in Ancient Rome: New Perspectives* (Ithaca: Cornell University Press, 1986); B. Rawson, *Marriage, Divorce, and Children in Ancient Rome* (Oxford, 1991); M. Henry, "Review Essays: Some Recent Work on Women and the Family in Greek and Roman Antiquity," *Journal of Family History* 14 (1989): 63-77; S. Dixon, *The Roman Mother* (Norman, OK: University of Oklahoma Press, 1988), and *The Roman family* (Baltimore: Johns Hopkins University Press, 1992); T. Wiedemann, *Adults and Children in the Roman Empire* (New Haven: Yale University Press, 1989); J. Gardner and T. Wiedemann, *The Roman Household: a Sourcebook* (New York: Routledge, 1991).

entity. Instead, it is necessary to pose to the evidence from the Hellenistic and Roman periods the question of how the Jewish family 'got to be the way it is.' It is the concerns signified by this question that this essay takes up. I will examine some data for "the family," and suggest some concepts and frameworks for thinking about "family" and families in early Rabbinic Judaism, in the Jewish communities of the towns, villages and cities of Roman Palestine. In doing so I am particularly interested in two things: a starting assumption of family that recognizes it as a site of male and female activity and as a site for the ideological construction of gender; and an expedition for evidence of the development of specific notions about what "family" was for and what "family" was to mean.

The "family" to be investigated is situated in Palestine in the period just following the political and military events of the first Jewish-Roman war, the destruction of the Jerusalem Temple, the second Jewish-Roman war and the ensuing military changes in Roman control of Palestine. The social, theological and ritual ramifications of these crises and the resulting modifications to and reconstructions of Jewish life have been treated from various perspectives.[9] These political changes also provide a context for thinking about what changes might have transpired in local understandings of family, and in the various roles that "family" as a social and ideological entity might be called upon to play.

Such historicizing is not meant to provide any reductionist argument for the direct and causal relation of crises of political power upon changing family structures and meanings. In fact, such change has yet to be proven. Rather, by recalling this historical context in which "family" might be viewed, I mean to raise the entire question of how the study of family might be properly contextualized.

This paper is divided into five interrelated sections. The sections include both methodological and theoretical criticisms, and studies of relevant evidence for families in Roman Palestine and early Rabbinic Judaism. The methodological reflections aim to call attention to some problems in the conceptual frameworks often used to study "the family;" in pointing out these problems, I hope to suggest possible alternatives.

From "Family" to "Families"

Most scholars of "the family" in late antiquity have assumed that we already know what the family is, and so have proceeded to catalogue differences and anomalies among families, within the same culture and

---

[9]I.e. economic effects (Büchler), changes in local leadership (Cohen), modifications in ritual (Bokser), late first century eschatological literature (Stone), and village life (Goodman).

between different cultures. The family is often assumed to be a universal human structure, with relatively superficial modifications that nonetheless are worth noticing and explaining. This dominant approach embodies an always-already perception of the family. This kind of study –particularly as it has been manifested in the study of family and families in the Roman period – should not be misleadingly stereotyped. The past few years have seen a renewed interest in "the family" in the Roman world. In general, the research strategy has been to investigate the many aspects of the social institution of "the family," as if the categorical existence and meaning of the cultural concept of "the family" were already ascertained and understood. Thus, consideration of the family as a social institution has been separated from consideration of the family as a cultural concept. To be sure, one scholar of the Roman family noted that "even at the level of ordinary discourse, *family* is an elusive term."[10] In practice, however, Bradley set aside the recognition of elusivity, at least temporarily, to allow for the collection of empirical data to detail the various aspects of families of different classes.

To justify this project, Bradley quotes L. Stone's definition of an agenda for research on family history, an agenda worth reviewing. "The history of the family," according to Stone,

> embraces not only the demographic limits which constrain family life but also kinship ties, family and household structures, marriage arrangements and conventions and their economic and social causes and consequences, changing sex roles and their differentiation over time, changing attitudes toward and practice of sexual relations, and changes in the affective ties binding husband and wife, and parents and children.[11]

This approach has informed much study on families in Rome, Egypt, Palestine and elsewhere during the Roman period, and the result has been the proliferation of descriptive studies of specific aspects of family life. This new scholarship includes methodological advances in: demography and family size, marriage and divorce patterns, ages at marriage and death, Imperial legislation for and regulation of the family, the relations between slaves, servants and household members related both biologically, contractually, and through marriage, as well as the variations cf all these elements for families situated in different classes. Scholars have studied the evidence for relationships between husbands

---

[10]K. Bradley, *Discovering the Roman Family: Studies in Roman Social History* (New York: Oxford University Press, 1991). I use Bradley as an example because he is in my opinion one of the best and most careful scholars of Roman social antiquity. My critique of the conceptual problems in his use of family is not meant to undercut my appreciation and use of his studies in the social history of family.

[11]L. Stone, *The Past and Present Revisited* (London and New York, 1987).

and wives, fathers and daughters, mothers and sons; the declining importance of *manus* in contracting marriage, and the subsequent emphasis on biological families; and the influence of family law and custom in constraining the lives of female family members. This generation of social historical and literary studies has greatly and helpfully increased our knowledge about families in Roman antiquity. But the new information about families has left out an array of important questions about the functions that "the family" played in these societies, and particularly about the varying kinds of meanings imposed upon "the family." The empirical details of families' lives are often decontextualized from cultural meanings and power relations.

One particularly positive feature of this scholarship has been to point out through empirical research that "the family" is not a singular entity. The bulk of these studies have illustrated sufficiently that throughout the provinces of the Roman empire, the entity commonly portrayed as "the family" is more aptly expressed in the plural. The evidence from Roman antiquity displays a variety of types of families and alludes to the dissimilarity that characterized the experience of a family by different members, and by members of families in different classes. This plurality has ramifications for future study. As Saller and Kertzer note in a recent review of scholarship on Roman families, "The diversity has important consequences for the historian: it may make *the* history of *the* Italian family impossible to write, but it may lead to a more complex and sophisticated, and ultimately more satisfying, understanding of family life."[12]

This leads to the first point: family is a plural concept. In Palestine in the first few centuries CE, families would have taken various forms and would have been characterized by varied arrangements and configurations. While specific studies are lacking, we can surmise from available written and archaeological evidence a variety of diverse family situations. In Palestine, families – mother, father, their children and other family members – may have lived in the same or adjacent household compounds; or, their family may have been structured around males who traveled away from home to find agricultural and other kinds of work.[13] Some families were certainly augmented by slaves, servants, or hired workers; other families may have sent male children away as apprentices to learn trades.[14] Some families may have been organized around polygamous double marriages, in which one or more wives were

---

[12]R. Saller and D. Kertzer, "Historical and Anthropological Perspectives on Italian Family Life," in Saller and Kertzer (1991), 2.

[13]D. Sperber, *Roman Palestine 200-400* (Ramat Gan: Bar Ilan University, 1978)

[14]Bradley (1991); suggested also by tannaitic references to slaves and servants.

married to the same husband.[15] Families lived variously in villas, stone buildings, caves, tents, wooden structures with thatched roofs.[16] Families were rich, or poor. Some families might align with other families in order to pursue similar trades. Families lived in a wide variety of built environments– hamlets, villages, towns and cities; they lived in a variety of different kinds of rooms and spaces.[17] We must suppose that these variations would have made differences in what these families were and what they did.

That families were different and that regional variations of customs made a difference in the everyday activities of families and family members may sound like a truism. But it is a truism not usually incorporated by scholarly research, which has tended toward broad generalizations about "the family." The tannaitic Sages themselves seemed to recognize regional cultural differences, and tried at least in one instance to account for the effects of these differences upon family members and their roles. For instance, the articulation of a household work code for wives in t.Ket 5.4 (Z. 266) states that a husband cannot force his wife to perform household labors prescribed by that code in regional locations where such labors were not customarily done by women and wives. Excavation and analysis of the material culture of Galilee in the Roman and Byzantine periods has suggested even this very small region, the heartland of early rabbinic activity, was characterized by diverse relations to Greco-Roman culture, at least. Gush Halav, for example, in the Upper Galilee, sports a culture that incorporates the standards of Roman-Hellenistic culture, as witnessed by the evidence of art, architecture and aesthetics, to a far lower degree than nearby Lower

---

[15]The recent evidence for polygamous marriage in the archive of Babatha, published in N. Lewis and J.C. Greenfield, eds., *The Documents from the Bar Kokhba Period from the Cave of Letters* (Jerusalem: Israel Exploration Society, 1989) has demanded re-evaluation of the role of polygamy in Roman period families in Palestine and Arabia. For an older view, see L. Jacobs, "The Extent of Jewish Polygamy in Talmudic Times," *Journal of Jewish Studies* 9 (1958): 115-138.

[16]On domestic architecture, see Y. Hirschfeld, *Dwelling Houses in Roman and Byzantine Palestine* (Jerusalem: Yad Itzhak Ben Zvi, 1987), (Heb). Textile fragments of tent cloth were reported found at Tell el-Full, see N. Lapp, ed., *The Third Campaign at Tell el-Ful: The Excavations of 1964* (Cambridge, MA: American Schools of Oriental Research, 1981). On cave dwelling, see P.W. Lapp and N. Lapp, *Discoveries in the Wadi Ed-Daliyeh* (Cambridge, MA: American Schools of Oriental Research, 1974) and Y. Yadin, *The Finds from the Bar Kokhba Period in the Cave of Letters* (Jerusalem: Israel Exploration Society, 1963).

[17]Contra A. Killebrew and S. Fine, "Qatzrin: Reconstructing Village Life in Talmudic Times," *Biblical Archaeological Review* 17 (1991): 47-57. "The typical nuclear family unit focused on a large room called a *traqlin* in rabbinic literature." The supposition of "typicality" is problematic and in need of reformulation.

Galilean areas. The findings at Gush Halav are in stark contrast to the material culture of sites such as Sepphoris in Lower Galilee, with their theater, villas, and numerous Roman and eastern/Imperial style mosaics, or coastal sites such as Caesarea.[18] Any discussion of families in Roman Palestine must start from the empirically grounded point that "families" come in the plural; furthermore, recognizing that Galilean culture was not monolithic, we might surmise that regional distinctions made differences in family life, differences that must be acknowledged, even as more specific evidence for the ramifications of these differences is lacking.

While descriptions of differences among and between families are interesting as such, this research strategy declines to investigate the relations of families to other social institutions and to the production of culture. This strategy perpetuates a notion of the family as a private entity, detached from social relations. The exclusive use of sociological and social historical methods has meant that the stimulating questions regarding the relationship between sociological and historical verities of family life, on the one hand, and cultural notions about families, on the other, have remained at the sidelines of inquiry. This kind of research also ignores questions concerning the kinds of social meanings generated to explain the family and to explain its social meanings.

Multiple Perspectives, Multiple Meanings

The issue of how social meaning for families is produced has several aspects. Perception of "family" depends on the location from which one looks. Family looks different from the perspective of the *ba^cal ha-bayit* than from the perspective of the wife than from the perspective of the minor daughter. For example, tannaitic texts mention several times the family of Rabban Gamaliel and his slave Tabi: since these two characters occupied such different social locations and statures, we might suppose with good reason that each would have experienced the same

---

[18]E. Meyers, "Galilean Regionalism as a Factor in Historical Reconstruction," *Bulletin of the American Schools of Oriental Research* 221 (1976): 93-101; *ibid*, "The Cultural Setting of Galilee: the Case of Regionalism and Early Judaism," *ANRW* II. 19.1: 686-702, 1979; *ibid*, "Galilean Regionalism: A Reappraisal," In *Approaches to Ancient Judaism 5*, ed. W.S. Green (Atlanta: Scholars Press, 1985), 115-131. On Gush Halav, see E. Meyers, and C. Meyers, with J. Strange. *Excavations at the Ancient Synagogue of Gush Halav*. Winona Lake, IN: Eisenbrauns and American Schools of Oriental Research, 1990. The findings from Sepphoris are not yet published in final form; my observations are based on preliminary reports, excavation experience and discussion with the excavators.

family/household differently.[19] Or, we may ask what "family" may have meant to a hypothetical young widow whose husband died fighting Roman soldiers during the Second Judean-Roman war and who was then to reside at the residence of her deceased husband's family, awaiting levirate remarriage or redemption. "Family" would have meant something entirely different to members of the early Christian movement in Palestine, who to some extent may have reconfigured notions of family through the exigencies of conversion and the demands of new religious community.[20] However, our direct textual evidence for perceptions of Jewish families in Roman Galilee is limited to the written perceptions of those men who numbered among the tannaitic sages or whose words and views were recounted by them.

Second, family is not a natural entity, but subject to intervention and influence by those holding social powers. An example from Rome is instructive. Augustus instituted laws aimed at regulating family sexual moralities, the *lex Iulia de maritandis ordinibus* (18 BCE) and the *lex Papia Poppaea* (9 CE). A portion of this law, the *ius trium vel quattuor liberorum*, encouraged higher rates of familial reproduction, and exempted from male guardianship any freeborn woman who gave birth to three children, or any freed woman who gave birth to four children.[21] These examples of Imperial attempts to influence family patterns and behavior show that the family was considered to be an appropriate site for legal regulation; along these lines, we might ask how the religio-legal documents of the tannaitic Sages similarly contain their visions of, and interventions into the regulation of, family life.[22] The tannaitic Sages carefully molded systems of social rules; these included rules to regulate the formation and dissolution of marriages, and rules to remand a wife's

---

[19]m. Succah 2.1 and elsewhere. The households of R. Gamaliel and of his father appear repeatedly as a source of tradition and custom (i.e. m.Shekalim 3.3, m.Shabbat 1.9, m.Eduyot 3.10), and beckon further study.

[20]As suggested by E. Schüssler-Fiorenza, *In Memory of Her* (New York: Crossroad, 1983), and others. Newer research on the community at Qumran also points to the reconfiguration of "family."

[21]*Codex Justinianus* 5.66, 8.57, 8.58. See J. Gardner, *Women in Roman Law and Society* (London: Croom Helm, 1986). For brief synopses of this legislation see the relevant entries in A. Berger, *Encyclopedic Dictionary of Roman Law* (Philadelphia: American Philosophical Society, 1980).

[22]This is not to suggest any specific conclusions about the power and influence of the tannaitic sages in Roman Galillee, even in the second and third centuries; this problem is far from resolved. It is to emphaisize the innovation of even thinking of the family as worthy of legal regulation and monitoring. See D. Cohen, "The Augustan Law on Adultery: The Social and Cultural Context," in Saller and Kertzer (1991), 109-126. More generally on the historicity of regulation, see M. Foucault, *The History of Sexuality. Volume 1* (New York: Vintage, 1990).

or daughter's earnings to the husband/father. Furthermore, tannaitic texts contain remnants of debates over issues such as a father's obligations to maintain and support his male and female children.[23] The conjunction of so many debates over the policies that would organize and regulate family life suggests that "family" comprised a set of significant, even problematic, issues to the tannaitic Sages.

The issue of gaze, of who describes the family, is related to the multiplication of our perceptions of family, a multiplication characterized in part by an overlay of ancient notions of family. By admitting the evidence of different perspectives, it becomes less and less accurate to discuss "the family." The family becomes not just plural, but multiple. That is, whereas *plural* refers to the existence of various ways to organize Jewish families in the social world of Roman Palestine, *multiple* suggests that several simultaneous meanings may have been projected onto the canvas of the social entity called the family. If perceptions of families differ from person to person, ruling class to ruling class, and if descriptions of family life expand, "family" begins to multiply until it would seem difficult to pin down any specific concept of such a thing. Yet, since "families" do historically exist, it is necessary to examine the mechanisms that slow the movement of this ever proliferating "family" and stabilize it into a more unified construct.

The Cultural Idea of Family

This question moves us to the next methodological and theoretical point. "The family" is a cultural concept, a socially constructed notion of what a group of connected individuals should be and how this group should function in society. This aspect of constructedness is what I have meant to signify by placing the word family in quotation marks. From one perspective the family is a tangible entity which we can mark off by descriptions of marriage practices, the demographics of family size, the legalities of inheritance, and so forth. Simultaneously, "the family" is a cultural concept, a set of social values, a symbolic code for all sorts of

---

[23]A chapter of my dissertation, '*The Work of Her Hands': Gendering Everyday Life in Roman-Period Judaism in Roman Palestine (70-250 CE), Using Textile Production as a Case Study*, Duke, 1993, discusses the Roman period innovation of the laws regarding the earned wages of a wife and daughter, and analyzes in depth the debates concerning maintenance of children, especially in light of the evidence of Papyrus 18, of a Jewish family whose marriage document appealed to "Greek custom" (*hellenikos nomos*) to guarantee such support. See Lewis and Greenfield, 80-81; N. Lewis, R. Katzoff, and J. Greenfield, "Papyrus Yadin 18," *IEJ* 37 (1987): 229-250; A. Wasserstein, "A Marriage Contract from the Province of Arabia: Notes on Papyrus Yadin 18," *JQR* 80 (1989): 93-130, and R. Katzoff, "Papyrus Yadin 18 Again: A Rejoinder," *JQR* 82 (1991): 171-176.

social relations.[24] As J. Casey reminds his readers in the conclusion to *The History of the Family*:

> The problem ultimately for the student of the family is that of remembering that he [sic] is dealing with a concept, a creation of men's minds and of their culture, rather than with a material thing...To pretend that the family is something else, a biological relationship or a household, is to risk impoverishing the investigation. It is natural that we should want to know a little more about where our Western family, centered round the conjugal couple and its offspring, came from. But to take the categories familiar to us—the household, the husband-wife and parent-child relationship—and order the data of the past round them may be to pre-empt the terms of the enquiry. To understand the past demands more of an effort on our part to understand it on its own terms.[25]

Casey's insight that "the family" is a conceptual reality, in addition to a sociological reality, suggests a more complex research path. If "family" is a product of culture, then we might profitably ask how various cultural notions of family serve social functions, arise from social needs, create social needs, and/or allude to other kinds of relations. For example, ideas about "the family" might encode concerns and beliefs about other sorts of issues. One example of this kind of analysis from Second Temple Studies comes from a treatment of the social and political meanings for family, marriage and intermarriage in the Persian period, during the establishment of the new Jewish community in Yehud. A. Segal argues that at the beginning of the Second Temple period, the creation of families through intermarriage no longer served the "national interest" of royal alliance making.

> Instead, the old ideal of national family unity could be promulgated without opposition from above, though it was challenged in a new way, by the sheer number of intermarriages that had taken place among the ordinary people. Since the Second Commonwealth was a deliberate attempt to repattern the original kingdom without the sinful practices that had led to destruction, the new social experiment was planned to allow only pure Israelite marriages. The result was an idealized conception of the people, resting on the

---

[24]As I write this paragraph I cannot help but think about the recent debate in our own country over "family values." The dynamics of this debate highlight the tension between the plural realities of family lives and the ideological articulation of notions of those realities. Second, debates about "family" would seem to encode all sorts of notions about the role of women as workers and as caretakers, the construction of masculinity that casts men as breadwinners, the primacy of elite families as role models for all, and so on.

[25]J. Casey, *The History of the Family* (Oxford: Basil Blackwell, 1989), 166.

most widely understood basis of national definition, family
structure.[26]

Here, a concept of family serves as a visible emblem of a
community's new conception of itself and its relation to other nations
and ethnic groups. The intricate relations of the conception of family to
national interests of the elite should alert us to other ways that Jewish
statements about "family" might function. Granted, a family might be
composed of any number of members, pursue a set of daily and cyclical
activities, and so forth. But what social meanings are to be ascribed to
this group? Studies on families have shown empirically that the
culturally constructed notion of "the family" also changes historically.
Situationally, "family" acquires different meanings from different social,
political, and religious contexts and desires, although these meanings
should not be seen as easily reducible to these contexts. To further
complexify the problem at hand, multiple notions of and meanings about
the family will co-exist: "the family" may mean many things all at the
same time. In light of this approach to interpreting family by asking the
question "what is family for", and investigating how notions of family
are crafted and fashioned to fit in with other social values and social
desires, I will look now at some textual evidence for how an idea of
family becomes linked with specific theological values in the Mishnaic
texts of the late second/early third century CE.

A perpetual answer to the question of what the Jewish family in the
Roman period was for is to say that family life, usually conflated with
marriage and the production of children, served to produce legitimate
heirs, to ensure a kind of geneological purity, and to perpetuate the
family line.[27] Perpetuation refers not just to the reproduction of children,
but to reproduction on a grander scale: the reproduction of family lines,
family claims, and family estates. The reproductive aspect of families is
emphasized over all other aspects, such as the ongoing work of daily
production of food, distribution and exchange of resources, transmission
of culture and the socialization/education of the young, and providing a
structure by which individuals can live together and can be linked to

---

[26]A. Segal, *Rebecca's Children: Judaism and Christianity in the Roman World*
(Cambridge, MA: Harvard University Press, 1986), 20.

[27]Josephus, *Ag Ap* 2.199-204 and Sir 26:19-21 are consistently cited as explanations
of the importance of Jewish family life during the Second Temple period. Yet, the
passage from Josephus states that sexual relations between husband and wife are
solely for the procreation of children. The portrait of the sober, conservative and
sexually restrained married couple seems to be part of Josephus' argument for
the social respectability. This begs the question of the purposes for which families
are represented in literary sources.

larger groups.[28] This answer stresses the aspect of family life which manages and provides for the transmission of name and the transmission of property. These kinds of explanations follow a functionalist reasoning, i.e., inheritance laws incumbent on Jewish families (according to halakhah) function to fulfill a certain social need– the transmission of family holdings. But the reasoning is somewhat circular: *families* exist to transmit *family* holdings and *family* pedigree. The very term *family* remains unproblematized: the explanation of the role (transmission) serves to bolster the family as a social institution. This kind of reasoning ignores questions about why families, and which families at that, would hold a stake in transmitting wealth, or in policing the purity of their lineage. It imagines these functions to be universal and natural needs and fails to treat them as social constructs.[29]

A reading of m. Taᶜanit 4.8 illustrates less functional and more obviously theological notions of family.

> **There were no better days for Israel than Fifteenth Av and Yom Kippur. For on those days, the daughters of Jerusalem go out in white garments, borrowed so as not to embarrass those who had none. All the garments require ritual immersion.**

---

[28]This list of family/household functions emulates R. Wilk and R.Netting, "Households: Changing Forms and Functions," in *Households: Comparative and Historical Studies of the Domestic Group*, eds. R. Netting, R. Wilk, and E. Arnould (Berkeley: University of California Press, 1984). In principle I have tried to limit my recourse to statements and definitions authorized by anthropologists of the family. The field of ancient religious studies has become inundated with references to anthropological models as explanations for ancient phenomena, often done without recognition of the contested nature of various models in their own disciplines. In truth, the outlines and practices of "family history," "anthropology of the family and household" and other disciplinary studies of family are very much under debate. Another point is that most research on "family" has been masculinist, and hence is in need of review and revision. See for example, B. Thorne and M. Yalon, eds., *Rethinking the Family: Some Feminist Questions* (New York: Longman, 1982), which analyzes the effects of masculinist scholarship in constructing family theory. D. Herlihy, "Family," *American Historical Review* 96 (1991): 1-16 critiques historical practices. M. Poster, *Critical Theory of the Family* (New York: Seabury Press, 1978) claims that social scientists have no coherent theoretical analysis of the family. See also, D.P. Levine and L.S. Levine, "Problems in the Marxist Theory of the Family," *Social Analysis* 15 (1984): 50-58; S. Yanagisako, "Family and Household: the Analysis of Domestic groups," *Annual Review of Anthropology* 8 (1979): 161-205; and J.E. Smith, "Review Essay: Family History and Feminist History," *Feminist Studies* 17 (1991): 349-364.

[29]The critique of functionalist explanations of family is discussed in J. Collier, M. Rosaldo, and S. Yanagisako, "Is There a Family? New Anthropological Views," In *Rethinking the Family: Some Feminist Questions*, ed. B. Thorne with M. Yalon (New York: Longman, 1982), 25-39.

> And the daughters of Jerusalem go out and dance in the
> vineyards. And what did they say? Young men, please raise your
> eyes and see whom you would choose for yourself. Do not set
> your eyes on ornamental beauty; set your eyes on family
> (*mishpahah*).

Family lineage, (*mishpahah*), is to be valued over fleeting qualities.
This value is perpetuated by the young women of the text. They not only
chant this reminder to the young men viewing them; they exchange their
garments in order to disrupt easy identification of their individual
beauty, clothing, and ornamentation. This section of m. Ta^canit 4.8 is
most often read in isolation and interpreted at face value to recount a
festival where young women and men meet in the vineyards, the young
women dance in their white dresses before the young men who will pick
out their brides. Safrai, for example, described this text as a "lifelike
example of a folk festival"[30] and much discussion of this text had
centered around its possible accuracy and authenticity to ask whether
Jewish betrothal festivals of this sort did exist.[31] While these questions
are interesting, the text can be read differently when placed into its
textual context. When read in context, the text produces a tannaitic
notion that is more complicated than a mere reminder to forego
ephemeral aesthetic pleasure for lasting stability. The text composes a
more idealized role for "the family." Organizationally, m. Ta^canit
concludes a tractate devoted to solving communal problems through the
ritual use of fasting. The passages that immediately precede 4.8 list the
multiple sorrows and destructions to be commemorated by the Fasts of
12 Tammuz and 9 Ab. These passages are filled with details about the
ascetic practices that would fill the entire week of 9 Ab: the interruption
of common daily routines by a refrain from haircuts and washing
clothes, and a restriction from food and drink on the eve of the fast.
Amid this register of ascetic practices and the hints of past communal
pains and destructions, the youthful festival described in m. Ta^canit 4.8
does come as a reader's surprise, with its seemingly ingenuous and

---

[30]S.Safrai, "Home and Family," in *The Jewish People in the First Century*, Volume 2,
ed. S. Safrai and M. Stern (Philadelphia: Fortress Press, 1976), 728-792.

[31]As in L. Archer, *Her Price is Beyond Rubies: the Jewish Woman in Graeco-Roman
Palestine* (Sheffield, U.K.: Sheffield Academic Press, 1990), 120, n5 and 151, who
claims the ritual to be antiquated by this period. She writes that "the sentiment"
of the Mishnaic account is pertinent, but decontextualizes "the sentiment" in
order to analyze the passage as joining Second Temple and Babylonian Talmudic
traditions to pair "family" with social station and the perpetuation of rigid
divisions in "racial and religious purity." Because she focused on perceiving
continuities with earlier and later Jewish texts, and because she stopped reading
after the line which reads "set your eyes in family" she missed the text's
production of a new notion of family.

joyous account of girlish camaraderie, nubility, and egalitarian solidarity, all set amid a rustic simplicity.

But the section that immediately follows this short passage, and the section which brings the entire tractate to a close, provides some suggestions for the treatment of this thematically interluding story of a ritual. I will reproduce m. Taᶜanit 4.8 once again, this time contextualized by the lines that follow it and that conclude the tractate.

Rabban Shimon ben Gamaliel said:

> There were no better days for Israel than Fifteenth Ab and Yom Kippur. For on those days, the daughters of Jerusalem go out in white garments, borrowed so as not to embarrass those who had none. All the garments require ritual immersion.
>
> And the daughters of Jerusalem go out and dance in the vineyards. And what did they say? Young men, please raise your eyes and see whom you would choose for yourself. Do not set your eyes on ornamental beauty; set your eyes on family.
>
> *Grace is deceptive and beauty is illusory; a god-fearing woman, she is to be praised.* And it [referring to Scripture] says: *Give her the fruits of her hands and praise her, according to her works, at the gates.* And hence it says: *Daughters of Zion, go out and view King Solomon, view the crown with which his mother crowned him on his wedding-day, and on the day of his heartfelt joy.* "On his wedding-day" – this signifies the giving of the law (matan tôrāh)."*And on the day of his heartfelt joy"*–this signifies the building of the Temple. May it be rebuilt quickly in our days. Amen.[32]

Textually located between the recounting of past destruction and a continuum stretching from the giving of Torah to hopes for the future rebuilding of the Temple, the description of a festival that creates new families takes on a different meaning than interpreters usually perceive. The first prooftexts do seem to build on the comparison of beauty and

---

[32]The translation is my own. The biblical citations are (in order): Prov 31.30, Prov 31.31 and Cant 3.11. I am aware of arguments concerning the post-Tannaitic dating of portions of m.Taanit 4.8. [See Jacob N. Epstein, *Introduction to the Text of the Mishnah* (Jerusalem: Magnes, 1964) 686-687 (Hebrew).] I think that the epistemological claims of some parts of traditional scholarship on early Rabbinic texts need to be reconsidered in light of critiques of positivist scholarship and inherited interpretive traditions (see my discussion of Jameson at the beginning of this essay). In lieu of any scholarly consensus, I recognize the ambiguity of dating this text to the Tannaitic period, but I refer readers to the ambiguities of dating virtually any of the Tannaitic texts to the so-called Tannaitic period. We must recognize the relative historical fictions that undergird our work. In sum: I choose to use this passage as a source for Tannaitic culture, even while I recognize that it might derive from other times or places.

ornamentation to *mishpahah*. But then the text takes a different turn; it interprets Scripture to present a concept of family. The text's final words hint at a new family, one linked not to lineage, contractual agreements, details of economic exchanges between families, and the other socio-legal mechanisms that structure the beginning of new families. This new family is tied to broader theological goals. Family is associated with religious qualities of fearing God, socially productive work acts and praiseworthy action. In a universalizing move, the "family"–signified by the marital union of a man and a woman– becomes a foundation of, and even inherent in, the giving of the Torah and the rebuilding of the Temple. "Family" is linked to Israel, to redemption, and to the rebuilt Temple of the future. The genesis of a new "family" links the religious past and the religious future. It is a novel "post-destruction" family: m. Ta^canit 4.8 moves family into a web of theological concerns and desires. It ascribes meanings to "family" above and beyond the mundanities of everyday life and the intestate securities of family legacies and traditions. The priority of kinship is extended beyond the specific station of specific families to include a kinship to all Israel and to the its central religious institutions. Family is to be associated with wholescale communal religious survival, as suggested by this representation of a yearly, continual festival that would create new marriages and new families.

This notion of family is not antithetical to the notion of the family as an instrument of familial reproduction. Rather, it would be understand better as additional, simultaneous social idea. "Family" may function as a medium of the social reproduction of status and station, and the transmission of holdings, and it simultaneously may function as a means of prioritizing and tying together religious values and desires in the period of reconstruction following the destruction of the Jerusalem Temple. These religious values become embedded in notions of family. "Family" as a concept appears changed in this text, and the changes may indicate tannaitic perceptions of a new social condition, and a subsequent re-crafting and re-fashioning of ideas about families.

[Gendered] Families

The next point is now in order. The study of the family is in many ways intimately connected to the study of men, women, and gender relations. As. B. Thorne points out, the underlying structures of the family are closely related to the perpetuation of the sex/gender system whereby two dichotomous genders are formed, labor is divided by sex (in ways that emphasize and exacerbate the gender dichotomies) and sexuality is highly regulated.[33] Gender relations are closely associated with families, through the various laws of marital contract, inheritance, and through the daily experience of differential work assignments. However, studies of families have in many cases ignored the participation of women and the role of gender relations, instead speaking of the abstraction of a gender-neutral family. I have chosen not to investigate a topic called "women in the family." Instead, I wish to suggest a comprehension of the family that is always-already gendered. This comprehension would recognize that "family" is embedded in gender relations, and would seek to identify the relation of "the family" to the perpetuation of specific kinds of gender systems. Moreover, I hope to have taken these recognitions as a foundation for this paper, in effect making the study of "the family" into the *a priori* study of the [gendered] family.[34]

One way to accomplish this is to re-examine the prevalent use of distinctions between public and private space to explain ancient society. Interpreters of this period have made extensive use of a model of society that divides the world into two supposedly complementary – but opposite – halves. Society is construed as divided into public and private, or domestic, spheres; the public sphere – law, politics, institutions – are coded masculine while private worlds – homes and families – are conceived as feminine. This model comes from naturalized Western stereotypes of gender and society; it comes as well from early feminist attempts to explain variances in women's status by using the division of space into the domains of public and private/domestic as a testing device to evaluate the relative oppressions of women in different societies.[35] Despite the barrage of critiques made against this scholarly

---

[33]B. Thorne, "Feminist Rethinking of the Family," in B. Thorne and M. Yalon, *Rethinking the Family* (White Plains, New York: Seabury Press, 1982), 8-9. The phrase sex/gender system refers to the explanation of the cultural construction of biological sexual differences into cultural categories of gender, as articulated by G. Rubin, "The Traffic in Women: Notes on the 'Political Economy' of Sex," in *Toward an Anthropology of Women*, ed. R. Reiter (New York: Monthly Review Press, 1975), 157-210.

[34]For this project applied to modern Jewish families, see D.R. Kaufman, "Engendering Family Theory: Toward a Feminist-Interpretive Framework,: in *Fashioning Family Theory: New Approaches*, ed. J. Sprey (Newbury Park, CA: Sage, 1990): 107-135.

[35]M.Z. Rosaldo, "Woman, Culture, and Society: a Theoretical Overview," in *Woman, Culture, and Society*, ed. M.Z. Rosaldo and L. Lamphere (Stanford: Stanford University Press, 1974), 23. The model was widely appropriated by feminist scholars in many disciplines.

imposition of a particularly modern frame upon ancient society,[36] and despite the feminist criticism and subsequent revision of the public/private model,[37] use of this paradigm continues almost unabated.

Contemporary scholarship has approached the study of ancient religion and society by assuming a division of society into two spheres: public and private. However, while the exact definitions of the social institutions designated as public and private vary, the general agreement that family belongs in the private realm has remained constant.[38]

---

[36]A. Wallace-Hadrill, "The Social Structure of the Roman House," *Papers of the British School at Rome* 56 (1988): 43-97: "Post-industrial society has become accustomed to a divorce between home and place of work: status is generated at work not home, so that the home becomes endowed with a 'privacy' alien to the Roman." Interesting in this regard is a look back at L. Epstein, *Marriage Laws in the Bible and Talmud* (Cambridge: Harvard University Press, 1942), vii: "Of all human relations, paradoxically enough, the marriage relation is at once the most private and the most public. On the one hand, society recognizes the inviolable privacy of the home and affords it certain measures of protection against outside interference; but on the other, it takes unto itself the right to interfere in that privacy by setting up rigid laws restricting the individuals in choosing their mates for the establishment of a home." The scholarly tendency to rely on public/private distinctions is itself historically situated and seems much more prevalent in recent and current scholarship of Jewish religious history than in the scholarship of past generations.

[37]Rosaldo herself reponded to mounting criticism and re-conceived the model. M.Z. Rosaldo, "The Use and Abuse of Anthropology: Reflections on Feminism and Cross-Cultural Understanding," *SIGNS* 5 (1980): 389-417: "Our analytical tradition, in short, has preserved the nineteenth-century division into inherently gendered spheres and, in doing so, has cast one presumably basic social fact not in moral or relational terms but, rather, in individualist ones, wherein the shape of social institutions is implicitly understood as a reflection of individual needs, resources, or biology...Home versus public life appears to have a transhistoric sense, at least in part, because it corresponds to our long-standing ideological terms contrasting inner and outer, love and interest, natural and constructed bonds, and men's and women's natural activities and styles. As we have seen, there is some cause to think that our acceptance of these dichotomous terms makes sense; but at the same time, it would now appear that understandings shaped by oppositional modes of thought have been – and will most likely prove themselves to be – inherently problematic for those of us who hope to understand the lives that women lead within human societies...But if this account [of public/private dichotomy] "makes sense" in universal terms, I would go on to claim that when we turn to concrete cases, a model based upon the opposition of two spheres assumes–where it should rather help illuminate and explain – too much about how gender really works." See also D.O. Helly and S.M. Reverby, *Gendered Domains: Rethinking Public and Private in Women's History* (Ithaca: Cornell University Press, 1992).

[38]For example, J.R. Wegner, *Chattel or Person? The Status of Women in the Mishnah* (New York: Oxford University Press, 1988) construes the public realm as the synagogue; hence work, market relations, economic transactions are all placed

According to this model of society, the entire subject of this paper would fall into a realm labeled "private", and into a realm understood as somehow separate from the social relations of work and economy that characterize the "public" realm. Because the two realms are gender coded so that the public realm is predominantly male and the private realm is predominantly female, "family" would appear to be the preserve of women. This formulation, however, ignores and makes invisible the presence and contribution of men in families and households. It ignores the role of male elites in creating legal structures that shape families and family life, and the role of both men and women in creating, legitimating, and perpetuating certain notions and practices of family life. The assignment of family to a "private" realm distorts Jewish family life in Roman antiquity by pre-determining its position in society, as well as its social and theological meanings. In doing so, such an assignment removes from visibility some very important issues.[39]

It is generally agreed that ancient societies entertained notions of private and public acts and activities, and that in some cases these were coded as either and exclusively masculine or feminine.[40] It is also generally agreed that the pre-modern household did not know the stereotyped ideology that divides (public) work from (private) family that is so pervasive in late-capitalist societies.[41] Yet, the construction of gendered space would vary by class. An historical review of the concept of family by Herlihy suggested that late ancient peoples "came only slowly to conceive of the domestic community as sharply separated from the larger society."[42] In light of these combined challenges, Wallace-

---

into the private realm with the family and women. However, in a broader cultural-historical perspective, institutions such as synagogues would be construed as part of a privatized sphere from the perspective of Roman institutions.

[39]There is an extensive scholarly literature on the question of the efficacy and epistemology of the public/private dichotomy. See for starters, C. Bose, "Dual Spheres" in *Analyzing Gender: A Handbook of Social Science Research*, ed. B. Hess and M. Ferree (Newbury Park, CA: Sage, 1987); H. Moore, *Feminism and Anthropology* (Minneapolis: University of Minnesota Press, 1988); M.Z Rosaldo, "Woman, Culture, and Society: a Theoretical Overview, in *Women, Culture, and Society*, ed. M. Rosaldo and L. Lamphere (Stanford: Stanford University Press, 1974); M. Rosaldo, "The Use and Abuse of Anthropology: Reflections on Feminism and Cross-Cultural Understanding" *SIGNS* 5 (1980): 389-417.

[40]For instance Philo, *Spec Leg*, III. 169-177; Columella, *Re Rus*, XII.

[41]The difference between this ideology and historical realities must be reiterated. See for example, A. Kessler-Harris, *Women Have Always Worked: A Historical Overview* (Old Westbury, New York: The Feminist Press, 1981) and the large literature on women's working lives in the nineteenth and twentieth centuries that produced this ideology of dual spheres.

[42]D. Herlihy, "Family," *American Historical Review* 96 (1991): 1-17.

Hadrill's suggestion that the dualistic conception of public and private/domestic be replaced by a framework of a "spectrum that ranges from the completely public to the completely private" is more appropriate as a starting point for a better view of how families worked day-to-day.[43] In fact, a new focus on work activities of "the day-to-day" might take up the challenge of investigating the family and family living space as a work environment shared by both male and female family members.

Work and Inter-relationality

Most people in antiquity worked, and most people spent most of their lives working to produce and reproduce daily needs. Family cannot be perceived as a feminine zone and it cannot be perceived separately from work activities and work precincts. In J. Kelly's words: "Work and home were bound together, and so were the daily work lives of women and men, children and adults."[44] Archaeological and architectural evidence from the excavated material culture of Roman Palestine are particularly illuminating here. After all, it is not sufficient to take the broader historical conclusions as evidence for a new understanding of Jewish families in Roman Palestine. Rather, these may be used as guides to find explanations that are most particularly accurate to Jewish families in Roman Palestine. The (so-called) residential architecture of Meiron, Upper Galilee witnesses the combination of work activities with the other activities of sustenance and production that we more typically associate with families. The excavations at Meiron reported several strata of an extensive residential area, dated to the Middle and Late Roman periods. These archaeological periods are coterminant with, and continuing after, the activity of the tannaitic Sages. The findings from these excavations and others provide data on everyday life in a Jewish community at that time.[45]

At Meiron, insula MI contains two adjacent residences.[46] In the larger of these "homes", the ground floor consists of eight rooms and a

---

[43]"The Social Structure of the Roman House," 43-97.

[44]J. Kelly, "Family and Society," in *Women, History, and Theory* (Chicago: University of Chicago, 1984), 128. See also C. Meyers, *Discovering Eve: Ancient Israelite Women in Context* (New York: Oxford University Press, 1988).

[45]E. Meyers, J. Strange, and C. Meyers, *Excavations at Ancient Meiron, Upper Galilee, Israel 1971-72, 1974-75, 1977* (Cambridge, MA: American Schools of Oriental Research, 1981). Also, G. Foerster, "Excavations at Ancient Meron (Review Article)," *Israel Exploration Journal* 37 (1987): 262-269.

[46]The stratigraphy of insula MI is complicated by piecemeal additions and changes made to the structure, but the strata of occupation were III (Middle Roman: 135-250) and IV (Late Roman: 250-365). In the interests of providing

courtyard. The type and quantity of debris excavated in the four northernmost rooms (Rooms A,B,C and D) suggest that over these rooms was a second story which functioned as the sleeping quarters.[47] Insula MI resembles in some ways residences excavated at other northern Palestinian sites, such as Capernaum, Khorazin, and Qatzrin.[48] According to the excavators, the population of Meiron was largely Jewish; Insula M1 would have housed a family of some economic means.[49]

The materials excavated from MI identify some functions of each of the rooms. One room (Room E) contained a stone workbench (8005), a semi-circular stone installation (8007), and an iron-handled bronze planer or scraper. Such finds indicate that this room and the adjacent Room D were workshop areas. The excavators of Meiron have suggested tentatively that the workshop was a cooperage which produced wooden barrels, perhaps for the Galilean olive and olive oil trades. Another room (Room A) functioned as a kind of passage way from the entrance courtyard to the inner courtyard. Along the northern wall were low benches for sitting. In this area was found a spindle whorl, which alludes to the preparation and spinning of thread.[50] Additional rooms (Rooms F and C) contained stone grinders and artifacts necessary for the production and preparation of food. In the same occupation levels, three ovens were found. Additional evidence for the daily tasks of production were found in the basalt food grinder and needles made of bone and bronze excavated in the southern part of the courtyard (K). These suggest

---

context for this building, strata IV contains the building of the synagogue at Meiron, and the peak of village life there. The site is largely abandoned during the Byzantine period. The term *insula* has several meanings for Roman period architecture. At Meiron it refers to semi-contiguous residences contained by the four sides of a block. More commonly it describes the multi-family and multi-story buildings, exemplified in Ostia, Italy.

[47]Thick plaster excavated from rooms A and C was extraneous to the walls of the first level, hence is interpreted as the floor or wall covering of the upper floor. Many of the fine small objects from M1 were found in these loci; these were taken to suggest the sleeping or personal quarters of some residents.

[48]V. Corbo, *Cafarnao: Gli Edifici della Citta* (Jerusalem: Franciscan Printing Press, 1975); Z. Yeivin, "Excavations at Khorazin," *Eretz Israel* 11 (1961): 144-157 (Heb); Yizhar Hirschfeld, *Dwelling Houses in Roman and Byzantine Palestine* (Jerusalem: Yad Yizhak Ben-Tsvi, 1987) (Heb).

[49]Iconic remains of other religious-ethnic groups were not found there, in contrast to say, Sepphoris or Beth Shean which show evidence of a more religiously and ethnically varied population.

[50]Spindle whorls move about easily and are often displaced from the places where spinning might have taken place. That spindle whorls were found in Room A is suggestive but not conclusive evidence for textile production in that room.

that the work of food preparation and sewing took place there.[51] In the smaller dwelling next door, rooms contained an oven (Room G) and various grinding tools (Room H). In these rooms were also found four bone needles.[52]

The number of different work projects found in residence MI illustrates clearly that in the architecture of family, residential space and work space overlapped.[53] This kind of overlap appears also in Tannaitic passages that describe the production of olives inside the home (m. Toh 9.6). The interior of the home does not represent "private" space, as distinct from work space, nor is it easy to discern which rooms and spaces had public and/or private uses and meanings. This is not to say that all "work" was done at "home." Such a statement would certainly be belied by ample archaeological evidence for workshops and work areas located at a remove from residential dwellings. Olive presses, pottery kilns, and installations for wine making were often situated outside the more built-up areas of a town or village.[54] And the smoke and odors from some industries would provide warrant their distance from residences.[55] Rather, it is to argue that conceptualizations of distinct public and private zones simply do not serve to describe meaningfully nor accurately how members of a household were organized into the architecture of the household. Such dichotomous zones falsely militate

---

[51]It has been suggested that perhaps the basalt grinder was not used for food but perhaps for dye production or cosmetic production.

[52]In the common entrance area, MI.5, were found two spindle whorls, of ceramic and glass. The locus (5002) is windblown rock and tumble, and sits very close to contaminated surface loci. 5002 is not considered a critical locus by the excavators.

[53]Suggested also by a building at Nabratein: a central courtyard is surrounded by small chambers, and the excavators interpret the remains as indicating a trading depot amid the household functions of the building. See C. and E. Meyers, "Talmudic Village Life in the Galilean Highlands," *Bulletin of the Anglo-Israel Archaeological Society* (1982): 11-14. This kind of architectural and activity related overlap of work and residential space may be seen as well at Qatzrin, as Ann Killebrew and Steven Fine point out.

[54]See for example, Khirbet Shema, excavated by E. Meyers, A.T. Kraabel, and J. Strange, *Ancient Synagogue Excavations at Khirbet Shema: Upper Galillee, Israel 1970-1972* (Durham, NC: ASOR and Duke University Press, 1976). At Khirbet Sumaqa, 12 workshops for tanning, dyeing, and some unidentifiable industries were located around the site; S. Dar, "Horvat Sumaga– Settlement from the Roman Byzantine Periods," *Bulletin of the Anglo-Israel Archaeological Society* 8 (1988-89): 34-48. But, note the wine press and oil press at the early Roman villa at Kh. Mansur el-ᶜAqab, Y. Hirschfeld and R. Birger-Calderon, "Early Roman and Byzantine Estates near Caesarea," *Israel Exploration Journal* 41 (1991): 81-111.

[55]F. Vitto, "A Look into the Workshop of a Late Roman Galilean Potter," *Bulletin of the Anglo-Israel Archaeological Society* (1983-1984): 19-22.

against seeing the household, family, and activities of daily life as central facets of ancient society and religion.

The textual and archaeological evidence for this period suggest that Jewish families in Galilee be characterized in part as a working group. This characterization is strengthened by the representations in various Tannaitic passages of the economic relations of daily family life. Work and economy were very much a part of familial social relations, and very much part of conceptualizations of families. Tannaitic texts dwell repeatedly on work done by husbands, wives, sons and daughters, by slaves, by those designated as "workers." The marital economy of work and wages was subjected to legal attention and regulation, and constituted by the principles *ma'ăśēh yādêhâ* (the work of her hands) and *mězônôt* (maintenance). These attentions provide witness to the Sage's quandaries about the ownership of the earned wages of wives and minor daughters; the *halakhah* that would transfer their profits to the fiscal control of the husband/father,[56] as well as the attention to the obligations of women's unpaid household work[57] would suggest specific ways that Sages meant to organize the relations of family members to one another, as delineated through their work and economic activities. The Sages' attentions witness not only the "problems" they discerned in female's work, but the very activity of girls' and women's labors.[58] Because both men and women performed work that was paid and unpaid, it is particularly incorrect to construe males as sole breadwinners for most families in most classes.[59] Men worked at a wide range of agricultural and industrial tasks; the range of work portrayed by the Tannaitic texts as done by women is smaller, yet these portrayals incorporate aspects of mercantile work, production of textiles and foodstuffs, service work (wetnursing, midwifery, teaching, hairdressing and innkeeping) and agricultural labor. Significantly, several kinds of jobs were not assigned rigidly to either men and women, particularly tasks related to the production of textiles.

---

[56]m.Ket 6.1; m.Ket 4.4; m.Ket 5.8; t.Ket 5.8, 5.9; t.Ket 5.2; m.Ket 5.9; t.Ket 13.1 [12.4]; m.Ket 5.4; t.Ket 5.3; m.Nid 5.7, and elsewhere.
[57]m.Ket 5.5, t.Ket 5.4.
[58]I discuss these issues in detail in my dissertation, cited above.
[59]S. Pomeroy, *Goddesses, Whores, Wives, and Slaves: Women in Classical Antiquity* (New York: Schocken, 1975), 133, suggests that a wife and children are an important source of labor for a poor free man. The recent scholarship on women's work in Roman antiquity demands a revision of our generalizations. See R. Gunther, *Frauenarbeit, Frauenbindung: Untersuchungen zu unfreien und freigelassenen Frauen in der Stadtrömischen Inschriften* (München: W. Fink, 1987); E. Levy, ed. *La Femme dans les Sociétés Antiques* (Strasbourg: Institut d'Histoire Romaine, 1983).

The existence of occupations that were not rigidly divided by gender in the Tannaitic documents points to an important phenomenon in the Roman world, one that would seem to have characterized Jewish communities in Roman Palestine as well. Husbands and wives often worked at the same trade, as indicated by inscriptional evidence.[60] The textual evidence for such work practices in Palestine is limited to one reference to a husband and wife both engaged in selling olives.[61] However the widespread evidence for family trades in Rome, as well as in Egypt, and Asia Minor[62] augments the evidence for Palestine: the recollections of family based artisans associations of Abtinas and Garmu that produced showbread and frankincense for the Jerusalem Temple[63]; references to fathers teaching trades to their sons;[64] and Josephus'

---

[60]S. Treggiari, "Lower Class Women in the Roman Economy," *Florilegium* 1 (1979): 65-86. *brattiaria* and *brattiarius* (CIL vi. 9211, 6939); *clavaria* and *clavarius* (CIL v.7023); *conditaria* and *conditarius* (CIL vi.9277); *furnaria* and *furnarius* (CIL viii.24678); two *pomararii* (or perhaps read *pomarii*), (CIL vi.37819); two *purpurarii* (CIL vi.9846). N. Kampen, *Image and Status: Roman Working Women in Ostia* (Berlin: Mann, 1981), 125ff adds additional evidence for shared wife/husband occupations: CIL iii.2117 (lead work) and CIL v.7023 (production of nails). Treggiari interprets these few inscriptions to suggest a more widespread scenario, and given the close architectural proximity, in fact, overlay, of shopfronts and workshops to living quarters in Rome, I would concur. She writes: "The frequency with which a woman is paired with a man, usually a husband, in the same trade suggests that many of them worked alongside husbands, either because they adopted the husband's trade after marriage, or because men looked for wives who were already in the same (or a related) trade, which no doubt they generally derived from their fathers and perhaps mothers." Occupational choices, or lack of choices, for the non-elite and the non-slave, in the context of a fairly stratified, fairly rigid society, seems very determined by one's family.

[61]t.BQ 11.7.

[62]In Roman Egypt, both Bradley and Lewis argue that textile trades were handed down generationally. Families might apprentice their sons to other weavers; the sons would later return to the father's family workshop. See P.Mich III.170; P.Mich III.172; P.Wisc 4, cited in K.Bradley, "Child Labor in the Roman World," in Bradley, *Discovering the Roman Family* (New York: Oxford, 1991), 109. N. Lewis, *Life in Egypt Under Roman Rule* (Oxford: Clarendon Press, 1983), 135. Lewis does not cite any evidence for this, but presumably is referring to the papyri apprenticeship contracts. With regard to Asia Minor, consider the reference of Acts 18.2-3 to the married couple Aquila and Priscilla who work together as tent makers.

[63]m.Shek 5.1; m.Yoma 3.11.

[64]m.Eduy 2.9; m.Qidd 4.14. It is not specifically articulated in this text that fathers are teaching their sons the family trade, but note Mark 1.29: James and John worked as fishermen with their father Zebedee. The inscription for the artisans Marianos and his son Aninas, reveals two generations involved in the same trade. See inscription no. 77 in B. Lifshitz, *Donateurs et Fondateurs dans les Synagogues Juives* (Paris: Gabalda, 1967), 66.

reference to quarters in Jerusalem devoted to the residences and shops of particular kinds of artisans.[65] Gathered in this way, the ancient evidence would suggest that the interconnections of work and family provided the daily experiences of most free men and women.

The combined reading of material culture and religio-legal texts suggest another facet of family life. Roman Galilean architecture is characterized by tightly fit and overlapping architectural features. Families living next to each other in these residences shared walls, courtyard workspaces, water cisterns, and common rooftop areas. These interconnected architectural features and their shared common spaces seem to assume, and to insure, that Galilean life would have included a certain interrelationship between families. The architecture itself would have functioned as a nonwritten text that conveyed meanings about family life.[66]Presumptions of interfamily relationship are found as well in tannaitic passages that describe the lending of tools, utensils, and food materials between households. For example, in m. Sheviit 5.9 and m. Gittin 5.9 a woman lends to her neighbor several items, including sieves, handmills, ovens and vessels for grinding and sifting corn.[67] Interrelationality seems to be the assumption of *Erubin* and the regulation of the ways that members of families sharing a courtyard might eat together during the Sabbath. The regulation of this social practice presumes that families in adjacent and nearby houses ate

---

[65]Josephus, *BJ*, 2: 530. On the concentration of crafts in certain districts of cities. see R. Macmullen, *Roman Social Relations* (New Haven: Yale University Press, 1974), 132-135.

[66]On architecture as a text that conveys meaning, see essays in S. Kent, *Domestic Architecture and the Use of Space: An Interdisciplinary Cross-Cultural Approach* (New York: Cambridge University Press, 1990). Also, see D. Fiensy, *The Social History of Palestine in the Herodian Period: The Land is Mine* (Lewiston: Edwin Mellen Press, 1991), 145, points to a "network of social units: incorporating "the nuclear family, courtyard neighbors, neighbors of the same alley, and fellow villagers."

[67]These practices are discussed in context of how daily work acts might be affected by the regulations of the Sabbatical Year. The lending of tools would also be determined by the value of tools in Roman Galilean society. That is, could everyone afford to buy the tools required for the production of everyday life? Are tools relatively scarce? Are tools commonly borrowed and lent? And are the borrowers and lenders perhaps anxious about the transfer of valuable objects? These questions were suggested to me by Professor M.T. Boatwright. I am not aware of any substantive and reliable research on this topic.

Another example of interrelationality might be seen in the phenomena of several olive oil presses found in a single settlement in Roman-Byzantine Golan. However, this is a difficult interpretive issue, and it has not been determined whether these were communally or individually owned; see D. Urman, *The Golan: A Profile of a Region During the Roman and Byzantine Periods* (Oxford: British Archaeological Reports, 1985), 273.

together with some regularity, and that it was necessary to find a way to accommodate this social practice within the halakha for Sabbath and holidays.[68]

If we set aside the presuppositions of public and private spheres, then the economic family is not a discrete social unit characterized by interpersonal relationship and institutional marital markers. Instead, the Jewish family emerges as a working group. The terms public and private no longer explain "the family." This working family was subject to and part of the social relations of the economies and polities of Roman Palestine. To replace the model of individual family units sheltered from social relations, the conception of socio-economic interrelationality acts as a starting point for reflections upon Jewish families, and hence about Jewish society, in Roman Galilee.[69]

Conclusions

This essay has intended to contribute some preliminary frameworks for the study of family, families, and "family" in late antiquity. These frameworks should be appropriate to the arguably complex project of reconstructing the lives, gender relations, and ideological constructions of families identified as Jewish, Christian, or pagan; whether they live in Rome, Asia Minor, Syria-Palestine or elsewhere. Future study will need to grapple with the points that families existed in plural sociological and social historical forms; that perceptions of "family" depend on who is perceiving, and on the social location and ideological conditions of the perceiver; that "family" is a cultural construction, often implicated in a web of all sorts of social and religious concerns; and that families are inextricably connected to gender relations.

With regard to Jewish families in Roman Palestine and as portrayed in early Rabbinic texts, I have suggested that a passage in m. Taᶜanit 4.8 works to secure new families to Israelite pasts and Jewish futures; and to

---

[68]While the intricacy of specific configurations of courtyards in *Erubin* seems more fantastic and reflective of Tannaitic imagination, I would argue that one generative problem was the desire and practice of families to dine together, and to produce and process the foods for these meals. In analyzing these texts by examining what they seem to assume, I am adopting a methodological tactic suggested by E.P. Sanders, *Jewish Law from Jesus to the Mishnah* (Philadelphia: Trinity Press International, 1990), especially ch. 3, "Did the Pharisees Eat Ordinary Food in Purity?"

[69]After my initial suggestion of this mode of inter-relationality to characterize families in Roman Palestine, I came across similar usages and descriptions in D. Oakman, *Jesus and the Economic Questions of His Day* (Lewiston, DE: Edwin Mellen, 1986), 23: "At the village level, there is sharing of common implements and labor between households on the basis of balanced reciprocity."

ensure Jewish futures specifically through the theology of families. This post-70 idea of family is endowed with theological force as families become part and parcel of new rabbinic visions. The rebuilding of the Jerusalem Temple, and all that this trope signifies in early rabbinic Judaism, becomes linked to the this-worldly perpetuation of Jewish families. Furthermore, the built environment of domestic architecture is another layer of evidence for, and of the ancient experience of, family. The use of this kind of evidence refocuses scholarly eyes on the commonplace realia of daily life in Jewish communities of late antiquity. As well, it serves doubly as evidence for another "text" that would have provided notions of family life. Domestic architecture and the artifacts of everyday life would have shaped understandings and definitions of family for Jewish inhabitants of Roman Palestine; for instance, class distinctions apparent in residential building would have indicated class and status differences among families. For the most part, these are meanings whose specificity is lost to modern interpreters; yet the existence of such meanings inherent in the 'texts of everyday life' must at least be acknowledged. Finally, amid arguments for the plurality and multiplicity of families, I have nonetheless chosen to emphasize the material and economic relations of families as an underpinning of family life. My argument for socio-economic interrelationality bypasses the more common but problematic application of the notions of public and private space to explain family life in late antiquity. This exchange of one framework for another should obscure fewer of the cultural dynamics of family and gender. At the same time, the accuracy of the description of interrelationality might have varied by class; we can speculate that a more affluent or higher status family, or a family that owned its own household tools, might participate differently in an economy of borrowing and trading than families more dependent on such an economy.[70]

This study has argued that the project of family studies is more complex than previously regarded. Broad references to "the Jewish family in late antiquity" generally contain more unexamined stereotype than arguable fact. "Family" is simultaneously a socio-economic and historical entity, a cultural idea, and more. The same families that

---

[70]Higher class and status seem to be major influences on the creation of notions of privacy and segregation of women in the Roman world (and the related effects of this on the organization and social construction of family life, as well as the identities of higher status families). Recognizing interrelationality and the lack of "privacy" as constituent features of life in Roman Palestine provides a new context for interpreting passages such as m.Ketubot 7.6, which seems then not to "reflect" notions about the privacy of the family/marital couple, but to build a performative argument for such a notion of privacy.

produce and distribute and consume the material needs of daily life also participate in, indeed are one focus of, the production and perpetuation of religious and cultural values. In sum, the categories we use to organize and study the evidence for families and "family" in late antiquity need to acknowledge the complexities of our subject. As Kaufman articulates so well in her study of modern Jewish families, we need to approach future studies of Jewish families and family in late antiquity with "analytic categories as complex as the lives people really live."[71]

---

[71]D.R. Kaufman, "Engendering Family Theory," 125.

Part Two

PARENTS, CHILDREN, AND SLAVES

2

Parents and Children in the Jewish Family of Antiquity

O. Larry Yarbrough

We have no idea what Amelius and Maria thought at the birth of their son. We can only imagine what they might have felt when he died two years, two months, and five days later. All we know is that they named the child after his father and that when they placed his body in one of the Jewish catacombs in the city of Rome, they described him as "a very sweet...innocent and pious child."[1] Perhaps the elder Amelius had hoped his son would follow in his footsteps and become archon of the synagogue.[2] Perhaps, too, he intended for his son to carry on the family business. If these were his dreams, however, they were shattered by the boy's early death.

About the same time, across the sea which the Romans boldly claimed as theirs, another father's dreams for his son were being shattered, though the circumstances were decidedly different. The families themselves were different, too. For whereas Amelius and his namesake were in all likelihood of modest means and limited prospects, this father, who also named his son after himself, was of considerable means and almost unlimited prospects.

---

[1] For the text and translation of the inscription (which is now lost), see H.J. Leon *The Jews of Ancient Rome* (Philadelphia: Jewish Publication Society, 1960), 264.

[2] Other parents had such hopes for their sons. The funerary inscription of Marcus Cvyntus Alexus, erected most likely by his parents, described the twelve-year-old as "Archon-to-be of the Augustesians." He had already attained the status of "scribe." (Leon, number 284, p 306).

The father was Alexander Lysimachus, alabarch of Alexandria.[3] As chief customs officer of Egypt's eastern border, Alexander had many opportunities to amass a fortune, and apparently took advantage of them. The Jewish historian Josephus indicates that Alexander "surpassed all his fellow citizens both in ancestry and in wealth,"[4] citing as evidence his loan of 200,000 drachmas to the Jewish King Agrippa[5] and his paying to have the nine gates of Jerusalem plated with silver and gold.[6] But Alexander's wealth and status did nothing to prevent his losing a son. Indeed, they may have contributed to it, for he lost his son not to death, but to the Romans.

It is impossible to say whether the son, Tiberius Iulius Alexander, formally apostasized or simply neglected the ways of his people[7] in order more readily to make his way in the Roman equestrian career he had chosen for himself. It is also impossible to say what the father may have thought of his son's career. Perhaps he viewed it with pride and even used his own position to help further that of his son.[8] But if Josephus is correct in stating that Alexander "was superior to his son...in his religious devotion,"[9] he may well have had regrets at the turn Tiberius' life had taken, even if he did not regard him as "lost."[10]

Whatever the father may have thought about his son's neglect of his religious heritage, there can be little doubt about what his uncle must have thought about it. For in one of his many treatises on the Jewish law, "uncle Philo" wrote that any one who rejected the ways of the fathers should be summarily executed without benefit of trial.[11] Philo was of

---

[3]On the duties of the alabarch, see *Encyclopedia Judaica* 2.507. Alexander also oversaw the Egyptian land holdings of the emperor Claudius' mother-in-law. See *Antiquities* 19.5.1 (276).

[4]*Antiquities* 20.5.2 (100). According to *Antiquities* 19.5.1 (276), Alexander was a friend of the emperor Claudius.

[5]At the behest of Agrippa's wife Cypros "because he marvelled at her love of her husband and all her other good qualities." *Antiquities* 18.6.3 (159-160).

[6]*War* 5.3 (203)

[7]Josephus reports that Tiberius "did not stand by the practices of his people." (*Antiquities* 20.5.2 (100), trans. Feldman).

[8]Even if Alexander did nothing to help his son's career, his status (and contacts) doubtless provided opportunities which would otherwise have been unavailable.

[9]*Antiquities* 20.5.2 (100).

[10]During one of the riots in Alexandria, the Jews refused to listen to Tiberius, who was then prefect of Egypt, suggesting that he was not held in regard by the populace. See Josephus, *War* 2.18.7 (492-493).

[11]*Spec. Leg.* 1, 54-56. See also 1, 315-318, where Philo writes, "But as for these kinships, as we call them, which have come down from our ancestors and are based on blood-relationship, or those derived from intermarriage or other similar causes, let them all be cast aside if they do not seek earnestly the same goal,

course in no position to do anything about his nephew's actions – the Roman authorities would never have allowed so promising an officer to be dispatched on such trivial grounds. But Tiberius' career must have caused him deep pain and embarrassment.

There was, however, a poignancy to Philo's pain beyond what he might have felt as a "defender of the faith." It derived from the fact that Philo, more than any single Jewish writer of antiquity, wrote of the obligations parents had in the rearing of their children and of the responsibilities children had toward their parents. He must have wondered what had gone wrong in the family of his own brother.[12]

Philo, however, was not the first Jewish writer to treat the obligations parents owe to their children and the responsibilities children have toward their parents. The two themes can be found in the earliest strata of Israelite law and lore. It is not possible for us to trace here how and why they became a part of these traditions. It is enough to survey them in the forms in which they would have been known to Amelius, Alexander and their namesakes. Moreover, we cannot limit ourselves to, or even focus on, the traditions of the Bible, for these traditions were developed and expanded by many different writers both in the Jewish homeland and scattered throughout the diaspora. Still, we must begin with the Biblical material, for it formed the basis of later discussions. We look first at the obligations parents owed to their children and then turn to those children owed their parents.

I. Parents' Obligations to their Children

Before examining specific obligations parents owe to their children, we should note that having children was itself an obligation, derived from the commandment to "be fruitful and multiply" in Gen 1:28. The question of when and how one had fulfilled it and on whom the obligation rested was a matter of debate. The general consensus appears to have been that the requirement to be fruitful and multiply was for men only, though this interpretation was challenged by Johanan ben Baroka (120-140 CE).[13] To fulfill the commandment to be fruitful and multiply the rabbis decreed that a man must have two children. Here the

---

namely, the honour of God, which is the indissoluble bond of all the affections which makes us one." Trans. Colson, Loeb edition.

12The metaphor of the family is an important one for Philo, evidenced by his reference to some aspect of it in almost all of his treatises. I hope to treat this in a separate essay. [See also the essay by Adele Reinhartz in this volume].

13He notes the commandment in Gen 1:28 is addressed to "them." The discussion treated in this paragraph is found in *m. Yebam.* 6.6. See also *m. Ed.* 1.13 which cites Is 45:18.

debate was whether he must have two sons (the school of Shammai) or a son and a daughter (the school of Hillel).[14]

The Talmud identifies three commandments in the Torah delineating obligations parents owe to their children.[15] The father should redeem his son,[16] circumcise him,[17] and teach him the commandments.[18] The first of these pertains to the firstborn only; the others to all male children. Outside of rabbinic literature the obligation to redeem the firstborn and to circumcise male children receives little attention.[19] But if the first two obligations do not receive much attention, the last one certainly does.[20] Usually the emphasis is on what a father teaches his son, though there are indications that a mother or grandmother would provide instruction.[21] And on occasion there are indications that a daughter would be taught the commandments as well.[22]

The home was the setting for the earliest education, and, as *M. Pesah* 10.4 indicates, festivals must have been one of the primary occasions when children were taught – both by instruction and observation. The mishnah states that at the mixing of the second cup during the passover celebration,

> the son asks his father (and if the son has not enough understanding his father instructs him [how to ask]), 'Why is this night different from other nights? For on the other nights we eat seasoned food once, but this night twice; on other nights we eat leavened or unleavened bread, but this night all is unleavened; on other nights we eat flesh roast, stewed, or cooked, but this night all is roast'. And according to the understanding of the son his father

---

[14]If a couple had no children after ten years, the husband was still obligated to seek to fulfill the commandment, either by continuing to have sexual intercourse or divorcing his wife and marrying another. If she remarried, the second husband was allotted ten years also.

[15]*B. Qidd* 29a.

[16]Ex 22:29b.

[17]Lev 12:1-8.

[18]Deut 4:9, 6:7, and 31:12-13.

[19]I am not aware of any reference to the redemption of the first-born outside of rabbinic literature. References to circumcision as a paternal obligation are few. See, for example, Jub 20:3 where it is an obligation Abraham places on Ishmael, Isaac, Keturah and their children. In 4 Macc 4:25 there is a reference to mothers' being thrown from city walls along with their infants who had been circumcised.

[20]In all literary traditions – the Bible, the apocrypha, the pseudepigrapha, Josephus, Philo, and rabbinic literature.

[21]Prov 6:20-21 is illustrative of the mother's role in providing instruction; Tob 1:7b-8 refers to Tobit's grandmother Deborah teaching him since he was left an orphan by his father.

[22]See *Susannah* 3. See the debate regarding the advisability of teaching a daughter in *m. Sota* 3.4.

> instructs him. He begins with the disgrace and ends with the glory; and he expounds from *A wandering Aramean was my father*...until he finishes the whole section.[23]

Here in the home, therefore, children first learn the decisive stories which shaped the Jewish community. The directive to the father to adapt the story to his son's ability to understand is noteworthy . Similar advice is given in the instructions for the Day of Atonement. *M. Yoma* 8.4 indicates that although children are exempt from the fast set for this day, parents should exercise their children in it one or two years before they are of an age to participate fully, "that they may be versed in the commandments."[24] According to *m. Berakot* 3.3 children, although exempt from reciting the Shema and from wearing phylacteries, were required to recite the Tefillah and the Benediction after meals and to observe the law of the Mezuzah.

Typically, admonitions to teach a child are very general, as in the well-known saying "Train up a child in the way he should go, and when he is old he will not depart from it."[25] Prov 4:1-4 is more expansive. But, though it does tell us that instruction begins when the child is quite young, it says little about what "precepts" were to be taught :

> Hear, O sons, a father's instruction, and be attentive, that you may gain insight; for I give you good precepts: do not forsake my teaching. When I was a son with my father, tender, the only one in the sight of my mother, he taught me, and said to me, 'Let your heart hold fast my words; keep my commandments, and live; do not forget, and do not turn away from the words of my mouth. Get wisdom; get insight.

Tobit 4 appears to provide some clues regarding what a father would actually teach his son. Given in the form of a father's blessing before he sends his son off to obtain a wife, the passage lists a number of admonitions concerning everything from honoring his mother (vv 3-4) to giving alms (v 7) to blessing the Lord God on every occasion (v 19). But in reality this is more a literary topos than a reflection of life. Like the numerous other examples of the topos (from Genesis 49 to the *Testament*

---

[23]Trans. Danby.

[24]*M. Suk* 3.15 offers similar advice with regard to the shaking of the *Lulab*. According to *b. Ketubot* 50a a boy was ready to observe a 24-hour fast at the age of 13, a girl at the age of 12.

[25]Prov 22:6. (Unless otherwise indicated, all quotations are to the RSV.) Here there is no indication of what is to be taught, though the whole collection of proverbial sayings addresses this. Sirach provides numerous examples of this kind of admonition. The wisdom psalms provide a link between proverbial wisdom and the commandments. In *b. Qidd.* 30a, Prov 22:6 is taken as a reference to obtaining a wife for one's son.

of the Twelve Patriarchs), it provides occasion to rehearse general ethical teaching. Still, the issues treated in these blessings reflect the morality that must have been taught to the young.

At first glance, 4 Macc 18:10-19 provides just the information we are seeking. In this passage the mother of the seven sons about to be martyred reminds them of their father:

> He, while he was still with you, taught you the Law and the Prophets. He read to you of Abel, slain by Cain, of Isaac, offered as a burnt-offering, and of Joseph, in prison. He spoke to you of the zeal of Phineas, and taught you about Hananiah, Azariah, and Mishael in the fire. He sang the praises of Daniel in the lion's den and called him blessed. He reminded you of the scripture of Isaiah which says, Even though you walk through the fire, the flame shall not burn you. He sang to you the psalm of David which says, Many are the afflictions of the righteous. He recited the proverb of Solomon which says, He is a tree of life to those who do his will. He affirmed the word of Ezekiel, Shall these dry bones live? Nor did he forget the song that Moses taught which says, I kill and I make alive, for this is your life and the length of your days."[26]

This list of stories, psalms, and proverbs can hardly have been typical, however, reflecting as it does the extraordinary circumstances of 4 Maccabees – a call to faithfulness in the face of persecution. But in all likelihood the passage is reflective of *how* a father would teach his children and *what kinds of things* he taught: He would *teach* "the law and the prophets," *read* stories about biblical heroes, *sing* psalms, and *recite* proverbs.

At what age the father would begin to teach his children and for how long is difficult to determine. Philo claims that Jewish parents taught their children to acknowledge the one God from the time they were in swaddling clothes.[27] It appears that for the later rabbis a child was ready to study scripture at age 6 and Mishnah at age 12.[28] This discussion, however, focuses on the age at which a son was to be committed to the care of a teacher, so that the issue is one of a father's providing for his

---

[26]Trans. Anderson, in J.H. Charlesworth *The Old Testament Pseudepigrapha* 2.

[27]*Embassy to Gaius* 115. See also 210, "For all men guard their own customs, but this is especially true of the Jewish nation. Holding that the laws are oracles vouchsafed by God and having been trained in this doctrine from their earliest years (ἐκ πρώτης ἡλικίας), they carry the likenesses of the commandments enshrined in their souls." (Trans. Colson, Loeb ed.) Josephus (*Against Apion* 2.18) echoes this, claiming that Jews begin to learn their Law as soon as they are able to understand anything (ἀπὸ τῆς πρώτης αἰσθήσεως).

[28]B. *Ketubot* 50a. See also *m. Abot* 5.21, where the ages of 5 and 10 are given as appropriate for the study of scripture and mishnah respectively. There is some question about the date and source of the passage.

son's education and not teaching him himself.[29] Before schools were established and where they did not exist, we should probably assume that these were also the ages at which education in the commandments began. There is no explicit evidence for this, but since the rabbis' determination of the appropriate age to begin a child's education was based, in part at least, on the advice given by a nurse who had raised one of them, it must have been a widely held opinion based on practical observations.[30]

Although most of the treatments of what a child was to be taught emphasize the commandments and moral education, other matters are mentioned from time to time. As noted above, the rabbis considered it a paternal obligation to teach a son a trade.[31] The author of *Jubilees* repeatedly mentions that the patriarchs taught their sons writing.[32] An admonition to teach one's children writing also appears in *T. Levi* 13:2. In *Jubilees* no explicit reason for teaching writing is given; in the *Testament of Levi*, however, children are to be taught so that they may ceaselessly study Torah.

Apart from any reference to educational content, parents were to discipline their children. This shows up especially in Proverbs[33] and Sirach,[34] in both of which corporal punishment is the primary means of discipline. The REB translation of Proverbs 22:15 captures the spirit well: "Folly is deep-rooted in the hearts of children; a good beating will drive it out of them." As a corollary of this dictum, the child should not be spoiled or pampered. Indeed, one should not even laugh with a child.[35] The most often cited reason for this insistence on disciplining children is

---

[29]The relation between a young man and his father and teacher becomes the topic of debate in *m. B. Mes* 2.11 and *B. Qidd.* 32b.

[30]*B. Qidd* 50a. Abbayye, a fourth generation amoraic scholar, was raised by a nurse, his mother having died in childbirth. In addition to learning from her the appropriate age for teaching children, he learned such things as what to do for scorpion bites and bee stings.

[31]They also discussed at some length relative merits of various trades.

[32]8:2; 11:16; 19:14. The last reference is especially interesting since it indicates that while Jacob learned to write Esau did not "because he was a rustic man and a hunter." The ability to read and write, therefore, was a means to distinguish between the rustic and the refined. In 8:2, learning to write appears to be associated with urban life.

[33]13:24; 19:18; 22:15; 23:13-14; 29:17.

[34]7:23-25; 22:3-6; 22:9-10; 26:10-12; 30:1-13; 42:9-11.

[35]Sirach 30:1-13.

that they are a reflection of their parents, so that "it is a disgrace to be the father of an undisciplined son."[36]

Such comments are balanced somewhat by others which speak of the joy of children. Ps 127, for example, refers to sons as "a heritage from the Lord," and compares them to "arrows in the hand of a warrior," concluding that the man who has a quiver full of them is happy. Similarly, one of the nine thoughts which gladdens the heart of Jesus ben Sirach is "a man rejoicing in his children."[37] He also advises the householder not to be a "lion" in his own house.[38] It is in Pseudo-Phocylides, however, that one finds explicit warnings about too heavy a hand in the disciplining of one's children. "Do not be harsh with your children," the author advises, "but be gentle." Indeed, to insure good relations between a father and his children, he adds that when a child offends against the father, he should let the mother, the elders of the family, or the chiefs of the people administer punishment.[39]

There were, of course, other obligations which parents performed for their children. Obviously, they fed and clothed them.[40] According to the author of the *Letter of Aristeas*, to fail to do so was the worst type of neglect.[41] For the rabbis, too, providing maintenance for one's children was important. But since there was no law mandating it, they spoke of it as a moral duty and not a legal obligation.[42] The passage from *b. Qidd* which listed the obligations mentioned in the Torah discusses two others drawn from the scriptures. From Jer 29:6 the rabbis decreed that a man should obtain a wife for his son and from Eccl. 9:9 that he should teach him a trade.[43] Some rabbis argued for a sixth obligation – teaching a son to swim. No scriptural support for this responsibility is adduced. The comment is simply made that "his life might depend on it."[44]

---

[36]Sirach 22:3. See also 42:11, "Keep strict watch over a headstrong daughter, lest she make you a laughingstock to your enemies, a byword in the city and notorious among the people, and put you to shame before the great multitude."

[37]25:7.

[38]4:30.

[39]207-209.

[40]Nursing an infant was seen as an obligation a wife owed her husband. See *m. Ned.* 5.5. According to *m. Git* 7.6, children were weaned between the 18th and 24th month.

[41]248.

[42]*B. Ketubot* 49ab. If *m. B. Qam* 10.1 refers to a specific case (a father's stealing to feed his children), it shows the lengths to which some were forced to go to fulfill this moral obligation. The passage also indicates that a certain leniency obtained in such events, since the children were not obligated to make restitution for what was stolen, unless it was mortgaged property.

[43]There were extended discussions about which trades were most appropriate.

[44]*B. Qidd.* 30b.

The education and training of children also took place outside the home. Though most of our knowledge of schools comes from a later period, there are indications that they existed at the end of the Second Temple period.[45] It is beyond the scope of this essay to discuss these schools, however, except to note that the obligation to teach a son Torah came to include sending him to school or otherwise providing him with a tutor.

We must also limit treatment of the place of children in the synagogue and the Temple, though for a different reason – there is precious little evidence even to speculate on it. According to Deut 31:12 young children (*taf*) were to be assembled along with the men and women to hear the law. It is not clear, however, precisely how this was carried out. With regard to services in the temple, *m. Hag* 1.1 indicates that all male children who can ride on their father's shoulders or hold his hand as they walk up to the Temple Mount were obligated to attend the three great festivals.[46] Though the passage does not explicitly say so, it is clear that the father bore responsibility for seeing that his son fulfilled this duty. Aside from the festivals, however, minors were apparently not allowed to enter the Temple court, except when the Levites were singing. On such occasions, moreover, they were not permitted to play instruments but only to sing – "to add spice to the music."[47]

There appears to have been greater latitude with regard to synagogue services. According to *m. Meg* 4.5-6 a boy who was not of age could read the Torah and give an interpretation but could not recite the Shema and Benedictions. His father (or teacher) went before the Ark to lead the prayers on his behalf. The performance, therefore, was as much for the father as the son and in most instances must have been a source of pride for the boy's parents. Indeed, if the Jewish inscriptions in Rome which refer to young children holding offices in the synagogues are an indication that at least some positions were passed down within a family and if, as seems likely, the families in which this was the case held special status within the congregation, to allow a minor to read would have been

---

[45]*Y. Meg* 3, 73d. *B. B. Bat* 21a refers to a time when children learned from their fathers or not at all, then a time when the father would take his son to Jerusalem to study, and finally to the time when Joshua ben Gamala (high priest from 63-65 CE) decreed that every town should establish a school. There are several detailed treatments of education. See, for example, F.H. Swift, *Education in Ancient Israel from Earliest Times to the Year 500*; N. Drazin, *History of Jewish Education from 515 B.C.E. to 226 C.E.* For an overview, see S. Safrai in *The Jewish People in the First Century* (Philadelphia, Fortress, 1976) 2, 945-970.

[46]The two definitions belong to the schools of Shammai and Hillel respectively.

[47]See *m. Arak* 2.6.

a way of honoring the parents and ensuring their continued beneficence toward the synagogue.

In most instances, however, children in the synagogue were probably to be seen and not heard. Indeed, there seems to have been some question about why one should bring children to the synagogue at all. Commenting on Deut 31:12, R. Eleazar ben Azariah (ca 90-130 CE) noted that men came to learn and women to hear, but wondered what the children were there for. He concluded that it was not for their own benefit but "to acquire a reward for those who bring them."[48] Just what the reward was, however, he does not say.

Now, what are we to make of all this? First, in almost all the sources treating the obligations parents owe their children the emphasis is clearly on moral and religious education. Training a child in the way he should go meant teaching him the scriptures, the law, and the moral code which defined him as a Jew. It also meant providing him with a trade by which to support himself (and, as we shall see later, to support his parents in their old age). This training began when the child was quite young and lasted until marriage, the point at which the tables were turned and the emphasis is placed on what children owe their parents rather than what parents owe their children. Even while in their parent's household, however, the children were hardly to be the focus of the family's attention. Children were there for the parents, not the parents for the children. To be sure, children might be a source of joy for the parents, but they were always to be reminded of their proper place. They were to be disciplined and kept at a distance, especially by the father. For children were a reflection of their parents, so that "bad" children reflected poorly on their parents, "good" children reflected well on them.

Such at least was the "ideal." What of the reality? Unfortunately, we have little evidence to form an opinion. Our writers tell us only of what they thought a child should be taught, not of what they actually were; they tell us of how a child ought to behave, not how they actually did. In pious households where the father was himself educated in the law, children were no doubt given explicit instruction, being told not simply what to do but why. After all, the father was reminded of his obligation to teach his children twice daily when he recited the Shema.[49] He would certainly have been attentive to his duty during the celebration of Passover, but may well have been equally involved in teaching his younger children to recite the prayers required of them and to learn to observe the law of the Mezuzah. In less observant households, especially those in which the father (and in many households the mother as well)

---

[48]*T. Sota* 7,9. Cited in George Foot Moore, *Judaism* 1, 315.
[49]I am grateful to my colleague Robert Schine for pointing this out to me.

was forced to work long hours to support the family, there would have been less time to devote to matters of moral and religious instruction and perhaps insufficient means to provide for study outside the home. In such households children would have learned only the rudiments, if anything at all.[50] At the same time, however, there were doubtless poor households for which the training of children was of prime importance, requiring great sacrifice on behalf of the parents. And there were surely wealthy households in which the moral and religious education of children was neglected so that parents could pursue their own interests and welfare.

Geography must have played a role as well. The literature we have examined is reflective of values obtaining in the Jewish homeland and the diaspora. So it is legitimate to speak of a Jewish perspective on the raising of children. But there must certainly have been differences between households in Judea and those in the cities of the Greco-Roman world. If nothing else, it would have been difficult for the poorer families in Rome, Alexandria, or any other of the major cities in which there existed a Jewish community for families to make a pilgrimage to Jerusalem so that a father might carry a young son on his shoulders up the Temple mount to celebrate one of the festivals.

Still, the very survival of Judaism throughout the Greco-Roman world is evidence enough that many Jewish parents took their obligations seriously. Like the father in 4 Maccabees they taught their children the law and the prophets, read them stories of biblical heroes, sang to them from the psalms, and recited proverbs. Perhaps this is what Amelius would have done had his son not died so young. Very likely, it is what Alexander did for his before he came under the influence of the Roman army. But if Alexander was unsuccessful in training his son in the way he should go, other parents, like those whose names appear on the inscriptions of the catacombs in Rome, were successful. And to no small degree, it is due to the efforts of such parents that Judaism survived.

II. Children's Obligations to Parents

In all the literature under examination, children's obligations to their parents may be subsumed under one commandment, "Honor your father and mother." The commandment first appears in Ex 20:12 and is

---

[50]Rabbi Akiba was said to come from a poor family and had no time to study as a child. See "Education and the Study of Torah" in S. Safrai and M. Stern (eds.) *The Jewish People in the First Century* 2, 949.

repeated, in slightly different form, in Deut 5:16 and Lev 19:3a.[51] In later writings the commandment to honor one's parents becomes a commonplace. Sirach 3:2, for example, declares that "the Lord honored the father above the children, and he confirmed the right of the mother over her sons," so that whoever honors his father and mother "atones for sins," "is like one who lays up treasure," "will be gladdened by his own children," "will be heard when he prays," and "will have long life."[52]

In Philo we find justification for the commandment: children are to honor parents because they share in the immortal act of creation,[53] stand in relation to children as rulers to ruled,[54] and provide numerous benefits.[55] Consequently, Philo argues, parents are to be honored second only to God,[56] a judgment which is shared by Josephus for much the same reason.[57]

With regard to how children are to honor their parents, Sirach informs us that it should be "in word and deed" (3:8). The examples he cites are helping a father in his old age (v 12) and showing forbearance if he is lacking in understanding (v 13). For Philo one honors one's parents by "trying both to be good and to seem good" (πειρώμενος ἀγαθός τε εἶναι καὶ δοκεῖν εἶναι), by showing courtesy to others of their generation,[58] and by "repaying the debt" (ἀνταποδιδόντες) they owe for the benefits they have received, which Philo interprets to mean taking care of one's parents in

---

[51]In Leviticus the verb is *yr'* (LXX φοβεῖσθω), which the RSV translates "revere." Commentators note that in Leviticus the mother is mentioned before the father, which was taken to mean that both were to be treated equally. *Pseudo-Philo* 11:9 paraphrases the commandment: "Love your father and your mother, and you shall honor them, and then your light will rise. And I will command the heaven, and it will give forth its rain, and the earth will give back fruit more quickly. And you will live many days and dwell in your land, and you will not be without sons, for your seed will not be lacking in people to dwell in it." (Trans. Harrington in *Old Testament Pseudepigrapha* 2.)

[52]*Sir* 3:3-7. See also 7:27 and *Ep Arist* 228. *Tob* 4:3-4 speaks of honoring one's mother.

[53]*Dec* 107 and *Spec Leg* 2.225-228.

[54]*Spec Leg* 2.226. On this see Balch, *Let Wives be Submissive*, chap 4.

[55]*Dec* 113-119 and *Spec Leg* 2.229-232.

[56]*Spec Leg* 2.235. He is apparently quoting here one of the "bolder spirits" (εὐτολμότεροι) to which he had referred in *Dec* 120. The reference is most likely to one of the Hellenistic moralists such as Hierocles, on whom see below.

[57]*Against Apion* 2.206. Interestingly enough, in *Mekilta de Rabbi Ishmael* (on Ex 20:12-14) the honor due to parents is *equal* to that due to God. This conclusion is drawn by comparing passages which speak of honoring, fearing and cursing parents and God (Ex 20:12 and Prov 3:9; Lev 19:3 and Deut 6:13; Ex 21:17 and Lev 24:17). In the Lauterbach edition (Philadelphia: Jewish Publication Society, 1933), see vol 2, 257-258.

[58]*Special Laws* 2.235 and 237.

their old age.[59] B. *Qidd* 31b is even more specific with regard to this last concern, stipulating that a son should honor his aged father by providing him with food, clothing, and shelter, and by escorting him when he goes out.

Closely related to the commandment to honor one's parents was the obligation to obey them. Consideration of this theme must begin with Deut 21:18-21, a legal discussion of the obedience children owe their parents:

> If a man has a stubborn and rebellious son, who will not obey (*sm^c*; LXX ὑπακούων) the voice of his father or the voice of his mother, and, though they chastise him, will not give heed to them, then his father and his mother shall take hold of him and bring him out to the elders of his city at the gate of the place where he lives, and they shall say to the elders of his city, 'This our son is stubborn and rebellious, he will not obey our voice; he is a glutton and a drunkard.' Then all the men of the city shall stone him to death with stones; so you shall purge the evil from your midst; and all Israel shall hear, and fear.

M. Sanh 8:1-5 indicates that the severity of this punishment was problematic for the sages and led them to regulate its enactment carefully. They ruled, for example, that the law did not apply to minors, that there could be mitigating circumstances should drunkenness be a factor in the son's behavior, that both parents must make the accusation, that the son must first be warned and punished by flogging, and that only when he continued to behave "evilly" could the capital punishment be administered. Indeed, it may well be, as Moore suggests, that the law requiring death to a son who rebels against his parents was not even in practice during the time under consideration and that the rabbis' discussion was meant only "to impress God's abhorrence of the abuse of parents."[60] Whatever the case with regard to the rabbis, Philo considered capital punishment preferable to cutting off the hand of one who assaults, disabuses, or dishonors his parents, since cutting off the hand of the offender renders him helpless and consequently at the mercy of his parents, so that the insult to them is only compounded, since they have to take care of the very one who offended them.[61]

Concern with a child's obligation to obey his or her parents is a major theme in the wisdom tradition. Indeed, it can be said to undergird the whole corpus, for throughout it admonitions are presented as if from a father to his children. But especially to the point here are the

---

[59]*Decalogue* 117. Animals provide the model for Philo here.
[60]*Judaism* 2, 135.
[61]*Special Laws* 2, 247-248. Philo, as apparently the rabbis too, appears to conflate Deut 27:16, Ex 21:15, and Lev 20:9.

admonitions explicitly referring to obeying one's parents.[62] Thus, for example, Prov 1:8 admonishes:

> Hear, my son, your father's instruction, and reject not your mother's teaching.

The same admonition appears in 6:20 as:

> My son, keep your father's commandment and forsake not your mother's teaching...[63]

In the *Testaments of the Twelve Patriarchs*, which, like the wisdom traditions, takes the form of a father's advice to his children, we also find admonitions to obey the father commands.[64] Outside of the rabbinic corpus, however, it is in 4 Maccabees that we find the most extensive reflection on the requirement to obey one's parents.[65] Here we have consideration of the extent to which a child is obligated to obey a parent. "The law prevails even over affection for parents," the author states in 2:10, "so that virtue (ἀρετή) is not abandoned for their sakes." The premise of this statement is clear: Obedience to the law takes precedence over obedience to parents. From it we may conclude that if a parent bids a child to do something which is against one of the commandments, the child is under no obligation to obey the parent. What is most striking about the discussion here in 4 Maccabees is that "reason" (ὁ λογισμός) is the determining factor, since "reason rules the emotions" (τῶν παθῶν ἐστιν ὁ λογισμὸς κρατῶν).[66] For the author of 4 Maccabees, that is, just as reason rules over pleasure and pain (1:20), so it rules over human relations.[67]

When the rabbis debated the extent to which one should obey one's parents, the deciding factor was not reason but the unconditionality of one's obedience to God. Thus, if a parent requests something which it is

---

[62]As in Deuteronomy 21:18 the Hebrew idiom used in these admonitions refers to "hearing" (or "giving heed to") the words (instructions, commandments, etc.) of the father or mother.

[63]See, for example, Prov 10:1; 13:1; 15:5, 20.

[64]See, for example, *T. Reuben* 4:5 "So then, my children, observe all the things that I command you" and *T. Issachar* 4:1 "Now, listen to me, children, and live in integrity of heart, for in it I have observed everything that is pleasing to the Lord." (Trans. Kee in *The Old Testament Pseudepigrapha* 1).

[65]4 Maccabees is usually dated to the first century C.E.

[66]The discussion of reason, which begins in 1:13, is concerned with "what reason is and what emotion is, how many kinds of emotions there are and whether reason rules over all these" (v 14).

[67]In addition to ruling over a child's relations with its parents, reason also rules over a husband's relations with his wife, a father's with his children, and over relations between friends (2:11-13).

not lawful to do, one disregards the request.[68] Even so, however, the commandment to honor one's father and mother demands that one refuse an improper request or point out its impropriety with appropriate humility.[69]

From these examples, it is clear that the commandment to honor one's parents, and thus the discussions of obligations children owe their parents, is addressed not to young children but to adults.

III. The Jewish Family in Greco-Roman Society

Our final consideration in this survey of the obligations parents owe their children and children owe their parents is the extent to which they may have distinguished Jewish families from others in the society around them. Here, too, we must limit our observations primarily to literary treatments of the themes and thus will describe the ideal rather than the real. But this in itself should be enlightening.

In almost every instance, the Hellenistic moralists provide parallels to the discussion of honoring one's parents found in Jewish literature. The neo-Pythagorean Pempelus is exemplary in numerous ways. In his treatise "On Parents," which is based on Plato's *Laws* 931, Pempelus speaks of honoring one's parents as demanded not only by nature but also by the Gods. Thus, if one does not honor one's parents one's prayers are not heard.[70] Pempelus also argues that honor is due to one's parents because they have given life and benefits and that these benefits should be repaid in both word and deed, especially when parents are aged.[71] The Stoic Hierocles[72] provides a list of the benefits one is to repay to one's parents which includes all the things in the list found in *Mekilta de Rabbi Ishmael:* food, a bed, clothing, and accompaniment when they go out.[73]

Like Philo and Josephus, Hierocles is also concerned with the proper ordering of the honors due to the Gods and to one's parents. He differs from them, however, in arguing that to honor one's parents ranks third, coming after the honor due to the God's and the honor owed to one's country. Nonetheless, Hierocles states that "[h]e...will not err who says,

---

[68]Examples in *m. B. Mes* 2.10, *b. Yebam.* 5b-6a.

[69]*B. Qidd.* 32a end.

[70]See Plato *Laws 931* C. Compare *Sir* 3:5.

[71]See above on *Sirach*, Philo, and Josephus.

[72]Second century C.E.

[73]*After what manner we ought to conduct ourselves towards our parents* 86-87 in the Taylor edition (Thomas Taylor, *Political Fragments of Archytas, Charondas, Zaleucus and Other Ancient Pythagoreans Preserved by Stobaeus and also Ethical Fragments of Hierocles* [London: C. Whittingham, 1822], 86-87).

that [parents] are certain secondary and terrestrial Gods" and that parents are "[the] most stable images of the Gods," since "they are the guardian Gods of the house."[74] More like Philo and Josephus in this regard is Aristoxenus the Tarentine, who argues that "after divinity and demons, the greatest attention should be paid to parents."[75] We need not resort to such lesser lights in the constellation of Greco-Roman moralists to establish the view that parents are to be honored like the Gods, however, for no less a person than Plato spoke of parents as "images" (εἰκόνα) of the Gods, declaring that nothing is more worthy of honor than they are.[76] Thus, it is not surprising that in numerous lists of maxims, one governing honor due to parents follows immediately upon the maxim ordaining the honoring of the Gods.[77]

Many of the same parallels between Jewish and Hellenistic moral literature can be found in descriptions of children's obligation to obey their parents. The evidence is plentiful, for as Aulus Gellius[78] informs us, "whether a father should always be obeyed, whatever the nature of his commands" *(an semper inque omnibus iussis patri parendum sit)* was a frequent topic of debate among both Greek and Roman philosophers.[79]

Gellius identifies three responses to the question:

> The first is, that all *(omnia)* a father's commands must be obeyed *(parendum)*; the second, that in some he is to be obeyed, in others not; the third, that it is not necessary to yield to and obey one's father in anything.[80]

The last opinion Gellius dismisses as "altogether shameful" *(nimis infamis)*, since the reasoning behind it is "both silly and foolish" *(frivola et inanis)*.[81] He rejects the first also, since fathers do sometimes command their children to do wrong.[82] The "intermediate way" *(media sententia)*, he concludes, is "the best and safest" *(optima atque tutissima)*, warning, however, that when a father commands one do something wrong, he

---

[74]Taylor 84-85.
[75]Taylor 65. Aristoxenus (born ca 370 B.C.E.) was a pupil of the Pythagorean Xenophilus and later of Aristotle.
[76]*Laws* 931A and DE.
[77]See, for example, Isocrates *To Demonicus* 13-14, and 16; ps. – Plutarch *The Education of Children* 10 (*Moralia* 7E).
[78]Ca 123-169 C.E.
[79]*Attic Nights* 2.7.1. Trans. Rolfe. Loeb edition.
[80]2.7.4-5.
[81]2.7.6-10. If a father commands one to do wrong, he should not be obeyed; if he commands one to do right, one does not obey because it is a *command*, but because it is *right*. Although Gellius regards this argument as a "mere quibble" *(argutiola quippe)*, it is the only one he discusses at length.
[82]2.7.11-12.

must be denied "gently and respectfully, without excessive aversion or bitter recrimination" *(leniter et verecunde ac sine detestatione nimia sineque obprobratione acerba reprehensionis).*[83]

Others, however, were not so quick to dismiss the claim that one should obey one's father in all things. Epictetus, for example, declared that one of the duties (τὰ καθήκοντα) required of those who pursue the philosophic life was "to give way [to one's father] in all things" (παραχωρεῖν ἀπάντων) and "to submit when he reviles or strikes you." This, Epictetus continues, was an obligation owed to all fathers regardless of their moral qualities, since "nature" (φύσις) gives one a father without making him either good or bad.[84]

The Neopythagoreans spell the argument out even further. Perictyone, for example, states that one should obey one's parents "whether their rank in life is small or great"; that one should "never oppose them in any thing they may say or do"; and that one should "submit to them even when they are insane." Such, he observes, is the conduct of those who are "pious."[85]

The most extensive treatment of Gellius' "intermediate way" of addressing the question of obedience is Musonius Rufus' treatise *Must One Obey One's Parents Under All Circumstances?* (Εἰ πάντα πειστέον τοῖς γονεῦσιν).[86] The question which appears in the title of this work was put to Musonius by a young man whose father forbade him to study philosophy. In his response, Musonius argues that while obedience (πείθεσθαι) to one's mother and father must be reckoned as "good" (καλόν),[87] it is not disobedient to refuse to do something "wrong or unjust or shameful" (κακὰ ἢ ἄδικα ἢ αἰσχρά).[88] One is disobedient only if one "refuses to carry out good and honorable and useful orders" (εὖ καὶ καλῶς καὶ συμφερόντως).[89] Obedience, however, is not simply obeying orders to do good, Musonius continues, for since parents desire what is

---

[83]2.7.13.

[84]*Encheiridion* 30. Trans.. Oldfather, Loeb edition.

[85]From the treatise *On the Harmony of a Woman* (145.7ff Thesleff. Trans. Taylor, *Ethical Fragments* 63-64). See also Aristoxenus' comment: "When parents, therefore, are angry, it is requisite to yield to them, and to appease their anger, whether it is shown in words or in deeds." (*On the Reverence Due to Parents* 4. Trans. Taylor, *Ethical Fragments* 66).

[86]Text and Translation in Cora E. Lutz *Musonius Rufus: "The Roman Socrates"* (New Haven: Yale, 1947) 100-107. References are to page and line of the Greek text of this edition.

[87]100,23-24.

[88]102,15. Musonius gives the example of a "money-loving" father ordering his son to steal.

[89]102,17-18.

good for their children, obedience is really a matter of doing good whether the parents command it or not.[90] In turning directly to the issue at hand – whether the young man is to disobey his father and take up the study of philosophy – Musonius raises a further consideration. Children owe obedience not only to their own fathers, but also to Zeus, "the common father of all men and gods" (ὁ κοινὸς ἁπάντων πατὴρ ἀνθρώπων τε καὶ θεῶν).[91] And it is to this father, Musonius declares, that one owes the greater allegiance. Thus, he tells his inquirer, "If you obey your father, you will follow the will (μέλλεις) of a man; if you choose the philosopher's life, the will of God."

Now, these treatments of honoring and obeying one's parents are wide-ranging. With regard to some, we can detect clear cultural, if not literary, dependence. Josephus and Philo, for example, were certainly aware of the moralists' treatment of the theme and were probably dependent on specific treatises addressing it. But what can we make of the requirement that children honor their parents found in Exodus and Plato? Neither is dependent on the other. They were both concerned with creating an "ideal" legal system, but in this particular case we probably have to do with nothing more than what must be an almost universal component of morality and culture.[92] Similarly, in the Jewish wisdom traditions, in Epictetus, and in Musonius, honoring and obeying one's parents are discussed in terms of what is "wise" and "good," so that to honor and obey one's parents is one of the virtues characteristic of the life of the wiseman and the philosopher. But here again, the connections between the traditions which they represent are loose.

Our concern in looking at these examples from the Hellenistic moral literature has not been to determine whether there was formal or literary dependence in either direction, however, but to determine the extent to which the Jewish descriptions of family life may have been a distinguishing feature of Jewish life. For the most part, we must conclude that Jewish families were not distinctive, at least with regard to the ideal. For both Jewish and Hellenistic moralists argued that parents had obligations to their children and children to their parents. And the similarities on both scores are striking.

To mention these similarities is not to diminish the strong sense of family that obtained in the social worlds of Judaism. It is simply to say that the Jewish emphasis on the obligations parents owed to children and children owed to parents was part and parcel of the ancient world. There

---

[90]102,27-37.

[91]104,31.

[92]Plato in fact refers to the claim of parents to rule over their children as "universally just" (*Laws* 627A).

may well have been differences in the ways the ideal was brought to reality. But we have few sources for testing this thesis. This is one of the areas in which more work on the family in antiquity needs to be done.

Indeed, because of the introductory nature of this essay, I conclude by noting a number of other areas in which further research should prove fruitful, for although most general works on Judaism in the first centuries before and of the common era provide surveys dealing with the family, there are no comprehensive treatments drawing on recent work.[93]

1. Among the most important of the recent treatments of parents, children, and related issues are Thomas Wiedemann's *Adults and Children in the Roman Empire*,[94] two collections of essays edited by Beryl Rawson,[95] Keith Bradley's *Discovering the Roman Family: Studies in Roman Social History*,[96] and the more specialized work of Susan Dixon, *The Roman Mother*.[97] Though none of these studies deals exclusively, or even primarily, with the Jewish family, they posed questions in new ways and provide data and analyses which will help to shape questions which may be brought to bear in the study of Jewish texts. Since, moreover, so many of the elements derived from Jewish literature have parallels in the Hellenistic material, we cannot dismiss these studies, though we must also think carefully about how best to use them in examining the Jewish family and to guide us when Jewish literature is silent. There are competing methodologies, presuppositions, and approaches in recent work on children in antiquity so that it is not simply a matter of which data are relevant but also of which interpretations of the data are most cogent.

2. To attain a greater degree of precision in imagining the living conditions of Jewish families, recent work on Israelite

---

[93]Among the general works are G. F. Moore, *Judaism* (Cambridge: Harvard, 1966) 2, 119-140; S. Safrai, "Home and Family" in S. Safrai and M. Stern (eds) *The Jewish People in the First Century* 2, 728-792.

[94]New Haven: Yale, 1989.

[95]*Marriage, Divorce, and Children in Ancient Rome* (Oxford: Clarendon, 1991) and *The Family in Ancient Rome* (Ithaca: Cornell, 1986). Rawson herself is working on a major study of the family in ancient Rome which will bring together her work over the past few years.

[96]Oxford: University Press, 1991. Bradley's work draws heavily on inscriptions and should prove especially useful. The essays contained in this collection provide a fascinating examination of Roman family life.

[97]Norman: Oklahoma, 1988.

houses should be examined. The recent article in the *Anchor Bible Dictionary* by John S. Holladay, Jr[98] and Yizhar Hirschfeld's *Dwelling Houses in Roman and Byzantine Palestine*[99] are good points of departure. Similar studies of architecture and housing in Greco-Roman cities should also be taken into account.[100] If Leon is correct in arguing that the inscriptions of the Jewish catacombs reflect a community of modest means, we are probably to imagine Jewish families living in *insulae*, which would have determined many things about the way they coped with life in the city.

3. The economic role of the family in ancient society is also important in determining the nature of relationships between parents and children. As noted above, fathers were obligated to teach their children a trade. In many instances the trade was doubtless that of the father himself. But the whole issue needs to be explored with our topic in mind. Studies of work, trades, and the economy should be examined, such as Moses Finley's *The Ancient Economy*,[101] and the chapter on child labor in Bradley's collection of essays on the Roman family just cited.

4. Though one can learn much from past studies of Jewish inscriptions, such as Leon's *The Jews of Ancient Rome*, looking at this evidence more closely and in the light of new insights should prove beneficial. Ross Kraemer's study of the inscriptions of Rome and Egypt which attest to the lives of Jewish women shows what results might be expected from further study.[102] Though the focus of this work is elsewhere, Kraemer provides a number of helpful observations about the roles of Jewish mothers – both what was and was not said about them.[103]

---

[98]See the entry under "House, Israelite" in 3, 308-318. His bibliography refers to a forthcoming book on *Israelite House: A Case Study in Applied Archaeoethnographic Analogical Reconstruction.*

[99]Jerusalem: Yad Yitzhaq ben Zvi, 1987 (Hebrew). I am grateful to Shaye Cohen for this reference.

[100]See, for example, John Stambaugh's *The Ancient Roman City* (Baltimore: John Hopkins, 1988).

[101]Berkeley: University of California, 1973.

[102]"Non-Literary Evidence for Jewish Women in Rome and Egypt" in *Helios* 13 (1986), 85-101.

[103]The role of the mother in Jewish families of antiquity warrants study. Though most of this essay has focused on the obligations of fathers, there are numerous references in the Bible, the apocrypha, the rabbinic corpus, and the inscriptions

5. Finally, the use of imagery of parents and children in apocalyptic literature warrants investigation. The most well-known passage is Mal 4:5-6 which refers to Elijah's turning the hearts of fathers to their children and the hearts of children to their fathers, lest the Lord come and smite the land with a curse. Other passages, however, reverse this saying, listing as one of the signs of the end the dissolution of relations between parents and children. 1 Enoch 100:1-2 is exemplary: "In those days...a man shall not be able to withhold his hands from his sons nor from [his] son's sons in order to kill them." The use of such imagery in apocalyptic literature illustrates just how significant relations between parents and children were in Jewish society. When apocalyptic writers sought to describe the woes of the last days, they could think of nothing worse than strife within the family; when they speak of the establishment of the new order, they could think of nothing better than the turning of fathers to their children and children to their fathers.

---

which should be examined systematically [see the essay by Ross S. Kraemer in this volume].

3

Parents and Children: A Philonic Perspective

Adele Reinhartz

Introduction

The literary records of the Greco-Roman world are replete with portrayals of or references to parents and children. It is only recently, however, that such comments have been used as a resource for the contemplation of parent-child relationships in Greco-Roman antiquity. While there have appeared several studies of children and childhood in classical Athens and imperial Rome,[1] surprisingly little scholarly attention has been given to the Jewish family in the Greco-Roman world.[2] Yet Hellenistic Jewish writers, like their gentile counterparts,

---

[1]See, for example, Mark Golden, *Children and Childhood in Classical Athens* (Baltimore: Johns Hopkins University Press, 1990); Thomas Wiedemann, *Adults and Children in the Roman Empire* (London: Routledge, 1989); Jane F. Gardner and Thomas Wiedemann, *The Roman Household: A Sourcebook* (London and New York: Routledge, 1991). Of related interest are Suzanne Dixon, *The Roman Mother* (London: Routledge, 1988) and Judith P. Hallett, *Fathers and Daughters in Roman Society: Women and the Elite Family* (Princeton: Princeton University Press, 1984).

[2]Some aspects relevant to children and childhood have been touched on in various introductory and specific works on Philo. See, for example, E.R. Goodenough, *An Introduction to Philo Judaeus*, 2d ed. (Lanham: University Press of America, 1986), 127-28; Alan Mendelson, *Secular Education in Philo of Alexandria* (Cincinnati: Hebrew Union College Press, 1982), passim; Dorothy Sly, *Philo's Perception of Women* (Atlanta: Scholars Press, 1990), passim.

made much mention of those of "tender age,"[3] and the adults who created and raised them. Pseudo-Phocylides, for example, whose work stems from first-century Alexandria,[4] offers advice on guarding the beauty – and the virginity – of one's children,[5] while Josephus, the first-century Jewish historian, expands upon some of the significant parent-child relationships of biblical narrative.[6]

The present study will explore the relationships of Hellenistic Jewish children and their parents by examining the work of one of the most prolific Jewish writers of the Greco-Roman world, Philo of Alexandria. Of course, Philo's primary concern is not to describe Jewish family life but rather to develop an allegorical interpretation of scripture.[7] Nevertheless, he devotes a series of treatises, entitled the *Exposition of the Law*,[8] to a more literal explication of Jewish narrative and legal texts which permits a glimpse, however blurry, into his social world.

Comments about children, and in particular, the parent-child relationship, appear in every extant treatise of the *Exposition*.[9] The *Life of Moses*, which apparently serves as the introduction to the series,[10]

---

[3]*Fug.* 39-40. The treatises of Philo are abbreviated according to the list in *Studia Philonica Annual* 3 (1991) 393-94. All citations and quotations from Philo are from *Philo in Ten Volumes (and two supplementary volumes)*, English translation by F.H. Colson et al., Loeb Classical Library (London: Heinemann, 1929-62).

[4]For discussion of date and provenance, see P.W. Van der Horst, "Pseudo-Phocylides," in *The Old Testament Pseudepigrapha*, ed. James H. Charlesworth, vol. 2 (New York: Doubleday, 1985), 567-68; idem, *The Sentences of Pseudo-Phocylides* (Leiden: Brill, 1978) 82; idem, 'Pseudo-Phocylides Revisited,' *JSP* 3 (1988): 15.

[5]*Pseudo-Phocylides*, lines 210-17 (*OT Apocrypha*, 581-82).

[6]See, for example, *Ant.* 1.215-219 on Sarah's relationship with Ishmael and *Ant.* 2.217-38 on the birth and childhood of Moses. All citations and quotations from the work of Josephus are from *Josephus in Nine Volumes*, ed. H. St. J. Thackeray et al., Loeb Classical Library (London: Heinemann, 1926-65).

[7]This is clear from the structure of many of his exegetical discussions, in which the literal exposition of a text is followed by an allegorical interpretation which explicates "an order of things which is not so apparent but is far superior to the order which is perceived by the senses" (*Abr.* 52). Cf. Harry Austryn Wolfson, *Philo: Foundations of Religious Philosophy in Judaism, Christianity, and Islam*, vol. 1 (Cambridge: Harvard University Press, 1947), 116.

[8]The intended audience of the *Exposition* has been a matter of some debate. E.R. Goodenough argued that the *Exposition*, like Philo's two-volume treatise *De Vita Mosis*, was a missionary document addressed to Gentiles. Cf. Goodenough, *Introduction*, 35; idem, "Philo's Exposition of the Law and his De Vita Mosis," *HTR* 26 (1933) 109-25. Victor Tcherikover ("Jewish Apologetic Literature Reconsidered," *Eos* 48 [1956] 178-79), however, argued that there is no evidence that Gentiles read any Jewish writings at all, let alone these particular works.

[9]Treatises on Isaac and Jacob, apparently part of the original *Exposition*, are not extant. Goodenough, *Introduction*, 40.

[10]See Goodenough, "Philo's Exposition," *passim*.

contains Philo's reconstruction of the sentiments and words of Moses' parents on the occasion of their infant's "exposure" on the river Nile (*Mos*. 1. 10-11). The "ages of man," as described by Solon and Hippocrates, form part of Philo's exposition of the number seven, in *On the Creation* (*Opif*. 104-5).[11] In his treatise *On Abraham*, Philo discusses various issues concerned with child sacrifice, in the context of Abraham's near sacrifice of his son Isaac (*Abr*. 167-199). In *On Joseph* Philo makes some general comments on the nature of children and youth and describes the strong love of Jacob for the son of his old age (*Jos*. 4, 225). Richest for our purposes are the treatises *On the Decalogue* and *On the Special Laws*, which treat in detail a variety of legal issues related to parents and children, including the biblical commandment to honor one's parents (*Dec*. 106-20; *Spec*. 2.224-41) and the laws of inheritance (*Spec*. 2. 125-39). The treatises which conclude the *Exposition* contain further reflections on such diverse aspects as infanticide (*Virt*. 131-34) and procreation (*Praem*. 108-9).

In the *Exposition* as a whole, Philo brings to bear on his interpretation of scripture many extrabiblical considerations and assumptions that apparently stem from his own particular intellectual, cultural, and political location in Alexandria at the turn of the eras.[12] This is true also of his discussions pertaining to parent-child relationships. For example, Philo's discussion of Gen 22 goes beyond an explication of the text to a comparison of Abraham's act with the various circumstances under which children were sacrificed among "the barbarian nations" such as India (*Abr*. 182). His detailed exposition of the fifth commandment extends the meaning of "honoring one's parents" to include the courtesy and honor that young people should show to their elders in general, an extension which, though not inconsistent with biblical morality, is nevertheless not mentioned in Ex 20:12 or Deut 5:16.[13] His vigorous condemnations of infanticide and exposure of infants, practices which according to Philo are detested by the "holy law," are attached to Ex 21:22 and Lev 22:27, which do not mention these issues at all. The fact that Philo's comments on parent-child relationships appear as biblical

---

[11]For discussion of the history of the idea of the "ages of man," see Philippe Ariès, *Centuries of Childhood: A Social History of Family Life* (New York: Knopf, 1962), 15-32.

[12]This is the assumption behind the works of Heinemann and Goodenough, for example, who try to determine where, when, and to what extent, Philo was drawing from the non-Jewish aspects of his cultural environment. See E.R. Goodenough, *The Jurisprudence of the Jewish Courts in Egypt* (New Haven: Yale University Press, 1929) and Isaak Heinemann, *Philons griechische und jüdische Bildung* (Breslau: M. and H. Marcus Verlag, 1932).

[13]See Lev 19:32 and the rabbinic discussion in b. *Qidd*. 32b.

exegesis precludes their use as a clear window into the everyday lives of children and their parents in Jewish Alexandria. Nevertheless, his discussions, drawing as they do from the social, legal and intellectual world in which he lived, do shed light on his basic assumptions regarding this fundamental relationship and its social and legal ramifications as he saw them.[14]

Our discussion of Philo's views will begin with a brief survey of the terminology he uses to refer to children and their parents throughout the *Exposition*. This will be followed by a treatment of four specific issues: 1) the hierarchical structure of the parent-child relationship; 2) the responsibilities of parents towards their children; 3) the duties of children towards their parents; 4) love and affection between parents and children. Also included will be some reflections on related issues such as the role of the male-female hierarchy in the parent-child relationship, and the possible influence of the Roman laws concerning patriarchal power on Philo's understanding of family life. Finally, we will consider the hints provided by Philo's comments for our picture of the lives of Jewish parents and children in Alexandria.

Philonic Terminology

1. Children

When referring to those "of tender age," Philo uses either the neuter *teknon* (for example, *Spec.* 1.139) or, for infants, the neuter *brephos* (*Spec.* 3.117). In the majority of cases in which the LCL translation uses the English term "child" or "children," however, Philo uses the noun *pais*.[15] From the varied contexts in which this term occurs, it is apparent that *pais* is used by Philo primarily to refer not to the age of childhood, but rather to the condition of being an offspring, that is, of being the inferior party to the parent-child relationship. This is particularly striking in the many passages in which Philo emphasizes the duty of children to care for their aging parents, as they themselves were cared for in their youth

---

[14]Cf. Goodenough, *Jurisprudence*, 13-14 and passim, who argues that Philo's interpretations of the special laws, in *Spec.* 1-4, reflect the actual practices and procedures of the Jewish courts in Egypt. F.H. Colson, however, disagrees with this theory, on the grounds that there is little evidence to suggest that in fact Philo is deviating from the biblical descriptions of these laws in such a way which would suggest that he was attempting to accommodate and to reflect the law as practised in his own community. See Colson, *Philo*, vol. vii, xii-xiii, note (g).

[15]Less frequently, Philo will refer more generally to "those whom parents have begotten," as in *Spec.* 2.231: "parents have...received authority over their offspring" [*eph' hois egennesan*].

(for example *Dec.* 113-18) or the severe penalties prescribed by biblical law for striking a parent (*Spec.* 2.243-48).

When speaking specifically of sons and/or daughters, Philo often uses the masculine *huios* and/or the feminine *thugater.* In numerous passages, however, the masculine forms of *pais* are used interchangeably with *huios* or its plural, to denote male children specifically.[16] For example, in *Spec.* 4.184, Philo advises that "the ruler should preside over his subjects as a father over his children [*paidon*] so that he himself may be honoured in return as by true-born sons [*hupo gnesion huion*]..." This pattern of usage suggests that many of the passages which according to the LCL translation refer to a child or children, in fact speak of male children solely or primarily unless daughters are specifically mentioned.

2. Parents

A similar situation exists with respect to the terminology that Philo uses in reference to parents. In most discussions, Philo speaks generally of "parents" [*hoi goneis*, masculine plural]. In some cases he speaks specifically of the mother [*he meter*], as in *Virt.* 128ff., which speaks of the special bond between mothers and their infants, or of the father [*ho pater*], as in *Virt.* 192, which speaks of the father disinheriting a disobedient son. In such cases it would seem that the more specific noun is used in a situation in which the parent of the other sex is definitely excluded.

In some situations, *hoi goneis* is indeed meant to be inclusive. This is explicitly so, for example, in *Dec.* 51, in which Philo notes that the fifth commandment treats "the duty of honouring parents [*peri goneon*], each separately and both in common."

In many other cases, however, the context indicates that in using this term, Philo has in mind the male parent. In *Spec.* 3.153, for example, Philo commends the biblical law according to which "fathers [*pateras*] should not die for their sons nor sons for their parents [*goneon*]." That these two terms [*pater* and *goneus*] are interchangeable is suggested by *Spec.* 3.168: "He expressly forbade that sons should be slain instead of fathers [*goneon*] or fathers [*goneis*] instead of sons."[17]

From his usage of terminology it is clear that Philo does not refrain from addressing issues which relate to all parents and children in general, as well as to daughters specifically. It would seem, however, that the relationship which is of greatest interest and concern to Philo is that between father and son. His remarks to "parents" and "children" are in reality addressed primarily to males in their roles as fathers and sons,

---

[16]*Pais* can in fact be either masculine or feminine, though Philo uses primarily the masculine forms.

[17]See also *Spec.* 2.243-48.

although this does not always emerge clearly from the LCL translation.[18] The Philonic emphasis on the father-son relationship is consistent with Philo's general view on the superiority of male to female[19] as well as with the likelihood that men constituted Philo's intended audience throughout the *Exposition*.[20]

Issues

1. Parents and children: a hierarchical relationship

The basis for every Philonic discussion of family life is the assumption of the hierarchical nature of the parent-child relationship. This principle is discussed explicitly and in detail in his comments on the fifth commandment:

> In the fifth commandment on honouring parents we have a suggestion of many necessary laws drawn up to deal with the relations of old to young, rulers to subjects, benefactors to benefited, slaves to masters. For parents belong to the superior class of the above mentioned pairs, that which comprises seniors, rulers, benefactors and masters, while children occupy the lower position with juniors, subjects, receivers of benefits and slaves.(*Dec.* 165-66).[21]

Philo grounds this hierarchical relationship in the definition of parents as the creators of their children:

> I say...that the maker is always senior to the thing made and the cause to its effect, and the begetters are in a sense the causes and the creators of what they beget. (*Spec.* 2.228)

Furthermore, the role of parents as creators makes them similar in some sense to God as creator: they "copy His nature by begetting particular persons" (*Dec.* 51). According to Philo this similarity accounts for the place of the fifth commandment in the Decalogue as the transition point between the commandments describing the duties that human beings owe to God and those they owe to fellow human beings:

---

[18]The LCL often translates *pais* and *goneus* in a general rather than gender-specific way, though see *Spec.* 3.168, quoted above, in which *goneis* is translated as "fathers."

[19]For a discussion of Philo's views of male and female, see Judith Romney Wegner, "Philo's Portrayal of Women – Hebraic or Hellenic," in *"Women Like This": New Perspectives on Jewish Women in the Greco-Roman World*, ed. Amy-Jill Levine (Atlanta: Scholars Press, 1991), 41-66; Richard A. Baer, Jr., *Philo's Use of the Categories Male and Female* (Leiden: Brill, 1970); Sly, *Women*.

[20]The possibility that Philo's intended readership for all of the treatises is male is touched on by Sly, *Women*, 59-70.

[21]Cf. *Spec.* 2.226-27 for a similar formulation.

> ...we see that parents by their nature stand on the borderline between the mortal and the immortal side of existence, the mortal because of their kinship with men and other animals through the perishableness of the body; the immortal because the act of generation assimilates them to God, the generator of the All. (*Dec.* 107)[22]

For this reason, Philo insists, parents

> are to their children what God is to the world, since just as He achieved existence for the nonexistent, so they in imitation of His power, as far as they are capable, immortalize the race. (*Spec.* 2.225)

These passages imply that the hierarchical relationship between parents and children is grounded in and proceeds from the creative activity which likens parents to God. There are hints, however, that for Philo the idea of the superiority of parents to their children is in fact separable from, prior to, and indeed more fundamental than its philosophical rationale. One hint is to be found in the fact that elsewhere Philo criticizes the very comparison between human parents and God that he himself had emphasized in the passages quoted above. In *Spec.* 1.10-11, Philo warns his readers that

> a man should know himself and banish from the soul the grievous malady of conceit. For there are some who have prided themselves on their power of fashioning as with a sculptor's cunning the fairest of creatures, man, and in their braggart pride assumed godship, closing their eyes to the Cause of all that comes into being, though they might find in their familiars a corrective for their delusion. For in their midst are many men incapable of begetting and many women barren, whose matings are ineffective and who grow old childless. The evil belief, therefore, needs to be excised from the mind with any others that are not loyal to God.

This contradiction suggests that the philosophical rationale for this particular hierarchy as stated in *Dec.* 51, 107 and *Spec.* 2.225 is not fundamental but rather utilitarian. Its main function is to justify the location of the fifth commandment at the transition point between the commandments relating to God and those to fellow human beings.[23]

---

[22]Cf. *Spec.* 2.224-25. Yehoshua Amir ("The Decalogue according to Philo," in *The Ten Commandments in History and Tradition,* ed. Ben-Zion Segal [Jerusalem: Magnes Press, 1990]), 156-58) suggests that this point reflects a knowledge of Greek cosmology, since Plato also refers to divinity as the father who brings forth life.

[23]This suspicion is strengthened by the ambivalence implied in the following passage:

> Some bolder spirits, glorifying the name of parenthood, say that a father and a mother are in fact gods revealed to sight

A second hint which points in the same direction is the fact that the hierarchical relationship between parents and children is only one of the many hierarchies which are operative in human society as Philo understands it. In some cases, the parent-child relationship is itself seen as a model for other kinds of hierarchies, as in *Spec.* 4.184:

> The ruler should preside over his subjects as a father over his children so that he himself may be honoured in return as by true-born sons, and therefore good rulers may be truly called the parents of states and nations in common, since they show a fatherly and sometimes more than fatherly affection.

These other hierarchical relationships cannot readily be explained by the philosophical rationale of the innate superiority of the creator to the created. This would be the case with respect to the relationship between the master and his servant, the benefactor and the benefited, the old and the young (*Spec.* 2.226). Philo does not provide a philosophical rationale for these hierarchies; rather, he simply accepts them as self-evident.

These observations suggest that Philo's notion of the hierarchical relationship between parents and children is first and foremost an expression of an essentially dualistic view of human society, and as only one (albeit an important one) of many hierarchies. One of the sources of this notion is clearly biblical. Ex 20:12 and Deut 5:16 express the divinely given commandment to honor one's parents, without even hinting at the notion that parents should honor their children. Many other biblical passages imply the hierarchy between master and slave (for example, Ex 21:1-6) and the ruler and the ruled (for example, 1 Sam 8:10-18). A similarly hierarchical view of human society is expressed in classical

---

> who copy the Uncreated in His work as the Framer of life. He, they say, is the god or Maker of the world, they of those only whom they have begotten, and how can reverence be rendered to the invisible God by those who show irreverence to the gods who are near at hand and seen by the eye?" (*Dec.* 120)

Here Philo is careful not to commit himself to the views expressed by the "bolder spirits." (For brief discussion and Stoic parallels, see Colson, *Philo*, vol. 7, p. 612). Indeed, his repetition of the fact that these views belong to others implies that he is distancing himself from them. (Compare Philo's conclusion to *De Opif.*170-72, in which he refers to the views of others in a context which makes his rejection of these views very clear). In *Dec.*, this rejection is not made explicit. Indeed, these views are brought to support Philo's assertion that "parents are the servants of God for the task of begetting children...." (*Dec.* 119). In this passage too, therefore, it would seem that the principle of hierarchy in the parent-child relationship is fundamental, and is being rationalized by recourse to various arguments, not all of which he would agree with under other circumstances.

literature[24] as well as in Hellenistic literature such as the Stoic *kathekon* and in the early Christian *Haustafeln*. The household relationships as described in these texts clearly reflect the fundamental acceptance of the hierarchies of husbands and wives, parents and children, masters and slaves.[25]

Philo's notions of hierarchy, therefore, have obvious parallels both in biblical and Greco-Roman thought, and are clearly fundamental to his descriptions of the responsibilities of parents towards children and vice versa. It is to Philo's discussions of these responsibilities that we now turn.

2. Parents' Responsibilities towards their Children

In *Spec.* 3.111, Philo states that children are sent into the world in order to "partake of the gifts of Nature." According to *Virt.* 130, the first two of these gifts are birth itself, "through which the nonexistent is brought into existence," and breastmilk, "the happily timed aliment which flows so gently fostering the tender growth of every creature." These two gifts of nature in fact identify two of the most important responsibilities of parents towards their children, namely, to bring them into the world, and to nurture their growth.

a. Procreation

For Philo, procreation is the sole legitimate goal of the marital relationship. He roundly condemns those "pleasure lovers [who] mate with their wives, not to procreate children and perpetuate the race, but like pigs and goats in quest of the enjoyment which such intercourse gives" (*Spec.* 3.113). Similarly reviled are "those who sue for marriage with women whose sterility has already been proved with other husbands, do but copulate like pigs or goats, and their names should be inscribed in the lists of the impious as adversaries of God...."(*Spec.* 3.36). The regulations governing permitted and forbidden marriages among the priests "are intended to promote the generation of children" (*Spec.* 1.112); firstborn sons are to be "consecrated as a first fruit, a thank-

---

[24]See Aristotle (*Nicomachean Ethics* 1158a12), in which the relationship between father and son, as well as that between husband and wife, ruler and ruled, older and younger, is explicitly described as hierarchical.

[25]For discussion of the similarities and relationships among Stoic, Hellenistic Jewish, and early Christian formulations, see James E. Crouch, *The Origin and Intention of the Colossian Haustafel* (Göttingen: Vandenhoeck and Ruprecht, 1972), 74-101; Ehrhard Kamlah "Philos Beitrag zur Aufhellung der Geschichte der Haustafeln," in *Wort und Wirklichkeit: Studien zur Afrikanistik und Orientalistik,* Teil I, ed. Brigitta Benzing et al. (Meisenheim am Glan: Hain, 1976), 90-95.

offering for the blessing of parenthood realized in the present and the hopes of fruitful increase in the future" (*Spec.* 1.138).[26]

To bring children into the world is therefore not merely a privilege or a right, but a responsibility of every adult. Although Philo speaks generally of parents in the passages quoted above, it would seem that the emphasis on procreation as the single justifiable reason for sexual intercourse is addressed primarily to men, since they are warned not to marry barren women whereas women are not similarly cautioned regarding infertile men.[27] This responsibility, however, must be exercised within the context of a legitimate marital relationship, because

> anyone who has a harlot for his mother has no knowledge of, and can claim no affiliation to, his real father, but must accept the paternity of most or practically all her lovers and patrons....(*Spec.* 1.332)

The paternity of such children is so difficult to determine

> because their begetting and their birth has been adulterated at the fountain-head and reduced to confusion through the number of their mother's lovers, so that they cannot recognize or distinguish their real father....(*Spec.* 1.326)

Similarly unfortunate are the children of an adulterous relationship, though in this case the principal victim is the cuckolded husband "who will be forced to cherish the children of his deadliest foe as his own flesh and blood" (*Dec.* 129).

---

[26]See also *Praem.* 108-10 and *Mos.* 1.14. The emphasis on procreation is also present in the works of Roman writers such as Cassius Dio, who asserts: "It was for this purpose above all that the first and greatest of gods who fashioned us divided the human race into two, male and female, and implanted into us sexual passion and the need for intercourse, and made that intercourse fruitful; so that even mortality might become in a way immortal by the birth of new generations..." (56.3). Cf. Gardner and Weidemann (*Roman Household*, 96) who comment that Dio's thoughts on procreation are commonplaces of Greek philosophy. According to Heinemann (*Bildung*, 263-69), fertility is not seen as the sole purpose of marriage in the Bible or in rabbinic tradition. For a recent and detailed discussion of this point, see Jeremy Cohen, *"Be Fertile and Increase, Fill the Earth and Master It:" The Ancient and Medieval Career of a Biblical Text* (Ithaca: Cornell University Press, 1989), passim.

[27]That Philo knew of the possibility of male infertility is indicated by *Spec.* 1.10-11, in which Philo refers to the "many men incapable of begetting." The rabbis of the Mishnah and the Talmud explicitly interpreted Gen 1:28 as a commandment devolving upon the male rather than the female, despite the biological necessity of female participation in the act of procreation. For discussion, see Cohen, *"Be Fertile,"* 124-44.

b. Providing Nurture

Once a couple has brought a child into the world, their next important responsibility is to nurture that child in an adequate and appropriate manner. In the first place, this means making a commitment to raising that child. Philo condemns in very strong terms the practices of exposure of infants and infanticide, which was apparently not uncommon in the Greco-Roman world as a method of population control.[28] If parents cut their children off from the blessings of nature, Philo argues,

> they must rest assured that they are breaking the laws of Nature and stand self-condemned on the gravest charges, love of pleasure, hatred of men, murder and, the worst abomination of all, murder of their own children. (*Spec.* 3.112)

Exposure of infants is no better than outright infanticide, since exposed children "suffer the most distressing fate" as helpless victims of carnivorous birds and "beasts that feast on human flesh" (*Spec.* 3. 115).[29]

The human mother and her infant are to remain together (*Spec.* 4.139). For human mothers as for animals, any separation would lead to great distress,

> because of the maternal affection natural to them, particularly at the time of motherhood, when the breasts, whose flowing fountain is obstructed through lack of its suckling, grow indurated and strained by the weight of the milk coagulated within them and suffer a painful oppression. (*Virt.* 128)

The importance of breastfeeding is indicated by the absence of teeth in the newborn, since teeth

> would be a superfluous burden to the infant who would be fed on milk, and would also bring serious trouble to the breasts, the fountain through which the liquid sustenance flows, as they would be galled during the suction of the milk. [God] looked forward, therefore, to the proper time, that is, to when the infant is weaned from the breast, and brought out that supplementary growth of teeth, which He hitherto kept in storage, only when the infant would refuse to take food in the form of milk and could bear the more mature kind which requires the instruments which I have mentioned. (*Spec.* 3.199-200)[30]

---

[28]John Boswell, *The Kindness of Strangers* (New York: Vintage, 1988), 139-152.

[29]See *Spec.* 3.110-19; *Virt.* 131-34; *Mos.* 1.10-14. For a more detailed discussion of these passages, see Adele Reinhartz, "Philo on Infanticide," *Studia Philonica Annual* 4 (1992) 42-58.

[30]According to Gardner and Wiedemann (*Roman Household*, 102-3), it was considered highly virtuous for a Roman mother to nurse her own child. See Plutarch, *Cato the Elder* 20, 4-7. When wet-nurses were hired, special care was

c. Protection

Another important responsibility borne by the parents, specifically the father, is that of protecting his family (*Mos.* 1.257, 330). For this reason, notes Philo, God

> provides for orphans and widows because they have lost their protectors, in the first case parents, in the second husbands, and in this desolation no refuge remains that men can give; and therefore they are not denied the hope that is greatest of all, the hope in God....(*Spec.* 1.310)

On a practical level, the protection of orphans, particularly of young girls, becomes the responsibility of the head magistrate, who is given

> the charge of protecting the girls left thus desolate and superintending their development, and the expenses of providing anything required for their maintenance and education as befits maidens...(*Spec.* 1.125)[31]

d. Financial Support

Raising children, then as now, entailed considerable financial expense. Necessary expenses ranged from the redemption of the firstborn (*Spec.* 4.139) to the providing of a dowry (*Spec.* 1.125). In between, notes Philo,

> parents pay out a sum many times the value of a slave on their children and for them to nurses, tutors and teachers, apart from the cost of their clothes, food and superintendence in sickness and health from their earliest years until they are full grown. (*Spec.* 2.233)[32]

In sum, "children have nothing of their own which does not come from their parents, either bestowed from their own resources or acquired by means which originate from them" (*Dec.* 118).

Financial obligations do not end with the death of the father, who must provide an inheritance for his children. Philo explicates the biblical laws pertaining to inheritance (cf. Num 27:8-11), indicating that "the

---

taken to ascertain their good character, since it was thought that infants imbibed something of the character of their nurses with their milk. The only evidence of wet-nursing in a Hellenistic Jewish context concerns the hiring of a wet-nurse for a foundling infant (CPJ no. 146) and the annulment of an agreement to hire a wet-nurse for a slave-child (CPJ no. 147). For the texts and discussion of these papyri, see *Corpus Papyrorum Judaicarum* II, ed. Victor A. Tcherikover and Alexander Fuks (Cambridge, Mass.: Harvard University Press, 1960), 15-20.

[31]See Colson, *Philo*, vol. 7, 626, for a discussion of the Attic law which he takes as the basis for Philo's discussion on this point.

[32]Aristotle (*Politics* 1260a7-10) also sees similarities in the relationships between master and slave, man and child, and male and female. See also Goodenough, *Jurisprudence*, 70.

heirs of parents are to be sons, or failing sons, daughters" (*Spec.* 2.124).[33] Although the daughters of Zelophehad are permitted by Moses to inherit their father's property in the absence of any male siblings (*Mos.* 2.243-45), Philo is careful to emphasize the exceptional nature of this ruling:

> For just as in nature men take precedence of women, so, too, in the scale of relationships they should take the first place in succeeding to the property and filling the position of the departed.... (*Spec.* 2.124; cf. *Mos.* 2.242-43)

Unmarried daughters whose male siblings have received the inheritance, however, must have a dowry provided for them from the estate (*Spec.* 2.125).

In addition to providing materially for the child, the father, or the head magistrate if the father is deceased, must choose a suitable marriage partner for his daughters (*Spec.* 2.125). The husband was to be chosen on his "merits," although another important consideration was also financial: the prospective mate

> should be...of the same family as the girls, or, if that cannot be, at any rate of the same ward and tribe, in order that the portions assigned as dowry should not be alienated by intermarriage with other tribes but should retain the place given to them in the allotments originally made on the basis of tribes. (*Spec.* 1.126)[34]

e. Instruction

According to Philo, parents, in addition to their various other roles,

> are also in the position of instructors because they impart to their children from their earliest years everything that they themselves may happen to know, and give them instruction not only in the various branches of knowledge which they impress upon their young minds, but also on the most essential questions of what to choose and avoid, namely, to choose virtues and avoid vices and the activities to which they lead. (*Spec.* 2.228)

Such instruction includes both physical training in a gymnasium, through which the child "gains muscular vigour and good condition and the power to bear itself and move with an ease marked by gracefulness and elegance" as well as education of "the soul by means of letters and arithmetic and geometry and music and philosophy as a whole..." (*Spec.* 2.230).

Although the passages quoted above speak generally of parents and children, it would appear that Philo in fact perceives the father to the primary provider of instruction. *Spec.* 2.29 describes the father as the one

---

[33]See *Mos.* 2.234-45 and *Spec.* 2.125-139 for extended discussion of the laws of inheritance. See also Goodenough, *Jurisprudence*, 55-65.
[34]Cf. Num 36.6ff.

whose nature it is "to beget good intentions and noble and worthy actions, and then to foster [his] offspring with the water of the truths which education and wisdom abundantly supply" (*Spec.* 2.29). The influence of the mother on the moral and intellectual development of the child, if any, is described as negative. Philo blames the misdeeds of children on the

> familiarity with falsehood which grows up with the children right from their birth and from the cradle, the work of nurses and mothers and the rest of the company, slaves and free, who belong to the household. (*Spec.* 4.68)[35]

Similarly, the primary recipient of paternal education and instruction would appear to be the male offspring. Although *Spec.* 2.230 speaks of the physical and moral education of "children," *Spec.* 3.176 explicitly praises the debarring of women from the gymnasium, and *Spec.* 2.236 speaks of the virtuous instruction that a father will give his son.

f. Discipline

The kind and selfless ministrations of parents[36] do not always result in virtuous and kind children. Philo warns against the overindulgence of one's children,

> For when parents cherish their children with extreme tenderness, providing them with good gifts from every quarter and shunning no toil or danger because they are fast bound to them by the magnet forces of affection, there are some who do not receive this exceeding tender heartedness in a way that profits them. They pursue eagerly luxury and voluptuousness, they applaud the dissolute life, they run to waste both in body and soul, and suffer no part of either to be kept erect by its proper faculties which they lay prostrate and paralyzed without a blush because they have never feared the censors they possess in their fathers and mothers but give in to and indulge their own lusts. (*Spec.* 2.240)

What is one to do as the "good" parent of an "evil" child?[37] Philo exhorts such parents "to employ more active and severe admonitions to cure the wastage of their children..." (*Spec.* 2.241). After all, "parents have...received authority over their offspring" which has been awarded not by lot or by voting, but "by the most admirable and perfect judgment

---

[35]While this sounds like an ancient example of the "blame the mother" syndrome, in fact it is in keeping with Philo's assessment of woman as bringing "blameworthy" behavior into the world (cf. *Opif.* 151). For an analysis of this syndrome in modern western society, see Paula J. Caplan, *Don't Blame Mother* (New York: Harper and Row, 1989).

[36]Cf. *Spec.* 2.236.

[37]Philo appears to be quite preoccupied with this particular situation, judging by the length of his discussion. Cf. *Virt.* 189, 198-227.

of nature above us which governs with justice things both human and divine" (*Spec.* 2.231).

By this authority, asserts Philo,

> fathers have the right to upbraid their children and admonish them severely and if they do not submit to threats conveyed in words to beat and degrade them and put them in bonds. (*Spec.* 2.232)[38]

Some fathers "of the most affectionate kind," notes Philo,

> formally disinherit their sons and debar them from their home and kinship, when the depravity which they show overcomes the peculiar and intense affection implanted in parents by nature. (*Virt.* 192)

In the case of truly rebellious children,

> the law permits the parents to extend the punishment to death, though here it requires more than the father alone or the mother alone.... For it is not to be expected that both the parents would agree to the execution of their son unless the weight of his offenses depressed the scales strongly enough to overcome the affection which nature has firmly established in them. (*Spec.* 2.232)

For the specific offense of striking one's father or mother, Philo, in accordance with Ex 21:15, prescribes the death penalty by stoning (*Spec.* 2.243). "This is quite just," comments Philo, "for justice forbids that he should live who maltreats the authors of his life." The death penalty is more appropriate than the lesser penalties suggested by

> some dignitaries and legislators who had an eye to men's opinions rather than to truth [and] have decreed that striking a father should be punished by cutting off the hands, a specious refinement due to their wish to win the approval of the more careless or thoughtless, who think that the parts with which the offenders have struck their parents should be amputated. (*Spec.* 2.244)

"But it is silly," continues Philo,

> to visit displeasure on the servants rather than on the actual authors, for the outrage is not committed by the hands but by the persons who used their hands to commit it, and it is these persons who must be punished.... (*Spec.* 2.245)

The death penalty should also be meted out to any who,

---

[38]Colson (*Philo* vol. 7, 450) suggests that the reference to degradation in this quotation may be to setting the children to degrading tasks, as in Plato, *Laws* 866. Goodenough (*Jurisprudence*, 69-70) notes that in this case Philo goes beyond the biblical text that he is explicating (Deut. 21:18-21). Whereas biblical law refers to beating as an initial form of discipline, Philo adds both imprisonment and degradation, failing which the child should be stoned.

even if while making no assault with his hands...uses abusive
language to those to whom good words are owed as a bounden
duty, or in any other way does anything to dishonour his parents....
(*Spec.* 2.248)[39]

The patriarchal focus of Philo's discussion led Heinemann, followed
by Goodenough, to suggest that Philo's views of parental discipline were
greatly influenced by Roman laws relating to *patria potestas*, that is, the
absolute power that the patriarch held over all members of his household
until his death.[40] In his notes to *Spec.* 2.232, Heinemann argued that both
Philo and Josephus are assuming *patria potestas*, which had already in the
first century been an aspect of Roman law and family life in Egypt.[41]
Goodenough agreed with Heinemann on this point, and emphasized that
"the parent is described in Roman terms throughout." For Philo, as for
the Romans, argued Goodenough, a father is the owner of his children,
since, like slaves, they are born into their parents' household, and cost
their parents money.[42] F.H. Colson conceded that Heinemann and
Goodenough "may be right in tracing here the influence of the Roman
patria potestas," though he took issue with Goodenough on specific
points.[43]

Unnoticed by Heinemann and Goodenough is one additional hint
which supports their suggestion concerning the power of the Jewish *pater
familias*. This hint appears in Philo's discussions of infanticide. Although
he refers in general to the 'guardians' (*Spec.* 3.112), 'fathers and mothers'
(*Spec.* 3.116) and 'parents' (*Virt.* 131) who expose or kill their children,
some of Philo's statements against infanticide appear to be addressed
primarily to men. He speaks sarcastically of the "good sirs," who expose

---

[39]It may be significant that Philo pauses for so long on this point. Does this
indicate an apologetic motif in an effort to account for the apparent harshness of
the law on this point? Goodenough (*Jurisprudence*, 73) suggests that Philo in fact
makes the law stricter than in the plain meaning of the biblical text.

[40]Cf., for example, Diodorus of Sicily, I, 77. For detailed discussion of *patria
potestas* in Roman law, see J. A. Crook, "Patria Potestas," *Classical Quarterly* 17
(1967): 113-22; W.K. Lacey, "Patria Potestas," in *The Family in Ancient Rome*, ed.
Beryl Rawson (London: Croom Helm, 1986), 121-44; William V. Harris, "The
Roman Father's Power of Life and Death," in *Studies in Roman Law in Memory of
A. Arthur Schiller*, ed. Roger S. Bagnall and William V. Harris (Leiden: Brill, 1986),
81-95.

[41]Isaak Heinemann, ed., *Die Werke Philos von Alexandria*, vol. 2 (Breslau: M. and H.
Marcus, 1910), 173; idem, *Bildung*, 234.

[42]Goodenough, *Jurisprudence*, 70-76. This is consistent with his argument about
the influence of Roman law on Philo's exposition of the Special Laws.

[43]For example, Colson disagrees with Goodenough's assumption that the Roman
penalty for striking one's father was amputation of the hand. See Goodenough,
Jurisprudence, 74; Colson, *Philo* vol. 7, 629.

their children (*Virt.* 133) and mate with their wives "like pigs and goats in quest of...enjoyment" (*Spec.* 3.113). While this may simply reflect the intended male audience of his writings, it may also indicate a special emphasis on men as the principal perpetrators of the crimes of infanticide and exposure of infants.

Further support for this possibility is found by the line of argumentation in *Virt.* 129-33. According to *Virt.* 129, Lev 22:27 prohibits the sacrifice of a newborn animal since such separation from her offspring would cause pain to the mother. From this law, Philo argues, the 'good sirs' should learn the duty of family love, implying that they – the fathers? – should not separate human infants from their mothers (*Virt.* 133). This argument suggests a similarity between the role of the father in Alexandrian Jewish society and that of the Roman *paterfamilias*, who apparently had the power, by picking up the newborn or refusing to do so, to decide whether that infant would live or die.[44]

These considerations suggest that Philo's understanding of parent-child relationships may indeed have been influenced by the Roman concept of *patria potestas*. It should be noted, however, that the hierarchical notions upon which this concept was based are not foreign to the biblical laws and narratives which Philo was elucidating in the *Exposition*.[45] Furthermore, as we have noted throughout our discussion, Philo's comments are paralleled in Aristotle's *Nicomachean Ethics*, in which the superiority of the parent to the child is seen as fundamental to the parent-child relationship. Hence it would seem that the notion of hierarchy was deeply embedded in the religious, ethical and legal traditions to which Philo was heir.

3. Responsibilities of children towards their parents

Our survey of Philo on parenting emphasizes both the seniority of parents in the parent-child hierarchy as well as the variety of roles that parents, as the "higher order," must assume. Philo does not leave us guessing as to the behavior required of those in the "lower order." Just as the duties of parents towards their children span their entire parental

---

[44]As Sarah Pomeroy ("Infanticide," 207), notes, infanticide was one form of family planning in the Greco-Roman world that was most likely to involve the father, because of *patria potestas*. This is discussed in detail regarding the Roman father by Harris, "The Roman Father's Power of Life and Death," in *Roman Law*, ed. Bagnall and Harris, 81-95. On the power of the *paterfamilias* in the Roman family, see Eva Cantarella, *Pandora's Daughters* (Baltimore: Johns Hopkins University Press, 1987), 115-16, and Sarah B. Pomeroy, *Goddesses, Whores, Wives, and Slaves: Women in Classical Antiquity* (New York: Schocken, 1975) 150-52.

[45]For discussions of male-female hierarchies in the Hebrew Bible, see the articles in *The Women's Bible Commentary*, ed. Carol A. Newsom and Sharon H. Ringe (Louisville, Ky.: Westminster/John Knox Press, 1992).

career, so, too, do the children themselves have clearly defined duties
and responsibilities towards their parents which extend long beyond the
period of childhood itself.[46] This situation is in keeping with the
indissolubility of the parent-child bond, since "children," Philo tells us,

> are separable parts of their parents, or rather to speak more truly,
> inseparable parts, joined to them by kinship of blood, by the
> thoughts and memories of ancestors..., by the love ties of the
> affection which unites them, by the indissoluble bonds of nature.
> (*Spec.* 1.137)[47]

The responsibilities of offspring towards their parents are seen by
Philo as at least partial compensation for all the trouble that parents go to
on behalf of their children, though such compensation can never be made
in full.[48] Furthermore, kind treatment of one's parents is seen as basic to
other human relations, as Philo suggests in *Dec.* 112:

> For to whom else will they show kindness if they despise the closest
> of their kinsfolk who have bestowed upon them the greatest boons,
> some of them far exceeding any possibility of repayment? For how
> could the begotten beget in his turn those whose seed he is, since
> nature has bestowed on parents in relation to their children an
> estate of a special kind which cannot be subject to the law of
> "exchange"?[49] And therefore the greatest indignation is justified if
> children, because they are unable to make a complete return, refuse
> to make even the slightest.

The primary context for discussion of the duties children owe their
parents is the fifth commandment, which enjoins children to honor their
fathers and mothers (Ex 20:12 [LXX]). Philo expounds at length on the
necessity for children to honor their parents and on what it means to do
so.

---

[46]While it is not clear exactly to what age Philo would limit the period of
childhood, his citation of Solon's periodization of human life implies that infancy
persists for the first seven years and is followed by youth, both stages of which
may be considered "childhood." See *Opif.* 104-5.

[47]Aristotle (*Nicomachean Ethics* 1161a16) comments that parents love children as
part of themselves. The metaphor of the body is used in a similar, but more
explicit way to convey the aspects of participation and hierarchy, in such New
Testament texts as 1 Cor 12, Rom 12:4-5 and Eph 4:16. All quotations from the
works of Aristotle are from the LCL translations.

[48]This seems to be a point of popular wisdom, and is also emphasized by
Josephus, in *Ant.* 4.262, as well as in Wisdom of Ben Sira 7:28. See Aristotle,
Nicomachean Ethics 1163b/17.

[49]According to Colson (*Philo*, vol. 7, p. 64), Philo is here alluding to Attic law
(found in Demosthenes), by which a citizen nominated to perform a "leiturgia"
might call upon a person not so nominated whom he considered to be wealthier
than himself to exchange properties with him.

> With all these facts before them [concerning the sums paid out by parents on behalf of their children], they do not do anything deserving of praise who honour their parents, since any one of the considerations mentioned is in itself quite a sufficient call to show reverence. And on the contrary, they deserve blame and obloquy and extreme punishment who do not respect them as seniors nor listen to them as instructors nor feel the duty of requiting them as benefactors nor obey them as rulers nor fear them as master. (*Spec.* 2.234)

Honor therefore entails respect, obedience, requital and fear. To this list, Philo in *Spec.* 2.235 adds goodness and the seeking of virtue:

> ...in no way wilt thou honour them as well as by trying both to be good and to seem good, to be good by seeking virtue simple and unfeigned, to seem good by seeking it accompanied by a reputation for worth and the praise of those around you.

Several of these duties, namely obedience, fear, courtesy, and nurture are accorded special attention.

a. Obedience

To gain the high excellence which their parents desire for them, states Philo,

> the children will be willing to hearken to their commands and to obey them in everything that is just and profitable; for the true father will give no instruction to his son that is foreign to virtue. (*Spec.* 2.236)[50]

Although's explicit emphasis here is on obedience, this passage raises the question of whether one is obligated to obey paternal instruction which is foreign to virtue. Philo nowhere addresses this question directly. In the context of Philo's worldview as a whole, however, one suspects that in a conflict between virtue and filial obedience, the former must prevail.[51]

b. Fear

In conjunction with the fifth commandment, Philo quotes Lev 19:3: "Let each fear his father and his mother."

> Here he [Moses] sets fear before affection, not as better in every way, but as more serviceable and profitable for the occasion which he has before him. For...persons subject to instruction and

---

[50]On the importance of obedience in the Roman family, see Gardner and Wiedemann, *Roman Household,* 64.

[51]For rabbinic discussion on what is entailed in honoring one's parents, and the limitations to this commandment, see b. *Qidd.* 31b-32b.

admonition are in fact wanting in sense, and want of sense is only cured by fear. (*Spec.* 2.239)[52]

In this sense the relationship between parents and children is similar to that between masters and servants, since the inferior party in both cases is to fear the superior party, and in particular the "active and severe admonition" which attend disobedience and dissolute behavior (*Spec.* 2.241).

c. Courtesy

Another duty which children owe their parents is that of courtesy. This duty extends beyond the parents to

> persons who share the seniority of the parents...One who pays respect to an aged man or woman who is not of his kin may be regarded as having remembrance of his father and mother...And therefore in the Holy Scriptures the young are commanded not only to yield the chief seats to the aged, but also to give place to them as they pass... (*Spec.* 2.237-38)[53]

Such courtesy is a "proof of filial piety" (*Spec.* 2.237) and expresses not only the awe that children should feel for those who remind them of their revered parents but also respect for those who have attained the old age to which the children themselves aspire (*Spec.* 2.238).

d. Care/Nurture

The most important duty that children owe their parents is to care for them in their old age. Like Aristotle, Philo emphasizes the duty of children to "return benefit for benefit" (*Dec.* 113).[54] This duty, encoded in the law of nature itself (*Dec.* 111) may be learned from the examples set by animals. For instance,

> Among the storks the old birds stay in the nests when they are unable to fly, while their children fly...gathering from every quarter provision for the needs of their parents; and so while they in the inactivity justified by their age continue to enjoy all abundance of luxury, the younger birds making light of the hardships sustained in their quest for food, moved by piety and the expectation that the same treatment will be meted to them by their offspring, repay the debt which they may not refuse – a debt both incurred and discharged at the proper time – namely that in which one or other of the parties is unable to maintain itself, the children in the first state of their existence, the parents at the end of their lives. (*Dec.* 116-17)

---

[52]Cf. also *Fug.* 3.
[53]See Lev 19:32; cf. also *Dec.* 167.
[54]Aristotle (*Nicomachean Ethics* 1165a21-27) also emphasizes the necessity of paying back our debt to our parents by supporting them.

If the birds and land animals such as lions and sheepdogs (*Dec.* 113-15) do this "without any teacher but their natural instinct," how much more so should human beings who have the benefit of explicit instruction.[55]

The length, detail, and tone of Philo's discussion of this point attest to its centrality in his view of the parent-child relationship. We can only guess at the reasons that underlie this emphasis. We do not know, for example, whether the neglect or abuse of the elderly was a problem in Philo's community. What is clear, however, is that Philo is addressing those adult children of aging parents who consider themselves to have outgrown the bonds of the filial relationship. Philo urges children of all ages to see themselves as the "repayers of a due" (*Dec.* 118), who are to honor, respect, fear, and obey those who gave them life, and to care for parents in their old age as they themselves were cared for in their youth. To fail in doing so is not only a breach of human trust but also an affront to God,

> For parents are the servants of God for the task of begetting children, and he who dishonours the servant dishonours also the Lord. (*Dec.* 119)[56]

4. Family affection

From the passages which we have discussed above, one might conclude that Philo saw the parent-child relationship primarily in legal terms, and was concerned solely with the obligations and responsibilities owed one to another and the sanctions that might devolve upon those who fail to fulfill them. It must be remembered, however, that most of the Philonic discussion of this relationship has its context in his exposition of the relevant biblical laws. Even in the course of such exposition, it is clear that love and affection, particularly of parents towards children, was considered by Philo to be not only a desideratum but in most cases a very powerful aspect of the state of parenthood.[57]

---

[55]Cf. a similar example in *Virt.* 131-34, in which Philo explicitly urges his reader to refrain from infanticide by learning from the examples of animals who care for their offspring.

[56]Similarly, Aristotle (*Nicomachean Ethics* 1165a24) comments that "Honour also is due to parents, as it is to the gods..." Philo's formulation is reminiscent of the christological statement in John 5:23, which asserts that "He who does not honour the Son does not honour the Father who sent him."

[57]The same point is apparent also in Philo's allegorical work. It is appropriate, suggests Philo, for the biblical matriarch Rebecca to call her son Jacob "child" [Genesis 27:43 LXX: *teknon*], since this title is "at the same time expressive of kindly feeling and suited to a tender age" (*Fug.* 39-40). Philo's comment, while serving his allegorical interpretation of Rebecca as Patience and Jacob as the Man of Practice (*Fug.*46-47), also implies a particular view of the parent-child relationship as one characterized by "kindly feeling" of the parent towards her

In *Spec.* 2. 239 Philo brings to our attention the fact that the law does not address the point of love between parent and child, since love of parents is "learned and taught by instinct and requires no injunction" (*Spec.* 2.240). It is not suitable, says Philo,

> to include in the enactments of a lawgiver an instruction on the duty of filial affection, for nature has implanted this as an imperative instinct from the very cradle in the souls of those who are thus united by kinship. (*Spec.* 2.239)[58]

In a similar vein, Philo explains why the law does not discuss inheritances that parents might receive from their children:

> ...the law, God-given as it is, and ever desirous to follow the course of nature, held that no sinister thought should be introduced. Parents pray that they may leave behind them alive the children they have begotten to succeed to their name, race and property, and the imprecations of their implacable enemies are just the opposite, that the sons and daughters may die before their parents. (*Spec.* 2.129)[59]

In these passages, Philo explicitly operates on the basis of the assumption of an affectionate and loving relationship between parents and children, and uses this assumption to account for the specific formulation of particular laws, and in particular, the omission of any commandment that children love their parents and vice versa.

In the course of other discussions, Philo reflects on the love of a father towards his children. He waxes particularly eloquent on a father's love for the child of his old age. In *Jos.* 4 he comments that

---

child. It may be argued that what Philo and his contemporaries actually meant by "love and affection" differed significantly from our own understanding of this affective bond. But see Golden, (*Childhood*, 82ff.) who affirms that, contrary to what many scholars have argued, Athenian parents did love their children in the ways that modern parents do, despite the high mortality rate and the practice of infanticide in classical Greece.

[58]See also *Spec.* 2.240. Whereas Philo's discussions of family affection imply the mutuality of this aspect of the parent-child relationship, Aristotle comments that the affection of the parent exceeds that of the child both in quality and duration. "For parents love their children as part of themselves, whereas children love their parents as the source of their being....and progenitor is more attached to progeny than progeny to progenitor...parents love their children as soon as they are born, children their parents only when time has elapsed and they have acquired understanding, or at least perception" (*Nicomachean Ethics* 1161b17-26). For similar reasons, Aristotle argues that "parental affection is stronger in the mother" (*Nicomachean Ethics* 1161b29).

[59]This possibility, however, is addressed by the law in a roundabout way, says Philo, by declaring the father's brothers to be the heirs of their nephews, "a privilege doubtless given to the uncle for the sake of the father" (*Spec.* 2.132). See also *Mos.* 2.245.

[Jacob's] love for this child of his later years [Joseph] –and nothing conduces to affection more than this – exceeded his love for his other sons; by special and exceptional attentions he fostered the fire of the boy's nature in the hope that it would not merely smoulder but burst rapidly into flame.

Similarly, the patriarch Abraham

had a most potent incentive to love in that he had begotten the boy in his old age and not in his years of vigour. For parents somehow dote on their late-born children, either because they have longed for their birth for so many years or because they do not hope to have any more, since nature comes to a halt at this point as its final and furthermost boundary. (*Abr.* 195)[60]

The love of father for son is particularly poignant in the face of mortal danger to the life of the son. Gen 22, the biblical account of Abraham's near sacrifice of his son Isaac, provides Philo with the opportunity for further reflection on this point. He notes that although Abraham was

devoted to his son with a fondness which no words can express, [he] showed no change of colour nor weakening of soul [at being asked by God to sacrifice his son], but remained steadfast as ever with a judgment that never bent nor wavered. Mastered by his love for God, he mightily overcame all the fascination expressed in the fond terms of family affection, ...he went forth with his son...as though to perform one of the ordinary rites. (*Abr.* 169-70)

Philo concludes his lengthy description of this event with a comparison of Abraham's act with similar sacrificial acts demanded of other fathers by their country or gods.[61] Abraham's act is superior to theirs for several reasons. First, he obeyed with alacrity, despite his personal anguish (*Abr.* 192). Second, he had no prior preparation for this possibility as human sacrifice was not a custom in his country (*Abr.* 193). Third, and perhaps most important judging by the length of Philo's discussion of this point, Abraham was to sacrifice his only "true" son (*Abr.* 194). Philo expands:

For a father to surrender one of a numerous family as a tithe to God is nothing extraordinary, since each of the survivors continues to give him pleasure, and this is no small solace and mitigation of his grief for the one who has been sacrificed. But one who gives his only darling son performs an action for which no language is

---

[60]The tone of these passages implies that Philo is here citing an aspect of popular psychology. We do not have the information to know whether this could reflect his own personal experience. For a summary of the biographical facts known about Philo, see Goodenough, *Introduction*, 1-8.

[61]For a more critical view of child sacrifice, see *Spec.* 1.312. The fact that Philo does not directly criticize this practice in *Abr.* testifies to an apologetic purpose. Whatever his views about child sacrifice in the abstract, Philo must after all defend Abraham who undertook his action in obedience to God's command.

adequate, since he concedes nothing to the tie of relationship, but
his whole weight is thrown into the scale on the side of acceptability
with God.... (*Abr.* 196)

Finally, Abraham, unlike other fathers, who avoid participating in or
even viewing the sacrificial act (*Abr.* 197), began to perform the sacrifice
himself. "Perhaps too," suggests Philo, warming to his topic, "following
the law of the burnt-offering, he would have dismembered his son and
offered him limb by limb" (*Abr.* 198).

Just as in this case Abraham's obedience to God had to override his
love for his son, so, too, in other cases did family affection have to be set
aside as a basis for behavior. Philo speaks strongly in favour of the
"excellent ordinance" according to which

fathers should not die for their sons nor sons for their parents, but
each person who has committed deeds worthy of death should
suffer it alone and in his own person. (*Spec.* 3.153)[62]

To those who are overly influenced by family affection, and "in their
excessive and overwhelming devotion [are] willing and glad to sacrifice
their guiltless selves for the guilty and die in their stead" (*Spec.* 3.154),
Philo answers:

your devotion is mistimed and the mistimed deserves censure just
as the rightly timed deserves praise....Those whom we call our
kinsfolk...are turned into aliens by their misconduct when they go
astray. (*Spec.* 3.155)

Although Philo clearly assumes that love and affection are the norm
in family relationships, he is not ignorant of situations in which this
norm, and the domesticity to which it should lead, are not operative. He
laments that

there are some who after marrying and begetting children unlearn
in their later days what they knew of self-restraint and are wrecked
on the reef of incontinence. Seized with a mad passion for other
women, they maltreat those who hitherto belonged to them and
behave to the children they have begotten by them as though they
were uncles rather than fathers, copy the unrighteousness shewn by
stepmothers to the first family and altogether devote themselves
and all they have to the second wives and their children, overcome
by the vilest of passions, voluptuousness. (*Spec.* 2.135)[63]

Although the law cannot "heal the frenzy goaded into savagery," it does
attempt to make amends by forcing the father to provide the double

---

[62]Cf. Deut 24:16. For the full discussion, see *Spec.* 3.153-68.
[63]Here Philo simply assumes the "unrighteousness of stepmothers," suggesting
perhaps that he is here expressing a popular stereotype.

portion of his inheritance to his oldest son by his first wife (*Spec.* 2.136). In this way, the law

> shows mercy and pity for the victims of injustice....For naturally we may suppose that the gratification felt by the son at obtaining the double portion is shared by the mother, encouraged as she is by the humanity of the law which refuses to allow her and her family to lie entirely at the mercy of her enemies. (*Spec.* 2.138)

In describing the biblical legal response to a situation in which there is a lack of affection on the part of the father, Philo is still assuming the necessity and normative nature of family affection as the basis of behavior of family members to one another.

Conclusions

In the foregoing pages we have considered Philo's views on the parent-child relationship as expressed in the treatises which comprise the *Exposition of the Law.* It is now appropriate to return to the question with which we started, namely, what do Philo's comments tell us about Jewish parent-child relations in first-century Alexandria?

The methodological obstacles to answering this question are serious and numerous.[64] Are we to regard Philo's words as descriptive or prescriptive? Are Philo's discussions of the *Special Laws* a direct reflection of the legal practices and dicta of the Alexandrian Jewish community, as Goodenough holds, or are they primarily apologetic and exegetical without a strong basis in his immediate social world? Do the parallels to Philo's views in the works of non-Jewish classical and Hellenistic writers have any bearing on whether and to what extent Jewish family life in the Roman Empire might have differed from or resembled family life among non-Jews?

To answer these questions fully would require a broader study than can be provided in these pages. Nevertheless, our survey permits us to hazard a few guesses about the nature of Jewish family life in Alexandria. These conjectures are based on the methodological assumption that the essential and definitive characteristics of the parent-child relationship as Philo describes it, as well as the specific areas pertaining to family life that receive the greatest emphasis in his

---

[64]For a discussion of similar methodological difficulties involved in the study of children and childhood in classical literature, see Wiedemann, *Adults and Children*, 1-3 and passim; Golden, *Childhood*, xiii-xix. We can only agree wholeheartedly with Golden's lament: "If only it were easier to know when these sources speak for others and when they speak just for themselves!" (*Childhood*, xvii).

discussions are at least to some degree reflections of everyday life in Jewish Alexandria.

According to Philo, the parent-child relationship is informed by three fundamental features: the presence of an indissoluble bond of love and kinship between parent and child; the inherent superiority of the parent to the child; the hierarchy of male and female. What is striking about this description of family life is not its uniqueness, but rather its commonplace nature. Neither the readers of Aristotle nor the readers of the "sacred books" of the Jewish commonwealth (cf. *Mos.* 2.45) would have been startled by Philo's views on parent-child relations.

While one should not assume a direct correlation between these views and the everyday reality of family relationships, it may be suggested that these three fundamental and widely accepted features may indeed have come to some expression in the experience of parents and children. Behind Philo's discussions of the many and complex responsibilities of parents towards their children, we can sense that childrearing, then as now, required much effort and dedication. In a cynical or perhaps frustrated moment, Philo suggests that "he who...under the stress of nature makes his children his first care...has passed from freedom into slavery" (*Hypoth.* 11.17). On the whole, however, Philo accepts and condones the tendency of parents to "have little thought for their own personal interests and find the consummation of happiness in the high excellence of their children...." (*Spec.* 2.236). One might imagine that children born within the marital relationship were very much desired and loved, and were in general treated with affection and tenderness by parents who did their best to provide for and nurture them, both physically and spiritually. The children, in turn, were expected to reciprocate by showing honor, fear, concern and courtesy towards their parents.

The male-female hierarchy, which associates women and the senses on the one hand, and men and the mind on the other (cf. *Spec.* 1.200-1), dictated different roles to mothers and daughters than to fathers and sons.[65] The physical nurturing of the child was primarily the

---

[65]Philo's description of the male as "closer akin to causal activity," in *Spec.* 1.200-1 as well as the connection he draws between the male, the rational and the mind recall Philo's account of the Creation of the world, which he attributes to "the active Cause," the "perfectly pure and unsullied Mind of the universe," namely, "its Father and Maker" (*Opif.* 8-9). Nevertheless, the hierarchy of male and female is not grounded in the opposition of active and passive, rational and irrational, mind and sense. Rather, it is the self-evident superiority of male to female that is portrayed as fundamental. The hierarchical relationship between men and women is of course most influential in Philo's discussion of the relationship between husbands and wives. See Heinemann, *Bildung*, 231-50. For discussions

responsibility of the mother, who, after all, is the only one who can provide breastmilk for her child, whereas the task of educating the child belongs to the father, who must provide academic, philosophical, physical, as well as moral instruction and discipline (*Spec.* 2.29, 236). Whereas sons were the recipients of a well-rounded education and their father's estate, daughters were protected, trained for their role of superintendence of and seclusion within the house, and provided with a suitable husband as well as a respectable dowry.[66]

The three fundamental characteristics of the parent-child relationship as described by Philo may have reflected the expectations regarding family life as well as its basic structure. In turn, the cases in which he departs from or expands at length on the biblical passage he is discussing may point to what he perceived to be exceptions or even threats to family life. On this assumption, it may be that neglect of family members, dissolute behavior, infanticide, adultery, "harlotry," and various other forms of nonprocreative sexuality[67] were not unheard of among Jewish adults and their offspring.

Finally, the many parallels in Greco-Roman literature, as well as the likely influence of such institutions as *patria potestas* on Philonic thought, raise the possibility that, despite Philo's protestations to the contrary, Jewish families were not fundamentally different either in structure or in their problems from the non-Jewish families in the Hellenistic world at the turn of the eras. Where they would have differed is in their expected adherence to specific practices such as circumcision and the redemption of the firstborn, for which Philo provides elaborate justification (cf. *Spec.* 1.1-11, 137-40).

Our analysis of Philo's views on parents and children has returned us repeatedly to the strict hierarchy of the begetter and the begotten which provides the framework for the parent-child relationship. Just as men and women must not break loose from the roles assigned to them by "nature,"[68] so, too, must children remain beholden to their parents even after they themselves have reached adulthood.[69] What distinguishes the parent-child hierarchy from the male-female hierarchy, however, is the

---

of male-female relationships in classical Greece and Rome, see Cantarella, *Pandora's Daughters*, passim, and Pomeroy, *Goddesses*, passim.

[66]On the seclusion of women, see *Spec.* 3.169-74 and Heinemann, *Bildung*, 233-35.

[67]This would include the practice of homosexuality, against which Philo directs many paragraphs in *Spec.* 2.50, 3.37-50.

[68]This is one of Philo's arguments against homosexuality, in which the "male type of nature" is debased and converted "into the feminine form, just to indulge a polluted and accursed passion" (*Spec.* 2.50).

[69]Unlike the male-female hierarchy, of course, the parent-child hierarchy is operative only until the death of the one of the parties to the relationship.

fact that individuals can experience both sides of the relationship, as the children of their parents and as the parents of their children. Indeed, when Philo addresses the "men" who should care for their parents as the animals do (*Dec.* 114), and the "good sirs" who need to value the lives of their newborn infants (*Virt.* 133), he may very well have in mind the same segment of the population.

We may therefore imagine the intended reader of Philo's remarks on family life as a member of the so-called "sandwich generation" caught between the competing demands of raising young children towards a life of virtue and repaying the debts owed to their own aging parents. Add to this the need to swim "in the ocean of civil cares," the desire on occasion to contemplate "the universe and its contents" (*Spec.* 3.1-3), and perhaps even the obligation to earn a living, and we have an image of Philo's ancient reader as someone that many of us can recognize. At the same time, both the content of and the assumptions behind Philo's remarks on parents and children more often than not only emphasize the distance that we, his modern readers, must travel in order to understand him and the world in which he lived.

4

Jewish Mothers and Daughters in the Greco-Roman World

Ross S. Kraemer

Introduction

In a provocative essay on women in the book of Judges,[1] Mieke Bal explores the absence of mothers to protest and protect the three victimized, murdered daughters in the book of Judges, concluding that the nurturing maternal qualities of murderous women reflect both women's displaced anger and men's fear of retaliatory mothers. Mother-daughter relationships have received relatively little attention in scholarly studies on family relationships in antiquity, including the research on Jewish family relations. While Bal's compelling analysis of the portrayals of mothers and daughters in Judges is not immediately germane to the study of Jewish family relationships in the Greco-Roman period, it has prompted me to undertake this preliminary inquiry into the representation of mother-daughter relationships in Hellenistic Jewish sources.

Part One: Surveying the Evidence or its Absence

The extant evidence for mother-daughter relationships in Hellenistic Jewish sources is sparse. Jewish texts from the Greco-Roman period, as

---

[1]Mieke Bal, "Dealing/With/Women: Daughters in the Book of Judges," in Regina Schwartz, ed., *The Book and the Text: The Bible and Literary Theory*, (Cambridge, MA and Oxford: Blackwell, 1990) 16-39, condensed from Bal, *Death and Dissymmetry: The Politics of Coherence in the Book of Judges*, (Chicago: University of Chicago Press, 1988).

well as earlier biblical writings yield only the tiniest snippets of narratives about mother-daughter relationships.

The Hebrew Bible

In the Hebrew Bible itself, Exodus 2:1-10 presents the coordinate effort of the mother and sister of Moses, but the focus of the story is clearly the dramatic salvation of the infant son and nothing is said about the relation between the two women. Prominent Israelite mothers are inevitably the mothers of sons, such as the four matriarchs of Israel, Hannah the mother of Samuel, Bathsheba, mother of Solomon, other mothers of kings and so forth. Inversely, the handful of prominent women seem rarely to have mothers. The judge and prophet Deborah, herself called a mother in Israel, has no parentage (although in Judges 4, the later narrative articulation of the poetic account in Judges 5, she acquires a husband). Genesis 11:29 identifies the father, but not the mother of the matriarch Sarah (here Sarai). The matriarch Rebekah is identified only by the name of her father, Bethuel (Gen 24:15),[2] although her mother does play a small part in the story here. When Abraham's servant proposes marriage between Isaac and Rebekah, her mother, whose own name is not given, appears as a minor figure in the marriage negotiations. She receives gifts from Abraham's envoy, and together with Rebekah's brother, she requests that Rebekah not leave immediately, but delay ten days. But the text suggests that when Rebekah consents to leave immediately, it is only her brothers and not her mother who bless her and send her to marry Isaac:

> So they sent away their sister Rebekah...
> And they blessed Rebekah and said to her,
>
> May you, our sister, become
> thousands of myriads...
>
> (Gen 24:59-60)

At best the text subsumes the mother's farewell in that of the brothers. Even the biblical Esther is an orphan bereft of mother and father, under the care of her male kinsman, Mordecai (Esther 2:7).

The closest articulation of a mother-daughter relationship in Jewish biblical texts is that between Naomi, Ruth and Orpah in the book of Ruth. But Naomi is clearly a mother-surrogate, the mother of Ruth and Orpah's now dead husbands. One other intriguing example, outside the

---

[2]Although Rebekah's mother remains unnamed, Rebekah repeatedly identifies herself as the daughter of Bethuel, son of Nahor, whom Milcah bore. Since Milcah was the daughter of Nahor's brother Haran, the repeated reference to her paternal grandmother appears to underscore the fact that Rebekah was Isaac's kin both patrilineally and matrilineally.

scope of my discussion, is the relationship between the narrator of Songs of Songs and her mother, which is still given little articulation.

The Greek Texts of Hellenistic Judaism

In the Greek texts of Hellenistic Judaism, mothers and daughters receive a little more notice, but not much. Judith is another example of the motherless heroine, identified by her father's illustrious lineage, and as her husband's wife (now widow).

In the perhaps less well-known tale of Susanna, the heroine's mother receives brief mention. In the opening verses, subsumed under the term "parents," she is credited with raising her daughter in the law of Moses. Susanna's parents, children and other relatives accompany her to her trial on trumped-up charges of adultery, and at the end, Susanna's parents, here described as "Hilkiah and his wife," praise God for Susanna's vindication.

Mothers and daughters receive the briefest of mentions in 3 Maccabees 1:18. When Ptolemy IV Philopater attempted to enter the inner courts of the Temple in Jerusalem, turmoil erupts in the city. "Young women who had been secluded in their chambers rushed out with their mothers, sprinkled their hair with dust, and filled the streets with groans and lamentations." But the imagery of secluded young women and their mothers, women on the eve of marriage and even nursing women all abandoning characteristic modesty and rushing into the city streets appears to be a literary device designed to highlight the severity of the crisis, and reveals virtually nothing about the nature of mother-daughter relations.

The book of Tobit, where all the female characters have names of their own, offers a few more interesting glimpses of mother-daughter relationships. In Tobit 7:15-17 Sarah's mother Edna comes to prepare the bridal chamber (actually just the 'other' room) for Sarah and Tobias. Bringing her daughter into the room, Edna weeps, but then dries her tears, and exhorts her daughter to take courage. Before she leaves the room, Edna prays that God may grant Sarah joy instead of sorrow, and exhorts her again.[3] Both Edna's tears and her prayer make eminent sense within the story, for Sarah has lost seven previous husbands to a lustful demon who kills each of them before they can consummate the marriage. But one may wonder whether this small scene between Edna and Sarah reflects social reality: where mothers bring their daughters into the

---

[3] Edna exhorts her daughter with the term θάρσει, courage. The same exhortation is found in funerary inscriptions, both Jewish and non-Jewish, urging the deceased to take comfort in the fact that no one is immortal. Perhaps this suggests that for Edna, marrying off her daughter is a little like burying her!

marriage chamber, weeping (for many reasons?) and praying for their daughters' welfare.

In a subsequent scene, after Tobias vanquishes the demon with the aid of a magical potion from the angel Raphael, and he and Sarah are about to depart for his father Tobit's home, Edna and Raguel give instructions to the bridal couple. Edna says to Tobias (10:12):

> In the sight of the Lord, I entrust my daughter to you; do nothing to grieve her all the days of your life.

In the version of the story found in the manuscripts Vaticanus and Alexandrinus, both Raguel and Edna express to Tobias their hope that they will have grandchildren from him and Sarah.[4] In Sinaiticus, only Raguel expresses this hope: Edna does not express the desire for descendants.[5]

The ties between Sarah and Edna are given a little more articulation than usual in Tobit. However, the whole book is generally unusual for its detailed portrait of family life, including wedding celebrations, funerals, meals, sleeping arrangements and other aspects usually conspicuous by their absence in Jewish texts of this period. The portrait of deep affection between parents and their children, and the notion that ties between in-laws are the equivalent of ties between parents and their biological children are both worth remarking.

While such details may point to the social world of Tobit's author, it is also important to note that both the structure and key elements of the story are derived from Genesis 24. In the biblical narrative, Abraham seeks a wife for his son, Isaac, from his own kin, as does Tobit for Tobias. In Genesis 24, the role of God's angel in guaranteeing the success of Abraham's servant is mentioned (24:7,40) but not developed. In Tobit, the role of the angel is paramount. Both stories are characterized by concerns about foreign wives, reluctance on the part of the bride's family to let her leave, nuptial gifts, formal blessings and so forth.

Of course, there are significant differences between the two. In particular, in Genesis 24, Isaac remains at home, while Abraham's

---

[4]Tob 10:11 and 10:13 – NRSV as 10:12.

[5]Fergus Millar summarizes the arguments for the probable priority of Sinaiticus here (in Emil Schürer, *The History of the Jewish People in the Age of Jesus Christ*, revised and edited by Geza Vermes, Fergus Millar, Martin Goodman et al, [Edinburgh: T & T Clark, 1986] 3:1, 228-229). While it is difficult to determine the significance of this seemingly small change, we may speculate that it suggests differing views about whether women as well as men are concerned to have descendants for their own sake, pointing perhaps to differing views about whether women as well as men are obligated to be fruitful and multiply.

servant travels to Aram-naharaim, and negotiates for Rebekah. It may be precisely those places where Tobit departs from the narrative in Genesis 24 that we may look for clues to social reality, including the enhanced attention to mother-daughter relations so sparingly noted in Genesis 24.

Perhaps the most interesting depiction of a mother-daughter relationship comes from the anonymous, apparently first century C.E. writer known as Pseudo-Philo, whose *Biblical Antiquities* contains some fascinating interpretations of women in various biblical narratives.[6] Among the many biblical tales the author retells is the fateful story of Jephthah's nameless daughter (Judges 11:29-40), whom her father sacrifices to God in fulfillment of his rash vow made on the eve of battle to sacrifice, if victorious, that which first comes out to greet him. In the biblical narrative, as Mieke Bal points out, Jephthah's wife, the mother of his daughter, is conspicuous by her absence and failure even to attempt the rescue of her child. While the author of the Biblical Antiquities is powerless to save Jephthah's daughter, he (or she?) imbues the daughter with great wisdom, and provides her not only with her own name, Seila,[7] but also with both mother and nurse to mourn her death.

In a lengthy lamentation, Seila addresses her mother, recalling all the bridal preparations her mother and nurse have made for her in vain.

> May all the blend of oil that you have prepared for me be poured out,
> and the white robe that my mother has woven, the moth will eat it,
> and the crown of flowers that my nurse plaited for me for the festival,
> may it wither up, and the coverlet that she wove of hyacinth and
> purple in my woman's chamber, may the worm devour it.[8]

Seila's consignment of her robe and coverlet to moths and worms suggests the transformation of bridal ceremonies into funeral rites, reinforced by her lament that Sheol has become her bridal chamber.

The portrait of mother and daughter here, limited though it is, suggests several things. As in Tobit, mothers are particularly associated with the preparation of their daughters for marriage, which is the fulfillment of a woman's life. "In vain," Seila tells her mother, "have you borne your only daughter, because Sheol has become my bridal chamber." Seila's mother has prepared certain elements of her daughter's nuptials, including special ointments, and a white robe. But Seila is tended not only by her mother, but also by her nurse, who has

---

[6]Now analyzed by Cheryl Anne Brown, *No Longer Be Silent: First Century Jewish Portraits of Biblical Women* (Louisville: Westminster/John Knox, 1992). English translation of the Latin by D.J. Harrington in OTP 2:297-377.

[7]Harrington (353 n.b) derives this from the Hebrew meaning "to ask," so that Seila is the one "asked for."

[8]*LAB* 40:6.

woven her garlands of flowers, and a blanket of hyacinth and purple, colors which have priestly associations. Though Seila's invocation of her mother might be taken to suggest strong ties between the two, the presence of the nurse points to a social setting of Pseudo-Philo in which nurses play a major role in the rearing of daughters, particularly since these elements are absent altogether from the narrative in Judges.

Another Greco-Roman tale of marriage, the story of the biblical Joseph and his Egyptian wife Aseneth, contributes little to the portrait of mother-daughter relations.[9] Although the mother of Aseneth is routinely present with her husband, the Egyptian priest Pentephres, all the family conversations take place between Aseneth and Pentephres. The mother, who is unnamed, never speaks, either to her daughter or to her husband, despite the fact that she sits next to her daughter during the crucial opening dialogue where Pentephres proposes to marry Aseneth to Joseph, and Aseneth refuses (4:5-5:2).[10] The mother plays an indirect role in the story, to the extent that Aseneth fears the rejection of both of her parents (12:11) for her destruction of their idols. At the resolution of the story, parents and daughter are reconciled at the marriage (20:5) of Aseneth and Joseph. But the mother's only active role in the entire story is to fetch her daughter from the upper rooms where Aseneth has observed Joseph's entry into her father's courtyard, and bring her to

---

[9]The original title of the work is not known, and the manuscripts assign it various titles. The more common *Joseph and Aseneth* has been preferred for its similarity to the titles of ancient Hellenistic romances, but I dislike it for its bias in favor of Joseph, who is in fact absent for much of the story. Two significantly different reconstructions of the text have been proposed by Marc Philonenko, *Joseph et Aseneth: Introduction, texte critique, traduction, et notes.* Studia Post Biblica (Leiden: E.J. Brill, 1968) and Christoph Burchard, *Joseph und Aseneth*, Jüdische Schriften aus hellenistisch-römische Zeit (Gutersloh, 1983). Burchard translated his own provisional text in *OTP* 2:177-247. English translations of Philonenko's text may be found in *The Apocryphal Old Testament*, ed. H.F.D. Sparks, (Oxford: Oxford University Press, 1984) 465-502 (by D. Cook); and in Ross S. Kraemer, *Maenads, Martyrs, Matrons, Monastics: A Sourcebook on Women's Religions in the Greco-Roman World* (Philadelphia: Fortress Press, 1988) 263-79.
Aseneth was the topic for the 1991-92 Philadelphia Seminar on Christian Origins, chaired by myself and Robert A. Kraft: it was also the focus of Kraft's doctoral seminar that same year. Although recent scholarship on Aseneth has tended to accept Burchard's provisional reconstruction, our work, still in progress, raised significant questions about this consensus. In correspondence, Burchard expressed his agreement with many of our concerns. For a brief discussion of the gendered dimensions of the different reconstructions, see Ross S. Kraemer, *Her Share of the Blessings: Women's Religions Among Pagans, Jews and Christians in the Greco-Roman World*, (New York and Oxford: Oxford University Press, 1992) 110-113.
[10]Versification follows the text of Philonenko.

greet Joseph (8:1). In contrast to Tobit, in *Aseneth* it is a male angelic figure who prepares Aseneth for the bridal chamber, not a human mother.

Finally, a brief allusion to mothers and daughters occurs in the Latin Assumption of Moses 11:12, where Joshua, speaking to Moses, asks:

> How then shall I be able to guide this people, as a father his only son, or as a mistress (domina) her daughter, a virgin that is being prepared to be given to a man, (a mistress) who was careful to protect her (daughter's) body from the sun, and her feet that they were not unshod to walk on the ground.[11]

This imagery provides additional confirmation of an image of the mother-daughter relationship focused around the preparation of the daughter for marriage. While this view is clearly androcentric, it may also reflect social reality, and a self-understanding held by many women themselves.

In many early Jewish texts, biblical and otherwise, intimate relationships between women, if they are visible at all, are between women and their servants, such as Judith and her steward; or women and their female companions (who may also be servants/slaves), such as Aseneth and the seven virgins with whom she was raised. This may also be true for Seila in the *Biblical Antiquities*, but there the virgin companions are among the features taken directly from the narrative of Judges, and so perhaps less an indication of the author's experience of intimate relationships between women.

Non-literary Evidence: Inscriptions

Mother-daughter bonds find only slight expression in Jewish funerary epitaphs. Rarely do mothers commemorate daughters, or daughters their mothers. The prevailing absence of such inscriptions, and their occasional presence both point to underlying social situations. Most ancient funerary dedications, Jewish and non-Jewish, were made by husbands for their wives, followed by wives for their husbands. Inscriptions by children for a parent suggest the absence of a surviving legitimate spouse.[12] The handful of extant inscriptions between mothers and daughters offer only the most minimal clues to relationships between Jewish mothers and daughters. For instance, in CIJ 141, from the Vigna Randanini catacomb on the Via Appia, a young woman named

---

[11]I am grateful to Professor Jan Willem van Henten for providing me with this reference, and with the translation.

[12]Women who are commemorated by their children rather than their husbands may simply have been widowed, but the absence of a spouse may also suggest that the woman was enslaved.

Dulcitia memorializes her mother, Melitium, who died at the age of 29.[13] That a woman of such age could have a daughter old enough to commission the inscription suggests much, as I shall develop below.

A few more literary burial inscriptions from the Jewish necropolis at Tel el-Yehudieh in Egypt allude poignantly to ties between mothers and daughters, although it is never easy to know when such inscriptions do more than employ expected social conventions. In *CIJ/CPJ* 1509, a woman named Horaia commemorates the successive deaths of her husband and her daughter, Eirene, lamenting that Eirene died unmarried. Though this small detail accords well with the limited literary evidence that mothers were especially concerned to see their daughters successfully married, we should note that at least one other Jewish inscription from Egypt bemoans the fate of a young boy who dies too young to have been married,[14] and that the fate of dying childless is lamented for both sexes. Sadly, Horaia herself died two days after her daughter, at the age of 30.

One other particularly poignant Jewish epitaph from Egypt, *CIJ/CPJ* 1510, commemorates a young woman named Arsinoe, who lost her own mother as a child, and who herself died giving birth to her first child. For these tragedies, the composer of her inscription calls her life hard and terrible.

Non-Literary Evidence: Papyri

Although Jewish papyri from Egypt illuminate various aspects of the lives of Jewish women, including their legal status, their economic roles and certain aspects of their social interactions, they shed virtually no light on relationships between mothers and daughters. However, a small number of non-Jewish letters from Egypt do testify to ancient mother-daughter relations. Since there are good reasons to think that the social dynamics of Jewish mothers and daughters were not unique to Jews, we should briefly discuss some of these papyri.

Fuks classified the first of these among the Jewish papyri, because the writer of the letter, Eudaimonis, was the mother of a participant in the suppression of the Jewish revolt of 115-117 C.E., a *strategos* named Apollonius.[15] In this particular letter, which the editor dates to July 16, 117 C.E., Eudaimonis writes to Aline, her daughter, who is married to

---

[13]Epitaphs from mothers to daughters include CIJ 108; 213; 678; 1509.
[14]*CIJ/CPJ* 1512.
[15]*CPJ* 442. *CPJ* 2, section 11, covers the papyrological testimony to the revolt, including a number of other papyri involving Eudaimonis, Apollonios and Aline, the daughter of Eudaimonis and sister/wife of Apollonios.

Apollonius, thus providing evidence for what appears to be a true sibling marriage.[16]

The letter seems to be written several weeks after Aline has left her mother in Hermoupolis for Apollinopolis. Aline is currently pregnant, and Eudaimonis expresses her hope that the outcome of the pregnancy will be successful and that the child will be a boy. While this may reflect general ancient preference for male children, it is important to note that Aline and Apollonios already have a daughter named Heraidous, who is living with Eudaimonis.

Eudaimonis reports that she has resumed weaving under difficult circumstances – it is hard to find help, and she is making do with Aline's slaves. Fuks takes this as evidence of the economic disruption caused by the revolt. She writes that Aline's sister Souerous has given birth, and that Aline's own daughter perseveres with her lessons, προσκαρτερεῖ τοῖς μαθήμασι, an interesting allusion to the education of girls. She then berates her daughter as follows: "Why did you send me 20 drachmai, when I have no leisure? I already have the vision of being naked when winter starts." Fuks takes this to mean that Eudaimonis considered the money too small to make a difference under the circumstances, though it seems not inconceivable that Eudaimonis here complains that she is so busy attempting to prepare for the oncoming winter she has no time to spend the money.

Eudaimonis' description of her own life, and her implicit assumption that such affairs interest Aline, and reflect the realities of Aline's life as well, conform to recent feminist reconstructions of women's lives in Greco-Roman antiquity. Eudaimonis' affairs are closely interwoven with those of other women: the female slaves who weave with or for her; the daughter recently delivered of a child; the granddaughter in her care; and two other women, Teeus and the wife of Eudemos, whose exact relationship to Eudaimonis or Aline is not clear, but who are obviously important. Teeus has written to Eudaimonis that she has left her own people and gone to be with Aline, while the otherwise unnamed wife of Eudemos continues to be of support to Eudaimonis.

The letter also testifies to women's participation in the ancient economy, here through the traditional activity of weaving, and to women's relative autonomy in travel, as witnessed by the journeys both of Aline and Teeus. The fact that Aline sends her mother money again suggests a measure of autonomy.

While the letter thus seems to accord well with our general perceptions that women in antiquity spent much of their lives interacting primarily with other women, it is also important to remember that this

---

[16]*CPJ* 2:227.

letter was written in wartime, when many men, like Apollonios, were away fighting (or had died in the battles), leaving women home to manage the ordinary affairs of both the private and public spheres. Many studies have shown that wartime frequently increases women's participation in public and communal affairs, and some of what we see in this letter may reflect the specific circumstances of the years around the revolt.

What may we say about the relationship between mother and daughter manifest in this letter? Clearly the two remain in close contact: they visit, they write, Aline sends money to her mother, and Eudaimonis cares for Aline's daughter during a time of crisis. Eudaimonis expresses her concerns for Aline's welfare, and carps about the money Aline has sent. Still, it is almost impossible to infer much about what we might characterize as "the emotional tenor" of the ties between the two.

It is also difficult to determine how representative their relationship might be for other mothers and daughters in similar social circles in early second-century Egypt, let alone for the many other mothers and daughters in the Greco-Roman period. If, as seems the case, Eudaimonis' children are married to each other, we may well need to take into account how such marriages affected the nature of relations between mothers and daughters.

Two other papyri, both from Oxyrhynchus in the third century C.E., written by daughters to their mothers, document the minutiae of ordinary life. In one,[17] a daughter sends her mother oil, dried figs and purple wool, asking that her mother make the wool into women's clothing. She asks that the mother send back her black veil and a shawl, and urges her mother to shake out her other *himation* to prevent it from spoiling. In the other,[18] Apia writes to her mother, Sarapias, sending clothing and greetings from a number of people. Interestingly, most of the persons Apia greets, or whose greetings she conveys to her mother are men, including her own brothers, and several whose relationships are not specified. Both papyri suggest that adult daughters and their mothers lived apart from one another, but maintained contact and continued to participate in the mundane aspects of each other's lives. When Apia admonishes her mother not to get all excited (μὴ μετεωρίζου, since "we are well," it may be tempting for us to imagine a familiar dynamic between mother and daughter, but whether such language points to family dynamics, or ancient conventions is difficult to say.

Finally, we should be cautious about extrapolating from the circumstances of women in Greco-Roman Egypt to women living

---

[17]*P. Oxy.* 2273.
[18]*P. Oxy.* 1679.

elsewhere in the ancient Mediterranean. The perception of strong ties between mothers and daughters in these three papyri may reflect the specific cultural contexts of Greco-Roman Egypt, which has by this time a long history of the relative autonomy of women.[19]

Non-Literary Evidence: The Babatha Papyri

In 1961, a team of excavators led by Yigael Yadin discovered a cache of personal papyri in the Cave of Letters in the Judean desert, which the previous year had yielded important finds from the Bar Kochba rebellion. These papyri constituted the personal archives of a Jewish woman named Babatha, whose precise association with the Bar Kochba rebellion remains a mystery. The majority are in Greek, with some Aramaic portions, particularly the attestations of witnesses. The find was reported in the *Israel Exploration Journal* in 1962, with brief descriptions of the contents of the archive, but the papyri themselves remained unpublished for more than a quarter century.[20] Unlike the Dead Sea Scrolls, this delay in publishing the most significant find ever to surface concerning a Jewish woman provoked no outcry, public or scholarly.

Unfortunately for the focus of this paper, Babatha's personal archive contains no documents which pertain directly to mother-daughter relations. From them, we know Babatha to have had at least one son, Jesus, by her first husband, also named Jesus. If she had other children, we know nothing of them. However, after the death of her first husband, when her son was still young enough to require the appointment of guardians, Babatha married a man named Judah, son of Eleazar, who already had another wife named Miriam. Judah and Miriam had a daughter, Shelamzion.

---

[19]On the general subject of women in Hellenistic Egypt, see Sarah Pomeroy, *Women in Hellenistic Egypt From Alexander to Cleopatra,* (New York: Schocken, 1984).

[20]Yigael Yadin, "Expedition D – The Cave of the Letters," *IEJ* 12 (1962) 227-57; H.J. Polotsky, "The Greek Papyri from the Cave of the Letters," in the same, 258-62. The find is described in Yigael Yadin, *Bar Kochba,* (New York: Random House, 1971). The papyri were published sporadically in Israeli, American and German journals over the next twenty-five years, including an assortment by Yadin and Polotsky in *Eretz Israel* 8 (1967); Naphtali Lewis, Ranon Katzoff, and Jonas Greenfield, "*Papyrus Yadin 18,*" *Israel Exploration Journal* 37 (1987) 4: 229-50; Lewis, "Two Greek Documents from Provincia Arabia," *Illinois Classical Studies* 3 (1978) 100-14. Some of these were also published in *SB*. The majority of the papyri were published in 1989: Naphtali Lewis, *The Documents from the Bar Kochba Period in the Cave of Letters: Greek Papyri,* Judean Desert Studies 2, (Jerusalem: Israel Exploration Society, Hebrew University, Shrine of the Book, 1989). Subsequent references are to this volume.

Among Babatha's papyri were several pertaining to Shelamzion, including the contract for Shelamzion's marriage (to a man also named Judah), a deed of gift dated eleven days after the marriage in which Shelamzion's father gives her half his property immediately, and cedes her the remainder upon his death; and a third document pertaining to disputes over that gift between Shelamzion and her male cousins.[21] Several weeks prior to Shelamzion's marriage, her father Judah borrowed 300 denarii from Babatha, which turns out to be precisely the cash portion of Shelamzion's dowry. Thus, as the editors surmise, it seems quite likely that Babatha provided the money for her step-daughter's dowry, while Miriam, Shelamzion's mother, was still very much alive.[22] That Babatha, and not Shelamzion's own mother, provided the funds for Shelamzion's dowry might also point to strong affective ties between Babatha and her step-daughter, although the papyri do not tell us why Babatha lent Judah the money, and perhaps the simplest explanation is that she had it, while neither Judah nor Miriam did.

As the editors note, though, the very fact that Shelamzion's papers were found together with those of Babatha suggests a close tie between the two women.[23] This may be all the more telling in light of the fact that after Judah son of Eleazar died, sometime before the summer of 131 C.E., several papyri attest to a conflict between Babatha and Miriam over the estate of their late husband.[24] In particular, it appears that Babatha took control of date orchards belonging to Judah when the estate failed to repay the loan for Shelamzion's dowry, or to restore Babatha's own dowry. In one document, Babatha accuses Miriam of cleaning out Judah's house after his death, while Miriam replies that she had previously warned Babatha to stay away from Judah's possessions, and denies that Babatha has any claims on the estate.[25] While we have little evidence for the relationship between Babatha and Miriam during the years they were co-wives, this document suggests that they were unlikely to have had a cordial relationship after they were widowed. In light of this antagonism, the evidence pointing to ties between Babatha and Miriam's daughter Shelamzion seems more significant. Perhaps

---

[21]P. *Yadin* 18, 19 and 20, respectively.

[22]Lewis, 24.

[23]Lewis, 26. Interestingly, I think all the editors have assumed that the papyri were brought to the cave by Babatha, who was also carrying papers belonging to Shelamzion. Since the vast majority of the papyri were clearly Babatha's and not Shelamzion's, this seems reasonable, but it also seems possible that the opposite is the case: that Shelamzion was carrying her step-mother's papers.

[24]P. *Yadin* 26; also the fragment in 34.

[25]P. *Yadin* 26.

Shelamzion sided with Babatha in the dispute, which was, after all, at least partly based on the loan for Shelamzion's own dowry.[26]

Lacking any real information about the relationship between Miriam and Shelamzion, we might still consider some possible implications of our limited data. Strong affective ties between Babatha and Shelamzion might also point to a poor relationship between Miriam and her daughter. We might also wonder which, if either, was the cause, and which the effect: whether Shelamzion and Babatha were close because Shelamzion and Miriam were not, or whether Babatha's entrance into the family disrupted previously strong ties. While the Babatha papyri illuminate a mother-daughter relationship indirectly at best, they do afford us some glimpses into the tensions which complex family relationships could have in this period.

Jewish Mothers and Daughters in the New Testament

Mother-daughter relationships have virtually no visibility in the writings of the New Testament. As in the Hebrew Bible, prominent mothers are routinely mothers of sons, and prominent women not identified as mothers seem to have no mothers of their own! The rare exceptions are not much help. The gospels of Mark and Matthew attribute the death of John the Baptist to the young Salome, who acts at the direct behest of her scheming mother Herodias.[27] These same two gospels also contain the story of Jesus' interaction with a Gentile woman who beseeches him to cure her possessed daughter.[28]

Part Two: Accounting for the Evidence (and its Absence)

How might we account for the paucity of evidence for mother-daughter relationships among Jews in the Greco-Roman period? Obviously, we cannot conclude that mothers and daughters had no relationships, but we also should not assume that the absence of evidence simply reflects the male distortion of women's lives, or disinterest in women's lives which is a major factor in the general absence of evidence for women in the ancient world. Rather, I suggest that this particular lack reflects the extent to which mother-daughter relationships were themselves devalued and discounted, even perhaps, by mothers and daughters themselves.

---

[26]It is also possible that by the time the archives were hidden in the cave, Miriam was dead, although nothing in the papyri allows us to establish this one way or the other.

[27]Mk 6:17-29; Mt 14:1-12. The story is essentially absent in Luke, who simply reports that Herod shut John up in prison.

[28]Mk 7:24-30; Mt 15:21-28. It is interesting that here, too, the story is absent in Luke.

Lacking much in the way of information about relations between Jewish mothers and daughters, the evidence for such a conclusion must be taken from what we know about mother-daughter relationships among non-Jews in the same period. This raises also the question of to what extent, if any, Jewish mother-daughter relations were likely to have been significantly different than those of non-Jews, especially given the findings of other papers in this volume that in many respects, Jewish family structures (if not also dynamics?) were remarkably similar to those of non-Jews.

In the last few years, a significant number of studies have appeared on the family in antiquity, with particular emphasis on the Roman period.[29] These studies identify a number of factors which would have discouraged the development of strong affective ties between parents and children in Roman society, including divorce; exogamy and patrilocal marriage; child-bearing and child-rearing practices; and maternal preference for sons. As we shall see, some of these are more applicable to relations between mothers and daughters than others. Many may be applicable equally to Jews and non-Jews. Some were pertinent only to free Roman citizens, while others affected slaves as well, though perhaps somewhat differently.

Divorce

Numerous Roman social historians have remarked on the relative frequency of divorce in ancient Roman society.[30] Ruptured conjugal ties

---

[29]Jane F. Gardner and Thomas Wiedemann, eds., *The Roman Household: A Sourcebook,* (London and New York: Routledge, 1991); Keith R. Bradley, *Discovering the Roman Family,* (New York and Oxford: Oxford University Press, 1991); Suzanne Dixon, *The Roman Mother,* (Norman, OK: Oklahoma University Press, 1988); idem, *The Roman Family,* (Baltimore: The Johns Hopkins University Press, 1992); Jane Gardner, *Women in Roman Law and Society,* (Bloomington and Indianapolis: Indiana University Press, 1986); Judith Hallett, *Fathers and Daughters in Roman Society,* (Princeton: Princeton University Press, 1984); Aline Rousselle, *Porneia. On Desire and the Body in Antiquity,* transl. Felicia Pheasant, (London: Basil Blackwell, 1988); idem., "Body Politics in Ancient Rome," in P.S. Pantell, ed. *A History of Women: 1. From Ancient Goddesses to Christian Saints,* transl. Arthur Goldhammer, (Cambridge, MA, and London: The Belknap Press of Harvard University Press, 1992), 296-336; Beryl Rawson, ed., *The Family in Ancient Rome: New Perspectives,* (Ithaca: Cornell University Press, 1986); Beryl Rawson, ed., *Marriage, Divorce and Children in Ancient Rome,* (Oxford: The Clarendon Press, 1991); Tim G. Parkin, *Demography and Roman Society,* (Baltimore: The Johns Hopkins University Press, 1992).

[30]Susan Treggiari, "Divorce Roman Style: How Easy and how Frequent was it?" in Rawson, *Marriage,* 31-46, makes the telling observation that frequency is a judgment of the modern scholar: "The suspicion arises that a writer who sees a high incidence of divorce in Rome means it is high in relation to what he thinks it should be or in relation to his own time," (44).

and the formation of subsequent alliances were common not only among the citizen elite (who were able to contract licit marriage) but also, though perhaps for different reasons, among the rest of population, even among those, such as slaves, who were not able to contract licit marital unions.[31]

For a woman legally married, divorce normally meant separation from her children, since under Roman law, children from a licit marriage essentially belonged to their fathers. Although Treggiari wisely points out that we cannot estimate the actual frequency of Roman divorce, it was frequent enough for us to surmise that it played a role in the attachments formed between elite Roman mothers and children, sons and daughters alike.[32]

In this regard, ironically, enslaved mothers might be seen to have had an advantage over their free counterparts, since the dissolution of their conjugal relationships did not (automatically) deprive them of their children. But enslaved women had no rights to their children, either, who belonged instead to the women's owners, and enslaved women were equally if not more likely to be separated from their children without any say in the matter. Free women whose children were born outside licit marriage were the only mothers whose children, in some senses, belonged to them,[33] and who were not likely to lose their children as a result of the dissolution of a conjugal relationship.

It is by no means clear which legal systems regulated the marital and familial arrangements of Jews in the Greco-Roman period, and it is not my intention to engage in that debate here, except to note that few Jews would have been bound by the laws regarding Roman citizens. Still, "traditional" Jewish regulation of marriage, divorce and child custody, whether derived from the Bible or from subsequent ancient Jewish sources shares several salient features with Roman law. Divorce was quite permissable, and children of legal marriages belonged to their fathers in the event of a dissolution of the marriage. Thus, free Jewish women, legally married by whatever standard, were similarly vulnerable to the loss of their children through divorce.

The situation of enslaved Jewish women owned by non-Jews was also similar to that of enslaved non-Jewish women, since their owners

---

[31]On licit marriage, see Gardner, especially 31-65.

[32]See e.g. Rawson, "The Roman Family," in Rawson, *Family*, 30. See also Bradley, "Dislocation in the Roman Family," in Bradley, *Roman Family* 125-55, on the general impact of Roman patterns of marriage, divorce and remarriage on Roman family life and expectations.

[33]Beryl Rawson, "Adult-Child Relationships in Roman Society," in Rawson, *Marriage*, 7-30; here p. 26. Such children, Rawson notes, were in fact legally autonomous, having neither a legal father, nor an owner.

could separate them from their children at will. Because the vast majority of Jews enslaved in the Roman period were owned by non-Jews, it is likely to have been irrelevant whether or not the woman was married according to any form of Jewish law.

The circumstances of Jewish mothers differed from that of non-Jewish Roman mothers only in one, interesting regard. Since Jewish law allowed polygamy, Jewish men did not have to divorce their wives to contract a second licit marriage. Theoretically, then, Jewish mothers might be slightly less vulnerable to be divorced, and thus to losing their children. Until recently, many scholars doubted that polygamy was practiced with any frequency in the Greco-Roman period, but the discovery of the Babatha papyri suggests otherwise.[34] By contrast, bigamy was illegal in ancient Rome, and Roman men had to divorce their wives in order to contract a second licit marriage.[35]

Exogamy and patrilocal marriage

Marriage in the Greco-Roman world separated mothers and daughters. Regardless of the specific cultural and legal contexts, brides were routinely expected to leave their natal homes at marriage and take up residence with their husband's family. Just how long mothers lived with their daughters depended on the average age at first marriage for girls, which seems to have varied in the Greco-Roman period. Aline Rousselle claims, for example, that Roman girls were routinely married before or at the onset of puberty, whereas Greeks generally waited until the evidence of puberty was firmly established, and that such differences continued well into the Roman empire.[36] The modest epigraphical and papyrological evidence suggests an average age at first marriage of about 15 for Jewish girls, although rabbinic sources generally assume an earlier

---

[34]Lewis, 23-24. The editors offer the tentative suggestion that a scarcity of suitable husbands due to the effects of the Bar Kochba rebellion might have increased the practice of polygamy in this period, and they speculate that "the status of a second wife was the best that a widow – even a young, well-to-do widow – could expect in Babatha's situation," 22. They do not consider the possibility that the best Babatha might have done was to remain single! Clearly, though, we know nothing about the motives of either Babatha or Judah in contracting their marriage.

[35]See Gardner 91-93.

[36]Rousselle, *Porneia* 32-33. Rousselle attributes the anatomical errors made by Roman doctors, and contested by Soranus, to the routine practice of marrying and deflowering young girls before first menses. See also Keith Hopkins, "The Age of Roman Girls at Marriage," *Population Studies* 18 (1965) 309-27 and Brent Shaw, "The Age of Roman Girls at Marriage: Some Reconsiderations," *Journal of Roman Studies* 77 (1987) 30-46.

age of 12, with betrothals even earlier.[37] Interestingly, if 15 was approximately the average age of menarche in the ancient world,[38] as some research has suggested, this would make the epigraphic and papyrological evidence consonant with Greek practice, while the rabbinic model accords more closely with Roman custom.

Regardless of cultural differences, it seems quite clear that the age of first marriage for girls was somewhere between twelve and eighteen. The average age for men at first marriage, again regardless of cultural difference, was significantly older: considerable evidence suggests that thirty was not unusual.[39] Philo of Alexandria considered a man "ripe" for marriage between the ages of 28 and 35.[40]

These demographic patterns are likely to have been of great significance for relations between free mothers and their children. Greco-Roman mothers, Jewish and otherwise, could expect to lose their daughters to marriage at an early age, often while those daughters were essentially still children, and before the daughter had become a woman in her own right. Sons, on the other hand, remained unmarried for far longer than daughters, and even when they married, were far more likely to continue living with or near their parents.

Judith Hallett and others have suggested that such realities contributed to the creation of stronger bonds between elite Roman mothers and sons than between Roman mothers and daughters,[41] and there is no reason to think that the same would not have applied to Jewish mothers as well, at least those of analogous social class. Mothers would have done well not to become too attached to daughters who would leave them and their households at an early age.

The pervasive concern for the virginity of brides at first marriage may also have created pressures on the mother-daughter relationship which was without analogue in mother-son relationships. While a daughter who lost her virginity prior to marriage shamed her father

---

[37]Ross S. Kraemer, "Jewish Women in the Diaspora World of Late Antiquity," in Judith Baskin, ed., *Jewish Women in Historical Perspective*, (Detroit: Wayne State University Press, 1991) 56-58, with references in the notes.

[38]D. Amundsen and C.J. Diers, "The Age of Menarche in Classical Greece and Rome," *Human Biology* 41 (1969) 125-32. Rousselle concludes that "[i]t would be presumptuous to hazard a guess as to the average age at puberty; it is better to accept the ancient physicians' own estimate of fourteen," "Body Politics," 303. See also Parkin 123.

[39]Richard P. Saller, "Men's Age at Marriage and its Consequences in the Roman Family," *Classical Philology* 82 (1987) 21-34; see also Parkin 125.

[40]*Creation* 103. Philo explicitly quotes Solon for his schema. By contrast, the Mishnah (*Abot* 5:21) gives 18 as the proper age for a young man to marry.

[41]Hallett 253.

particularly, it seems apparent that it was mothers who were responsible, on a daily basis, for guarding the purity of their daughters. Since ancient sources afford us only the most restricted understanding of how women experienced these constraints and concerns, it is difficult to say how this affected mother-daughter relationships, but it seems quite feasible that it provided one more incentive for a mother to be relieved when her daughter left the house, still a virgin on her wedding day.[42]

Little of this discussion, of course, bears on the experience of enslaved women whose children were also slaves, since such children were unlikely to contract licit marriage.[43]

Child-bearing and child-rearing

It would be unwise to assume that ancient attitudes toward children were essentially identical to those of twentieth century scholars. Recent studies suggest precisely the opposite, some of them even calling into question whether the idea of childhood itself as a distinct stage from adulthood is not in fact a modern cultural construct.[44]

In her recent study of the Roman family, Suzanne Dixon concludes that for Roman citizens, "the great cultural emphasis was undoubtedly on children as progeny who were able to continue the family name and cult, supply labor, inherit and maintain the family, support their aged parents, and supply them with proper funeral rites."[45] While these tasks may have been disproportionately the responsibilities of sons, rather than daughters, Dixon's description would seem reasonably accurate for free Jewish families as well,[46] with the probable exception of expectations

---

[42]Concerns for a daughter's purity are expressed in such Jewish sources as Sir 42:9-14, and Ps. Phocylides 215-217, which precedes its admonition to guard virgin daughters in locked rooms with a warning to guard young boys from the desires of adult men.

[43]They could contract licit marriage if they were freed, of course.

[44]Rousselle, *Porneia* 47-62; John Boswell, *The Kindness of Strangers: The Abandonment of Children in Western Europe from Late Antiquity to the Renaissance* (New York: Pantheon Books, 1988) 35-39, with extensive notes on the history of the discussion; T. Wiedemann, *Adults and Children in the Roman Empire* (London: Routledge, 1989).

[45]Dixon, *Roman Family*, 131.

[46]It is a little more difficult to know whether and how to apply Dixon's observations about slave children to Jews. "Slave children could be absorbed into the network of sentiment and patronage, but were also treated as a straight economic investment, to be developed or sold in most cases," 131. Dixon asserts that adults who reared abandoned children generally had specific gains in mind. Jews owned slaves in the Greco-Roman period, and apparently reared abandoned children at least on occasion (on which, see Ross S. Kraemer, "On the Meaning of the Term `Jew' in Greco-Roman Inscriptions," *Harvard Theological Review* 82 [1989]:1, 38-43. In general, though, Jewish experience of slavery was

about continuing household cults. Those expectations may easily have had their counterparts in expectations about continuing participation in Jewish communal religious life.

Although children were expected to provide their parents and families with respect, deference, support and commemoration, Dixon observes that Roman society exhibited a general disregard for the welfare of children. Children, both free and enslaved, were expected to work, and corporate punishment was unremarkable. Enslaved children were subject to harsher physical treatment, to which should be added sexual exploitation, for both girls and boys. All of this suggests that adults in the Greco-Roman world began with cultural assumptions about children very different than our own.

But beyond such cultural generalities, the specifics of bearing and raising children in the Greco-Roman world may have also contributed to a devaluing of the mother-daughter relationship. Some of these realities, of course, applied to parent-child relationships, generally, while others had a greater effect on mother-daughter ties.

Although actual figures are impossible to calculate reliably, it is undeniable that the experience, not only of spontaneous abortion, but also of infant and early childhood death was common, if not routine, in the ancient world. Classicists have argued recently that high infant and childhood mortality rates in general discouraged too much affection between parents and children, as a kind of prophylactic against inevitable grief.[47] Keith Bradley has even suggested that elite Roman parents gave their children to wetnurses, rather than having the mother nurse the child herself, as a strategy to distance the parents from the child during the period when children were most likely to die.[48] Bradley does not discuss whether this would have worked differently for the mother than for the father (whose closeness to the infant was never dependent on nursing). Presumably, it is not simply the employment of a wetnurse which distanced the parents from the child, but rather the fact that the wetnurse kept the child with her, perhaps even in her own household, minimizing early contact between the parents and the child.

Many scholars believe that girls were much more likely to be the victims of infanticide and exposure at birth. Ironically, this might be the product of a general preference for sons over daughters which might

---

more likely to have been from the vantage point of the enslaved, especially in the years from 63 BCE to the late second century CE.

[47]Bradley, "Wetnursing at Rome: A Study in Social Relations," in Rawson, *Family*, 220; *Dislocation*, 140; Dixon, *Roman Family* 99. Both Bradley and Dixon cite earlier work by L. Stone, *The Family, Sex and Marriage in England, 1500-1800*, (London: Weidenfeld and Nicholson, 1977).

[48]Bradley, "Wetnursing."

then suggest that those daughters who were allowed to live were particularly loved and valued.[49] Several ancient sources claim, though, that Jews did not practice abortion or infanticide, but rather raised all their children (a practice considered quite odd by Greco-Roman commentators).[50] While there is also some evidence to the contrary,[51] it is quite possible that infanticide and exposure were not routinely practiced by Jews.

Regardless, Jews were equally likely to have experienced the pain of infant and childhood mortality due to causes more "natural" than infanticide. While the available demographic evidence does not permit us to determine whether girls were more likely than boys to die in infancy or childhood, other factors suggest this would be a reasonable surmise. For instance, when food was scarce, women and girls were at the bottom of the priority list for food, both at the citywide distribution level, and probably within individual households as well, increasing girls' vulnerability to death from illness and starvation (at times). If girls were less likely to survive childhood, this might have provided further incentive for mothers, Jewish and non-Jewish alike, to minimize their attachments to their daughters.

Maternal Preference for Sons

Like their non-Jewish counterparts, Jewish mothers had ample reasons to favor sons over daughters. While daughters could be expected to leave their mothers at an early age, sons could be counted on to remain in the family sphere. They were expected to provide for their mothers in old age, and to serve as their legal guardians and protectors. These roles were particularly important given the typical great age discrepancy between Greco-Roman wives and their husbands, which vastly increased the likelihood that women who survived childbirth and avoided divorce were likely to end up as widows. Daughters, on the other hand, could be expected to provide little in the way of sustenance and support for their aged mothers.

---

[49]Rawson, "Roman Family," in *Family* 11, n.7.

[50]E.g. Tacitus, *Histories* 5,5; Hecataeus of Abdera apud Diodorus Siculus, *Library* 40,3. For detailed discussion and references, along with text and translation, see M. Stern, *Greek and Latin Authors on Jews and Judaism* (Jerusalem: Israel Academy of Sciences and Humanities, 1976-84)1:26-35, especially 33 note to 8 for Hecataeus; 2:19, 26, 41 for Tacitus. Among the Jewish authors who affirm this are Philo (*Spec. Laws* 3:110; *Virt.* 131f); Josephus, *Ag. Ap.* 2:202. Ps. Phocylides 184-85 inveighs against abortion and the exposure of children to vultures and wild animals. See commentary in Pieter W. van der Horst, *The Sentences of Pseudo-Phocylides* (Leiden: E.J. Brill, 1978).

[51]See the introduction to *CPJ* 421, a tax register from Arsinoe dated to 73 C.E.

Citing a number of ancient authors such as Plutarch, Hallett suggests that among elite Roman families, the mother-son tie was particularly strong because sons were also able to provide mothers with considerable indirect political power and prestige.[52] It seems highly likely that the same would have been true for mothers in elite Jewish families as well.[53] While ancient authors tended to see this as a one way street in which mothers were dependent on their sons, Hallett suggests more of a mutual interdependency, in which "elite Roman mothers could demand their sons' help in recompense for their own labors in their sons' rearing, and for their own resourceful efforts, often with male kinsmen, in their sons' interests."[54]

Many of the factors discussed here are likely to have operated in a spiraling fashion. Women whose maternal affection for their daughters was constrained by a range of factors from marriage practices, to divorce and infant and child mortality rates, might have insulated themselves by providing less love and affection and support to their daughters, thereby ensuring that their daughters would know little of loving, effective mothers. Unloved daughters themselves might make poorer mothers. Further, given the high rate of maternal mortality in antiquity, many daughters must have lost their biological mothers at an early age, either at their own birth, or at the birth of a subsequent sibling. Daughters born into slavery were also especially vulnerable to being separated from their mothers at an early age.

Attempting to assess the impact of these factors draws us into speculation about the psychological dynamics of persons in antiquity, Jewish or otherwise, always a tricky business. Even if it is correct to assume that patterns of parenting replicate themselves in subsequent generations, we should not forget that children in the ancient world could receive nurturing from persons other than their parents, including wetnurses, "foster" parents, step-parents and others.[55]

---

[52]Plutarch, *Coniug. Praec.* 36, discussed, *inter alia*, in Hallett, 246-57. Hallett claims that Roman mothers and daughters enjoyed "a special closeness," but she gives little evidence in support of this claim. The bulk of her discussion of mother-child relationships is devoted to that between mothers and sons, with only three pages on mothers and daughters.

[53]Hallett also suggests that Roman women would have been as close, if not closer, in age to their sons than to their husbands, and this might have generated a sexual attraction between sons and mothers which contributed to their closeness. This seems difficult to evaluate, and difficult to apply to Jewish families, lacking better information.

[54]Hallett 246.

[55]See for example, Bradley, "Dislocation."

In addition to all these factors, there are others we should consider. The relative powerlessness of most women in the Greco-Roman period may have further lessened women's attachments to their daughters, precisely the dynamic which Mieke Bal illuminates in her work on biblical texts. Women who feel powerless to protect their daughters against patriarchal abuses such as rape, forced marriage, and forced divorce among others, may well respond passively. Their inability to act communicates precisely such passive strategies to their own daughters, who then perpetuate such dynamics in a vicious cycle.

This is not to suggest that all mothers were passive. Jane Phillips identifies a handful of incidents in historical sources in which elite Roman mothers are reported to have manipulated the marital arrangements of their daughters for complex political and personal motives. Still, such actions essentially replicate the far better documented intervention of Roman fathers in the lives of their daughters and sons, and do not contradict our general sense that mothers were rarely able to protect their daughters.[56]

Conclusions and Directions for Further Research

Hellenistic Jewish sources provide little attestation to mother-daughter relationships. Literary sources furnish only the most minimal representations of mothers and daughters, in contrast to the depiction of fathers and sons, mothers and sons, and even fathers and daughters. Inscriptions and papyri offer scant testimony to the relationships between real, historical mothers and daughters. The extant evidence suggests that Jewish mothers were more interested in their sons than in their daughters, and that preparing daughters for licit marriage was the focal point of mother-daughter relationships among free Jewish families. We have no direct evidence, literary or otherwise, for the nature of mother-daughter ties among enslaved Jewish families.

One way to account for the paucity of evidence, as well as for the image of the mother-daughter relationship as concerned primarily with preparation for marriage, is as the product of male interests, authorship, experience and so forth. In this view, the androcentric lenses through which we are forced to see antiquity systematically distort the realities of women's lives. While I do not mean to disregard such an interpretation, I have suggested here that the sources may refract some aspects of social reality more accurately than it might initially seem. I have proposed that Jewish mothers, like their Greco-Roman counterparts, may well have had less investment in their relationships with their daughters than with their

---

[56]J.E. Phillips, "Roman Mothers and the Lives of their Adult Daughters," *Helios* 6 (1978) 1: 69-79.

sons, and less attachment to their daughters. Further, I have suggested that the reasons for those diminished investments and attachments may be found in factors common to the experiences of women in the Greco-Roman world generally, such as marital patterns; divorce; infant, child and maternal mortality rates and general cultural expectations about parent-child relationships. I have also argued that we must take into account whether mothers and their children were enslaved or free (and sometimes citizens or noncitizens). While I am not arguing that the experiences of Jewish mothers and daughters were identical to those of their non-Jewish counterparts, I am arguing that their experiences are more likely to have been similar than different.

The findings of this paper suggest numerous directions for further research. Since it is by now well-demonstrated that women in many cultures and societies participate in the perpetuation of patriarchal systems which denigrate and constrain women, it would be valuable to explore how this might have affected the relationships of Jewish mothers and daughters in the Greco-Roman world.

It would also be interesting to examine the portrayal of mother-daughter relationships in early Christian sources, to see whether, for instance, in ascetic strands of Christianity, or gnostic communities, such issues work themselves out differently, as a function of ascetic and/or gnostic beliefs.

The story of Thecla, in the text conventionally known as the *Acts of Paul and Thecla,* but which I prefer to call simply *The Acts of Thecla*[57] should prove particularly fruitful. Thecla's own mother, Theocleia, is presented as a mother who attempts to compel her daughter's acceptance of traditional, patriarchal culture: wishing to see her married to the rich and powerful Thamyris, instead of renouncing marriage and adopting an ascetic, peripatetic life. Thecla's deficient relationship with her natural mother is contrasted with the relationship between Thecla and the aristocratic Tryphaena of Antioch, who takes Thecla under her wing when Thecla is condemned to die at Antioch (having rebuffed the advances of the first man of Antioch, who attempted to rape Thecla on the city streets). On one level, Tryphaena merely does what any conventional respectable mother was expected to do: she guards her daughter's chastity. But whereas most mothers preserved their daughters' virginity for marriage, Tryphaena guarantees Thecla's virginity at death. Tryphaena does for Thecla what most ancient mothers do not seem to have been able to do – she shields her from sexual abuse. In exchange, Thecla prays for the salvation of Tryphaena's own dead

---

[57]English translation in Kraemer, *Maenads* 280-88; bibliography 407-8; see also Kraemer, *Blessings* 151-55.

daughter Falconilla, who died without the salvation of Christ. Tryphaena does for Thecla what Theocleia would (or could) not, while Thecla takes the place of Falconilla, and assures her salvation in heaven.

Other interesting Christian examples might include the mother/daughter relationship between Eve and Norea in the *Hypostatis of the Archons*, the absent mother of Perpetua in the *Martyrdom of Saints Perpetua and Felicitas*, and many others.

Finally, at the religious level, it should be interesting to consider whether the minimization of affective bonds between mothers and daughters might be reflected in the articulation and development of feminine imagery for the divine, particularly maternal imagery. Such imagery seems, in the Greco-Roman period, to have been strongest in religious traditions emanating from Asia Minor (the cult of the Magna Mater) and Egypt (the cult of Isis) – but in both cases, the divine mother is the mother of a son: only in the cult of Demeter does the mother-daughter bond receive religious recognition. Divine mother imagery within Judaism is a topic which clearly needs further research. Aside from the Wisdom traditions, in which Wisdom is again a mother of sons, two other contexts come to mind, Philo's use of such imagery (but again, as a mother of sons – as in the case of Rebekah comforting Isaac for the loss of Sarah) and the figure of Metanoia, the mother of all those who repent, particularly in the story of Aseneth. Perhaps at the religious level, diminished relationships between mothers and daughters deny or impoverish the range of spiritual metaphors available to women, reflecting their real social experiences.

5

Slavery and the Ancient Jewish Family

Dale B. Martin

The title of this essay may be misleading if it is taken to imply that there is something particularly "Jewish" about slavery as practiced by and among Jews of the Greco-Roman period.[1] In fact, the goal of this essay is to make the perhaps unremarkable point that Jewishness itself had little if any relevance for the structures of slavery among Jews. Jews both had slaves and freedpersons and were slaves and freedpersons. Slavery among Jews of the Greco-Roman period did not differ from the slave structures of those people among whom Jews lived. The relevant factors for slave structures and the existence of slavery itself were geographical and socio-economic and had little if anything to do with ethnicity or religion.

The usual problems posed by recalcitrant sources in ancient historiography are only compounded when dealing with Jewish slavery. Social historians writing about ancient slavery must often rely on sketchy or fragmentary evidence provided by sources like inscriptions and papyri. As historians of Judaism have noted, it is very difficult – often impossible – to tell from an inscription whether or not a person is Jewish. Jews seem to have buried their dead, for example, in much the same way as their neighbors.[2] Using names in inscriptions to decide Jewish

---

[1] I am grateful to Leonard Rutgers and Eric Meyers for important references and suggestions that have substantially improved this essay.
[2] Leonard Victor Rutgers, "Archeological Evidence for the Interaction of Jews and Non-Jews in Late Antiquity," *American Journal of Archeology* 96 (1992):101-118. For a particular example, see Ross Kraemer, "Hellenistic Jewish Women: The Epigraphical Evidence," in *Society of Biblical Literature 1986 Seminar Papers*, ed.

identity is precarious (though not completely useless, as will be apparent below), since many Jews bore Greek or Roman names, and some names assumed by previous scholars to be Jewish are now acknowledged as being borne by non-Jews as well. Therefore, unless Jews say they are Jews or place on their epitaphs (for example) some clear indicator of ethnicity or religion, such as a menorah, lulab, or other explicit symbol, we have no way of recognizing them as Jews.[3] There are probably hundreds of Jews, therefore, hidden among the thousands of Greek and Latin inscriptions of antiquity.

Doubling our dilemma, the situation with slaves is similar. Classical historians have little confidence that names on an epitaph can be used to decide servile status. Names once thought particularly "servile" are now seen to carry no formal status significance. Moreover, slaves and freedpersons were not required by law, as far as we know, to indicate their status on a tombstone, and such people seldom figure in the important social documents that comprise the bulk of the epigraphical sources. Many inscriptions and papyri, therefore, likely contain the names of slaves and freedpersons – but unbeknownst to us.[4] All this leads to the realization that Jewish slaves and slave owners are doubly invisible in many of our sources: we may know that they are slaves or owners but not that they are Jews; we may know they are Jews but not that they are slaves or owners. Persons about whom we can discern both their legal status (slave, freed, or free and whether or not they owned slaves themselves) and their ethnic status will be, due to the nature of the sources, rare.

Kent Harold Richards (Atlanta: Scholars Press, 1986), 183-200, at 194. According to a recent study by Byron McCane, however, Jewish secondary burial in Palestine did set them apart from non-Christian, non-Jewish (i.e. "pagan") neighbors, although McCane is convinced that Christian and Jewish burials could not be differentiated from one another until the fourth century. See "Jews, Christians, and Burial in Roman Palestine," (Ph.D. Dissertation, Duke University, 1992).

[3]Pieter W. van der Horst, "The Jews of Ancient Crete," *Journal of Jewish Studies* 39 (1988): 183-200, at 195-197; Ross S. Kraemer, "Hellenistic Jewish Women," 187-192; see also her "On the Meaning of the Term 'Jew' in Greco-Roman Inscriptions," *Harvard Theological Review* 82 (1989): 35-53.

[4]See my *Slavery as Salvation: The Metaphor of Slavery in Pauline Christianity* (New Haven: Yale University Press, 1990), 152; Argyro B. Tataki, *Ancient Beroea Prosopography and Society* (Athens: Research Center for Greek and Roman Antiquity, 1988), 496; Heikki Solin, *Beiträge zur Kenntnis der griechischen Personennamen in Rom* (Helsinki: Societas Scientiarum Fennica, 1971), 39-47; for tables that show how rare status indications in Roman epitaphs are: Pertti Huttunen, *The Social Strata in the Imperial City of Rome: A Quantitative Study of the Social Representation in the Epitaphs Published in the Corpus Inscriptionum Latinarum Volumen VI* (Oulu: University of Oulu: 1974).

To compound the problem even further, both Jews and, even more so, slaves were probably less likely to participate in that "Roman habit" of epigraphy than some other inhabitants of the Roman Empire – especially Romans themselves.[5] Although we have thousands upon thousands of Greek and Latin inscriptions from the Roman Empire, we have only, according to a recent reckoning by Ross Kraemer, about 1,700 Jewish inscriptions.[6] This is partly due to the aforementioned problem of *discerning* Jewish inscriptions, but it may also be due to a relative lack of zeal among Jews for the epigraphic immortalization so popular among the Romans. Slaves, because of financial and other constraints, may have been less likely than many free people to put up an inscription. In the end, any statement we make about ancient Jewish slavery must be tempered by recognition of these problems with the sources. We have, in the final analysis, little to go on.

In spite of the problems with our sources, however, they are useful for correcting a picture of Jewish slavery derived purely from traditional literary resources, scripture and rabbinic texts in particular. For example, one sometimes hears a great deal made about the difference, found in both scripture and the Mishnah, between the "Hebrew" slave and the "Canaanite" slave. As Paul Flesher explains, "Hebrew servants are Israelites who have become indentured servants. They are not permanent slaves. Despite the tie to their master, they stand independent of him. Conversely, foreign slaves are mere chattels. Legally, Scripture grants them a few more rights than other forms of property, but not as many as dependent persons."[7] In some previous scholarship these two categories of slaves found in the Mishnah have been taken to reflect actual social practice of Jewish slavery, even in first-century Palestine. The corresponding hypothetical social structure, then, was taken to set Jewish slavery apart from other forms of slavery in Mediterranean societies. Indeed, if the Mishnaic system portrayed actual slave structures in this regard, Jewish slavery would have differed significantly from other forms of slavery in the Greco-Roman world.

The system, however, was probably never in practice among Jews of the Greco-Roman period. For one thing, as Flesher has pointed out, the category differentiation occurs in only six of the 129 passages in the Mishnah that discuss slavery, and that only when the Mishnah is

---

[5]See Ramsay MacMullen, "The Epigraphic Habit in the Roman Empire," *American Journal of Philology* 103 (1982): 233-246, who does not, however, make this point about Jews.

[6]"On the Meaning of the Term 'Jew'," 37.

[7]Paul V. M. Flesher, *Oxen, Women, or Citizens? Slaves in the System of the Mishnah* (Atlanta: Scholars Press, 1988), 54.

concerned to carry forward scripture's own category distinction of native and foreign slaves. When the Mishnah uses its own system of slavery, with no desire to reflect the "Hebrew/Canaanite" categories of scripture, it uses as its categorical system a simpler one of bondman and freedman.[8] This indicates, I believe, that the Mishnah's framers spoke of Hebrew and Canaanite slaves only in order to remain true to the scriptural categories and not because those categories reflected any actual social structures of their own time. The second point to be made here, moreover, is that we have no evidence – from inscriptions, papyri, or other texts – that this two-tiered slave structure ever actually existed outside the textual world of the rabbinic sources themselves, which are notoriously problematic for historical reconstruction of first-century Palestine.[9] The distinction between native and foreign born slaves, as portrayed in scripture and the Mishnah, was probably never practiced in Greco-Roman Judaism; it was certainly never widespread.

Another previous misconception about Jewish slavery has to do with the very presence of slavery in Palestine. One used to come across the claim that slavery did not exist among Jews – at least in Judea – in the first century or thereabouts. The *Encyclopedia Judaica*, for example, relating this point to the previously mentioned differentiation between Hebrew and Canaanite slaves, says, "There is a strong talmudic tradition

---

[8]See Flesher, 36; see also Flesher, "Slaves, Israelites and the System of the Mishnah," in *The Literature of Early Rabbinic Judaism: Issues in Talmudic Redaction and Interpretation*, vol. 4 of *New Perspectives on Ancient Judaism*, ed. Alan J. Avery-Peck (Lanham, Maryland: University Press of America, 1989), 101-109; David Aaron, Review of *Oxen, Women, or Citizens?*, *Ioudaios Review* 2.016 (1992) [electronic medium].

[9]According to Niels P. Lemche, the scriptural laws concerning manumission of slaves, sabbatical years, and remission of debts were probably never actually enforced "at the time of the Old Testament," and when some sort of attempt was made to enact the sabbatical year many years later (1 Maccabees 6:49, 53) the result was economic catastrophe and famine. See "The Manumission of Slaves – The Fallow Year – The Sabbatical Year – The Jobel Year," *Vetus Testamentum* 26 (1976): 38-59; see also "The 'Hebrew Slave': Comments on the Slave Law Ex. xxi 2-11," *Vetus Testamentum* 25 (1975): 129-144. Lemche rejects the reconstruction of Nahum Sarna ("Zedekiah's Emancipation of Slaves and the Sabbatical Year," in *Orient and Occident: Essays Presented to Cyrus H. Gordon on the Occasion of his Sixty-fifth Birthday*, ed. Harry A. Hoffner, Jr. [Neukirchener Verlag des Erziehungsvereins, 1973], 143-149). In my opinion, Sarna takes both the biblical and rabbinic texts rather uncritically as reflecting contemporary social practice. For unconvincing attempts to harmonize later rabbinic statements about Jewish slavery with first-century witnesses, such as Philo, Josephus, and the New Testament Gospels, see Solomon Zeitlin, "Slavery During the Second Commonwealth and the Tannaitic Period," in *Studies in the Early History of Judaism* (New York: KTAV, 1978), 225-258.

to the effect that all bondage of Hebrew slaves had ceased with the cessation of jubilee years..., which would mean that from the period of the Second Temple the practice of slavery was at any rate confined to non-Hebrew slaves."[10] A similar article in *The Standard Jewish Encyclopedia* claims that "Hebrew" slaves were subject to only temporary servitude and that "even this limited form of slavery became impossible after the Babylonian Exile."[11] Shimon Applebaum, commenting about slaves in the Jewish community in Teucheira, Cyrene, in northern Africa, says, "There is no evidence whether these slaves were Jews or Gentiles. Jewish slavery had virtually disappeared in Judaea at this time [referring to inscriptions that are no later than 115 C.E. and mostly first century], but not necessarily in the Diaspora."[12] To back up this claim, however, Applebaum cites only a couple of references to the Babylonian Talmud (*Gittin* 65a; *'Arachin* 25a).

As I have hinted at already, the use of the Mishnah, not to mention the Talmud, to reconstruct social structures of first-century Palestine is highly problematic. We may indeed sometimes see reflections of actual social life in rabbinic texts. For example, there is a well-known discussion in the tractate *Semahot* ("On Mourning") focusing on the death of Tebi, the famous slave of Rabban Gamaliel: according to one point of view, Tebi's death, like the death of any slave, should not be mourned, contrary to Rabban Gamaliel's statement that Tebi is special.[13] The division of opinion about whether or not to accept condolences for the death of a slave occurs due to the fact that slaves in Jewish law constituted a problematic category. They were chattels, and therefore not legally agents (human beings in the full, legal sense), but it was recognized that they had wills; as human beings they were capable of volitional action.[14] Or, alternatively put, they were members of a man's household, but they were nevertheless considered "heathen" or "strangers" – and thus their deaths did not merit or necessitate

---

[10]Haim Hermann Cohn, "Slavery," s.v., *Encyclopedia Judaica* (Jerusalem: Keter, 1972), 14.1657, citing *Gittin* 65a; *Qiddushin* 69a; *'Arakhin* 29a; Maimonides, *Mishneh Torah (Yad Hazakah) Avadim* 2:10.

[11]"Slaves and Slavery," s.v., *The Standard Jewish Encyclopedia*, ed. Cecil Roth (Garden City, New York: Doubleday, 1959), 1730.

[12]*Jews and Greeks in Ancient Cyrene* (Leiden: E.J. Brill, 1979), 158. Most recent historians of Judaism seem to reject such views; see, for example, Martin Goodman, *State and Society in Roman Galilee, A.D. 132-212* (Totowa, New Jersey: Rowman and Allanheld, 1983), 38

[13]*Semahot* 1.9-11; *The Tractate "Mourning", Yale Judaica Series* vol. 17, trans. Dov Zlotnick (New Haven: Yale University Press, 1966); see also the comments and other references given by Zlotnick, p. 99, n. 10.

[14]This is studied in depth for the Mishnah by Flesher, *Oxen, Women, or Citizens?*

condolences. The rabbis were here addressing the same kinds of category problems as evidenced in Roman law in its attempt to classify slaves as both *res* (a thing) and *persona* (a human being).[15] The rabbis, of course, employ different mechanisms and a distinct discourse to deal with this problem of categories, but the activity demonstrates the similarity between the Jewish and Roman *structures* of slavery. In the end, however, we must be wary of using rabbinic sources for the reconstruction of Jewish social institutions of the Roman period. It is especially problematic to use rabbinic materials to argue that Jewish slavery did not exist in Palestine in this period.

We have firm evidence from other sources that slavery was indeed an important part of the household structures of Jewish families in Judea and elsewhere in the first century. Other sources suggest that Jewish structures of slavery reflect their immediate social and economic environments, not necessarily the theoretical systems of the rabbis or scripture. Although the evidence is sparse, we have instances of Jewish slave owners from inscriptions and papyri from Transjordan, Egypt, Italy, Greece, and Asia Minor. The same kind of evidence showing that Jews were themselves slaves comes from Jerusalem, the Galilee, Egypt, Italy, and Greece. The material presented below ranges in date from before the third century B.C.E. to the third century C.E.[16]

---

[15]Aaron Kirschenbaum, *Sons, Slaves and Freedmen in Roman Commerce* (Washington, D. C.: Catholic University of America Press, 1987), 15-16, n. 48; for Jewish and Near Eastern sources: Gillian Feeley-Harnik, "Is Historical Anthropology Possible? The Case of the Runaway Slave," in *Humanizing America's Iconic Book*, ed. Gene M. Tucker and Douglas A. Knight, 95-126 (Chico, California: Scholars Press, 1982).

[16]Although it is outside the chronological confines of the period of my concern, I should mention the late antique Roman laws concerning Jewish ownership of Christian slaves. From the time of Constantine II (in a law of August 13, 339) through the sixth century, various laws prohibited Jews from owning Christian slaves, converting their slaves to Judaism, or circumcising their slaves. The laws are not all consistent with one another, and changes were made repeatedly. For instance, in a law of 415, Honorius allowed Jews to keep Christian slaves on condition that they be allowed to remain Christians. The general thrust of the laws, however, was consistently to discourage Jewish ownership of Christian slaves, presumably in order to discourage conversions by those slaves to Judaism. These texts tell us several things: for one thing, in late antiquity Jews did own slaves, and often Christian slaves; secondly, since it appears that Jews converted and circumcised their slaves without necessarily consequently manumitting them, Jews were thereby also owning slaves who were (by having become) themselves Jews; finally, it is clear that the laws were never completely successful in prohibiting Jewish ownership of Christian slaves and that the practice continued throughout late antiquity. See the collection of these texts in Amnon Linder, *The Jews in Roman Imperial Legislation* (Detroit: Wayne State University Press, 1987), and commentary on pp. 82-85.

One papyrus document from Egypt (10 B.C.E.) records that a Jewish freedwoman named Martha had to pay one-half a debt of a man named Protarchos, who was probably her former owner. The editors of the text speculate, reasonably, that she probably inherited one-half his estate while his son inherited the other half.[17] A papyrus document from a much later period (291 C.E.) records the manumission of a Jewish slave woman named Paramone along with her two (?) children. The "synagogue of the Jews" pays the ransom for the woman to the brother and sister who owned Paramone; the synagogue, according to the document, thus acquires *paramonê* rights over the exslave, that is, she must continue to provide some services to the synagogue, as she normally would have to her "patron" (ex-owner) according to Greek and Roman practices of manumission.[18]

Two inscriptions from Delphi record the manumission of Jewish slaves. One liberates a mother and her two daughters, Antigonas, Theodora, and Dorothea. It should be noted that here, as will be the case most often, there is nothing "Jewish" about the names. The other inscription records the manumission, by sale to the god Apollo, of a man named Joudaios. In this case the rest of the inscription confirms what we would suspect on the basis of the name, that the man is Jewish. I believe the man to have been a Jewish slave in a Greek household; his name would have meant for them something like "the Judean" or "the Jew."[19] To move to Italy, in Naples (era of Claudius-Nero) a woman named Claudia Aster, who says that she is "a Jerusalemite, a captive," seems to have responsibility for the care of a tomb belonging to a twenty-five year old imperial freedman named Tiberius Claudius Masculus. Aster is probably a Jewish woman from Palestine. The man may also be Jewish, though we cannot tell from the inscription; they are both freedpersons of the imperial house.[20] An inscription from Aquileia, Italy records the

---

[17]*CPJ* 148 (Abusir el-Meleq, 10 BCE).

[18]*CPJ* 473. *Paramonê* rights existed in Greek systems of slavery; *operae* were those duties owed by ex-slaves in the Roman system. The two practices are different in some ways, but similar in that they extend a somewhat servile relationship past the time of manumission. See the discussion of this and other "redemption" instances by J. Albert Harrill, "Ignatius, *Ad Polycarp* 4.3 and the Corporate Manumission of Slaves," *Early Christian Studies* (forthcoming).

[19]*CIJ* 709 (Delphi, 170-157/6 BCE); *CIJ* 710 (Delphi, 162 BCE). See also the manumission of the Jew Moschos at Oropos, 3d century BCE: *CIJ* (1975), in the "Prolegomenon" by Baruch Lifshitz, p. 82, no. 711b.

[20]*CIJ* 556.

name of Lucius Aiacius Dama, a Jewish freedman, who also mentions that he was a *portor* ("ferryman"?; Frey suggests the French *batelier*).[21]

The situation in Rome presents its own problems, though they do not greatly affect the concerns of this study. We know from literary sources that there must have been many Jewish slaves and freedpersons in Rome. Josephus mentions in several places the thousands of Jews from Palestine who were captured and sold into slavery throughout the Mediterranean; certainly many of them must have ended up in Rome, though we cannot tell how many from his accounts.[22] Other writers also mention Jewish freedpersons and slaves in Rome.[23] Some scholars have pointed out, however, that among all the 500 or so Jewish funerary inscriptions from Rome, none explicitly names a Jewish slave or freedman. G. Fuks has thought of this as a curiosity needing explanation and suggested that Jewish freedpersons simply did not use the normal self-designation (*l.* or *lib.*) on their epitaphs when buried among other Jews due to the strong Jewish (or specifically "Zealot") ethic to "have no lord but God."[24] What

---

[21]*CIJ* 643; for another interpretation, however, see Jean Juster, *Les juifs dans l'empire romain: leur condition juridique, économique et sociale* (Paris: Paul Geuthner, 1914), 2.256, n. 6. Other inscriptions from Rome or Italy mention people who are *probably* Jewish: *CIJ* 70*, 74*, 75*, 77*. Still others mention people who are *possibly* Jewish (judging on the basis of names that *might* be Jewish): *CIJ* 68*, 69*, 71*, 73*. In many of these cases, Frey thought the name Sabbatis (or some variation on it) probably indicated Jewish status; others maintain that Sabbat- type names are not particularly Jewish: Louis Jalabert and René Mouterde, eds., *Inscriptions greque et latines de la Syrie* (Paris: Librairie orientaliste Paul Geuthner, 1939), 2.481; Naomi G. Cohen, "Jewish Names as Cultural Indicators in Antiquity," *Journal for the Study of Judaism* 7 (1976): 97-128, at 127 n. 136.

[22]See, for example, Josephus *War* 3.304-306, 540-542; 6.418.

[23]Philo, *Embassy to Gaius* 155; Tacitus, *Annals* 2.85; Empress Livia had a Jewish slave woman named Acme (Josephus, *Ant.* 17.5.7§141); Martial seems to have had a Jewish slave (7.35.2-3); see also Caecilius of Calacte (F. Jacoby, *Fragmente der griechischen Historiker* II B 183 T.1), whom Suda calls *tēn doxan Ioudaios* and *apo doulon*.

[24]G. Fuks, "Where Have All the Freedmen Gone?: On an Anomaly in the Jewish Grave-Inscriptions From Rome," *Journal of Jewish Studies* 36 (1985): 25-32. In an unpublished paper, J. Albert Harrill offers a new suggestion: "Jewish communities in Rome were concerned about the dependence of Jews (both symbolic and legal) upon pagan patrons, and offered group patronage in two major ways. First, Jews provided burial space and funerary rites to fellow Jews, and avoided the *lib.* status indicator, as a symbol of dependence upon pagans, in tombstone commemorations. Second, Roman synagogues engaged in an active campaign to redeem enslaved Jews with money drawn on common chests, thus enabling them to become legally 'independent' freedmen" ("The Social and Economic Position of Jewish Freedmen in Rome," paper presented to the SBL Group on the Social World of Formative Judaism and Christianity, Annual Meeting of the Society of Biblical Literature, San Francisco, California, November

Fuks thought of as a problem may be, however, no problem at all. As other scholars have pointed out, contrary to the beliefs of Frey, the Jewish catacomb inscriptions are all from late antiquity, mostly from the third and fourth centuries.[25] Non-Jewish, Christian inscriptions dating from the same period also contain very few explicit references to freed status (except for imperial freedpersons), even though we know that slavery was still practiced at this time.[26] Onomastic customs and designations of servile status seemed to have gone through important changes during the second and third centuries, with the result that we should *expect* the Jewish inscriptions to lack *libertus* designations. One therefore may need no explanation for the lack of freed and slave designations among the Jewish inscriptions; here again, the Jews were following the same practices as their Gentile neighbors.[27] The catacomb

---

23, 1992). Harrill's reconstruction is possible, but it must be admitted that the evidence for redemption of Jewish slaves by synagogues is scarce. There is none for Rome or Italy. Harrill cites the papyrus document from third-century Egypt manumitting Paramone and her children (*CPJ* 473 [=*P. Oxy.* 1205]) and a handful of inscriptions from first- to second-century Bosporus (*CIJ* 683, 683a, 683b, 690, 690a, 690b, 691). It seems to me doubtful that this evidence can be expanded to portray an "active campaign" by synagogues throughout the Empire to redeem Jews from slavery. In the last resort, if the work of other scholars on the dating of the Jewish inscriptions and the practice of self-designation by slave or freed status is correct, as argued just below, the "anomaly" that Harrill and Fuks seek to explain is no anomaly in the first place.

[25]For what follows in this paragraph I am endebted to the work of Leonard Rutgers, who is writing a dissertation at Duke University on the Jewish community at Rome. In an excursus he explicitly addresses Fuks's theory and demonstrates why it is unnecessary. See also his "Überlegungen zu den jüdischen Katakomben Roms," *Jahrbuch für Antike und Christentum* 33 (1990):140-157, at 142-154 for dating questions. See also A. Ferrua, "Sulla tomba dei christiani e su quella degli ebrei," *Civiltà Cattolica* 87 (1936):298-311, at 309-310; Heikki Solin, "Onomastica ed epigrafia: Riflessioni sull' esegesi onomastica delle iscrizioni romane," *Quaderni urbinati di cultura classica* 18 (1974):105-132.

[26]Iiro Kajanto, *Onomastic Studies in the Early Christian Inscriptions of Rome and Carthage = Acta Instituti Romani Finlandiae* 2.1 (Helsinki: Tilgmann, 1963): 1-141, at 6-9.

[27]Many Latin funerary inscriptions contain freedpersons with "Semitic" sounding names, and surely at least some of these are Jews. Some inscriptions mention a synagogue "of the Agrippesians," "of the Augustesians," or "of the Vernaclesians." Some scholars believe these to be synagogues of Jewish freedmen, as these designations may imply. See Nikolaus Müller, *Die jüdische Katakombe am Monteverde zu Rom, der älteste bisher bekannt gewordene jüdische Friedhof des Abendlandes* (Leipzig: G. Fock, 1912), 108; George La Piana, "Foreign Groups in Rome during the First Centuries of the Empire," *Harvard Theological Review* 20 (1927): 352; Peter Lampe, *Die stadrömischen Christen in den ersten beiden Jahrhunderten* (Tübingen: Mohr-Siebeck, 1989), 66-67. Harry J. Leon, *The Jews of Ancient Rome* (Philadelphia: Jewish Publication Society, 1960) rejects all such

inscriptions, therefore, cannot be used as evidence against the presence of slavery among Jews in Rome.

We have some similar evidence for Jewish slaves in Palestine. According to Acts 6:9, there was a "Synagogue of Freedmen" in Jerusalem (the Greek for "freedmen" is here a transliteration of the Latin *libertini*, with a Greek ending). Historically, scholars have assumed that these are Jews who returned to Jerusalem from abroad, possibly Rome. If they were freedmen of Roman citizens they would probably be citizens themselves, and thus may have enjoyed some of the "upward mobility" that some slaves of Romans knew.[28] Shimon Applebaum cites *CIJ* 1404 as providing an example of one such Jewish freedman. The inscription honors a freedman who built a Roman bath connected to a synagogue; according to Applebaum, he was a Jew returned from Roman slavery and so now held the enviable status of Roman citizenship.[29] We certainly find such a case in the person of Theodotos, whose ossuary inscription occupies a place among those of his rather large and apparently important family in Jericho. Theodotos, whose "Jewish" name was probably Nathanel, was a freedman of Agrippina the Younger (15-59 C.E.), wife of Claudius and mother of Nero. As Rachel Hachlili notes, "It is likely that he was taken as a 'political slave,' considering that he was from a prominent and important family." He later returned to his family in Jericho, where he was buried. The inscription indicates that "the events... were considered by the family to be important, indicating Theodotos' special status as a Roman citizen" – and, I would add, as a freedman of perhaps the most famous and powerful woman in the first century.[30] On the subject of women, I should mention the Beth She'arim tomb of Calliope, a freedwoman of a man named Procopios. According to Louis Robert (interpreting the Greek word *mizotera* in the inscription), Calliope was the *intendante*, or manager of Procopios's household, a position of responsibility most often held by male slaves or freedmen. Calliope (or perhaps a friend or relative making the arrangements)

---

arguments, insisting (too confidently, I believe) that there is no reason to take these men to be freed.

[28]See *Slavery as Salvation*, 30-42. The freedperson of a Roman citizen often, though not always, gained citizenship upon manumission. It seems to me uncertain, though possible, that these freedmen had been slaves of Roman citizens, as Applebaum assumes (*Judaea in Hellenistic and Roman Times*, 156).

[29]*Judaea in Hellenistic and Roman Times*, 160.

[30]Rachel Hachlili, "The Goliath Family in Jericho: Funerary Inscriptions from a First Century A.D. Jewish Monumental Tomb," *BASOR* 235 (1979): 31-66, at 33 and 46.

mentions it on her funerary inscription as something of a status indicator.[31]

We possess a few inscriptions and papyri from diverse locations that show Jews as slave owners themselves. The powerful Tobiad family, for example, dealt in slaves. In 259 B.C.E. Nikanor, a member of the household of Toubias, sold a seven year old Sidonian slave girl to Zenon, an official in the government of Ptolemy II Philadelphos. Two years later, Toubias sent four slave boys and a eunuch to Apollonios, the minister (*dioikêtês*) of Ptolemy II. Two of the boys were circumcised and thus may have been Jewish, though circumcision alone would not constitute adequate proof.[32] About 100 years later in Greece, Jews figure in the Delphic inscriptions as slave owners. Joudaios, son of Pinderos, sells a male slave, Amyntas, to Apollo, with the consent of his son, Pinderos.[33]

The sands of Egypt have yielded several papyri documenting Jewish slave owners.[34] In Edfu, on January 10, 162, Rufus, freedman of a woman named Sarra, pays the wine tax; Sarra is probably Jewish.[35] Other documents record payment of the "Jewish tax" by slaves. In the years 75 and 80 freedmen of another Sarra payed the tax. This woman seems to have been a Roman citizen as well as Jewish, since her freedman has the name Akyntas Kaikillias (Quintus Caecilius). In the year 107, Sporos, slave of Aninios, payed the tax, and in 116, Thermouthos, slave of a centurion named Aninios, did so. In these cases of the Jewish tax,

---

[31]Moshe Schwabe and Baruch Lifshitz, *Beth She'arim: Vol. II: The Greek Inscriptions* (Jerusalem: Massada Press, 1974), pp. 185-186, #200; Louis Robert, *Bulletin épigraphique, Revue des études grecques* 77 (1964): #503; "Inscriptions de l'antiquité et du Bas-Empire à Corinthe," *Revue des études grecques* 79 (1966): 733-770, at 767; for female managers: Robert, *Hellenica* 13 (1965): 105-108.

[32]*CPJ* 1 (Transjordan, 259 B.C.E.); *CPJ* 4 (Transjordan, 12 May 257 B.C.E.).

[33]*CIJ* 711 (Delphi, 119 B.C.E.).

[34]From a period earlier than my concerns we have papyri from Elephantine recording sales of slaves by Jewish owners. In one, Ananiah buys a woman, Tamut, from Meshullam in order to marry her. The marriage does not, however, imply her automatic manumission, for many years later Tamut and her daughter are again mentioned in a papyrus, this time as being manumitted. In another document, a slave boy named Yedoniah is given by one Jewish man to another for adoption. See E.G. Kraeling, *The Brooklyn Museum Aramaic Papyri* (New Haven: Brooklyn Museum, Yale University Press, 1953), papyri nos. 2, 5, 8, and p. 140; according to Kraeling, slaves at Elephantine were usually Egyptian (p. 145). For further discussion of these documents, see Zeev W. Falk, "The Deeds of Manumission of Elephantine," *Journal of Jewish Studies* 5 (1954) 114-117; "Manumission by Sale," *Journal of Semitic Studies* 3 (1958) 127-128. For other slaves of Jews at Elephantine, see A.E. Cowley, *Aramaic Papyri of the Fifth Century B.C.* (Oxford: Clarendon, 1923), #28.

[35]*CIJ* 378 (Edfu, 10 January 162).

the editors of *CPJ* believe that the Jewish masters had to pay the tax for their slaves even if those slaves were not themselves Jewish. Thus they take all these cases to be Jewish owners with possibly non-Jewish slaves. This may find support in the fact that in several cases the name of the owner looks "Jewish" while those of the slaves and freedpersons do not.[36]

Finally, we may note inscriptions erected by Jewish heads of households that follow typical funerary form in mentioning the members of their households, including freedpersons and/or slaves. In Italy, Gaius Julius Justus, a gerousiarch, erects a monument for himself, his unnamed wife, his freedmen and freedwomen, and his descendants.[37] From Smyrna in Asia Minor, an inscription survives in which Rufina, a female head of a synagogue (*archisynagogos*), announces that she has built the tomb for her freedpersons and *thremmata*. In the abstract, the latter term need not refer to slaves, since it can be equivalent to the Latin *alumni* and mean something like "foster children." On the other hand, it may refer to slaves, particularly "home born" slaves or those reared in the household (Latin *verna*). In this context, coming immediately after the term "freedpersons," it almost certainly refers to slaves.[38] Here we have, then, a Jewish woman who, like a few Greek and Roman women of her time and place, holds a role as the head of her own *familia* and accordingly provides for the burial of her slaves and freedpersons.

Although it is a sticky issue, mention should be made of the ancient category of persons known in our inscriptions as *threptoi*. Repeatedly, especially in certain areas and times such as Asia Minor in the second and third centuries C.E., one comes across inscriptions in which people provide burials or commemoration for their *threptoi*. The most "neutral" translation of the term is probably something like "those whom one has reared," and it has accordingly been translated as "foster children" or the like. At times, it appears to be equivalent to the Latin *verna*, referring,

---

[36]*CPJ* 171 (Edfu, 26 June 75), 179 (Edfu, 23 May 80), 180 (Edfu, 15 June 80), 212 (Edfu, 20 December 107), 229 (Edfu, 18 May 116); see also 206, 207, 218. Names of owners: Pesouris, Apanios Belaros, Antipatros, Aninios, Sarra; names of slaves and freedpersons: Zosime, Dekas, Kopreus, Sporos, Thermauthos, Akyntas Kaikillias (Quintus Caecilius), Rufus. This may be one of those cases in which names can provide some evidence without being taken to constitute proof. On the Jewish tax: Michael S. Ginsburg, "*Fiscus Judaicus*," *Jewish Quarterly Review* 21 (1930-31): 281-291. Other *possible* slaves of Jews: *CPJ* 490 (Side in Pamphylia, 8 July, 151; the sale of a Phrygian slave girl by a family that seems to be Jewish); 493 (Fayum, 2d century C.E.).
[37]*CIJ* 533 (near Ostia, no date but probably first half of the second century).
[38]*CIJ* 741 (Smyrna, no date).

that is, to slaves born and reared within the household.[39] Another possible Latin translation may be *alumnus/a,* which sometimes, though certainly not always, refers to a person of servile status. The term *threptos/ê,* in any case, is so ubiquitous in some areas that it is quite unlikely that it always refers to someone who is legally a slave or freedperson. Indeed, it may be that at some times and in some places there existed a "quasi-servile" status, something between actual slavery and freedom, occupied by these *threptoi.* Our information, however, is too skimpy to be certain. At any rate, inscriptions exist that appear to use the term (or a similar one) to refer to persons who are actually slaves, though perhaps slaves occupying a special place in the household.[40]

I have already noted the tomb built by Rufina, the Jewish *archisynagogos,* for her freedpersons and *thremmata.* *Thremma* is sometimes the equivalent of *threptos,* and here it probably refers to the same social situation, that is, to slaves reared in the household of Rufina.[41] Another Jewish woman named Chreste in an inscription from Panticapaeum (Cimmerian Bosphorus) fulfills a vow to manumit her *threptos* Heraclas; here it is certain that the man is either a slave or something very like a slave of the woman.[42] Such instances suggest that at least some of the other inscriptions that mention *threptoi/ai* of Jews are thereby referring to slaves, such as the funerary monument erected at Rome by a Jewish "father" and "mother" for their *threptê* Eirene, who died at the age of three years, seven months, and one day.[43]

---

[39]*Verna* usually, but not necessarily, indicates servile status: P.R.C. Weaver, "Misplaced Officials," *Antichthon* 13 (1979) 70-102, at 78 and n. 35; for a reference to a *verna* (possibly not Jewish), see *CIJ* 35*.

[40]For discussion of these issues see A. Cameron, "*Threptoi* and Related Terms in the Inscriptions of Asia Minor," in *Anatolian Studies Presented to W.H. Buckler,* ed. W.M. Calder and Josef Keil (New York: Longmans, Green, 1923), 27-62; T. G. Nani, "*Threptoi,*" *Epigraphica* 5-6 (1943-44): 45-84; Martin, *Slavery as Salvation,* 10 and 185 n. 38.

[41]*CIJ* 741; compare "*thremma*" and "*threptos,*" s.v., Liddell-Scott-Jones, *Greek-English Lexicon.*

[42]*CIJ* 683; see the similar, though fragmentary, inscription *CIJ* 684. Other dedication/manumission inscriptions: *CIJ* 690 (*possible* Jew releasing a slave according to a vow; Gorgippia, 41 C.E.); 691 (*possible* Jew dedicating a *threptos,* and thereby probably effecting his manumission; Phanagoria, Cimmerian Bosporus, 16 C.E.?). See also *CIJ* 65* and 78* (*possible* Jews, in the latter case a brother and sister, releasing a slave-*threptê,* Cimmerian Bosporus, 2d-3d century C.E.).

[43]*CIJ* 21 (Rome via Nomentana, no date); see the discussion of this inscription by Ross Kraemer, "The Meaning of the term 'Jew'," 38-41. See also *CIJ* 3 (Rome via Salaria, no date) and 144 (Rome via Appia, no date). *CIJ* 641 (Pola, Italy, no date) is the funerary inscription of an *alumna* who died at age 27, erected (probably) by her foster-mother (owner?). A "*threptos* of the most illustrious patriarchs" named

This brief survey of inscriptions and papyri has yielded few certainties about ancient Jewish slavery. Taken in sum, however, it suggests that slavery among Jewish families differed little if at all from slavery among those non-Jewish families surrounding them. The evidence for Palestine, however, has been thus far in my presentation even more scarce than for Jews living elsewhere in the Roman Empire. Fortunately, some literary evidence exists that may fill in the gaps. Furthermore, it is on the basis of this literary evidence that we can get a better idea not only of the existence of slavery in Palestine, but also of the kinds of slavery that existed there and its function within society as a whole.

In this regard, Josephus proves to be an invaluable source, providing evidence especially for the roles of slaves of the upper class. As is the case for imperial Rome, the most visible slaves and freedpersons in Judea were those of the royal family. At Herod's funeral 500 of his slaves and freedmen were in attendance, according to Josephus, and the Greek suggests that these may have been only a part of his *familia* (*War* 1.673). Later in the century, the freedmen of Agrippa, just like those of the various important political families of Rome, are completely implicated in the connivings and intrigues of royal machinations. The one we hear the most about is Marsyas, who borrowed money for Agrippa in Rome from Protos, a freedman of Berenice, Agrippa's mother (*Ant.* 18.155). Marsyas, of course, *may* not be a Jew, but we have no reason to believe he is not. After all, he does speak Hebrew.[44] Besides these, there are many other references in Josephus to slaves and freedmen involved in the political maneuverings of the royal families.[45]

The royal families, moreover, were not the only ones with slaves. Philip, King Agrippa's lieutenant (*eparchos*), sends messages by his freedmen (*Life* 48 and 51). Justus, a native of Tiberias, has a slave who is killed in battle (*Life* 341). One cannot pretend these are special cases or that only "non-Jewish Jews" had slaves. Even the high priests in Jerusalem had slaves and sent them, according to Josephus, to collect the tithes at the threshing floors, much to the offense of Josephus himself.[46]

Severus is mentioned in an inscription from Tiberius: Baruch Lifshitz, *Donateurs et fondateurs dans les synagogues juives répertoire des dédicaces grecques relatives à la construction et à la refection des synagogues* (Paris: J. Gabalda, 1967), 63. For another possible case, see Gert Lüderitz, *Corpus jüdischen Zeugnisse aus der Cyrenaika* (Wiesbaden: Dr. Ludwig Reichert, 1983), no. 12.

[44]*Ant.* 18.228; for other references to Agrippa's freedmen: 18.168, 203-205, 247.

[45]*War* 1.233, 585, 620, 641; 2.180; 3.373.

[46]*Ant.* 20.181, 206-207. The New Testament Gospels also mention slaves of the high priest: Matthew 26:51; Mark 14:47; Luke 22:50; John 18:10, 18. It makes little difference in this regard whether the gospel accounts are historical in themselves.

Finally, Josephus's statement that the Essenes did not keep wives or slaves is evidence that what was considered remarkable was not that there were Jews who had slaves but that there was a group of them who, as a matter of principle, did not (*Ant.* 18.21). The evidence seems clear: definitely from the time of the Tobiads, when Arion served as slave *oikonomos* for Joseph the Tobiad in Alexandria, through the Jewish War the slave structures of Jews in Palestine were not discernably different from the slave structures of other provincials in the eastern Mediterranean.[47] It was mainly the upper class families who had slaves and freedpersons, and large slave *familiae* were maintained by those Jews whose economic and social position enabled them to do so.

We may still be able to squeeze a bit more material from our sources and say something about the different activities of slaves in Roman Palestine. As we would expect, many slaves probably worked as personal servants to their owners. If they were slaves in small, less affluent households, they might be expected to work alongside the master in the fields or shepherding flocks while also working as household servants, serving meals, for example, to the master and his immediate family, a picture of slavery that emerges from a text in Luke's Gospel (17:7). The Gospels also portray large households, staffed by many slaves in a variety of positions. In Matthew 18:23-35, for example, the different slaves of a large household lend one another money and even maintain their own families. This picture reflects the same kind of

---

They certainly reflect a Palestinian pre-history to the text as it stands, which in turn indicates that it was at least quite believable that the high priest *would* have had slaves who acted in these ways, that is, as playing roles in something like his own "bodyguard" or private militia. Rabbinic sources also refer to slaves of the high priest, even to the extent of noting that slaves in important positions, such as Temple slaves, partook of a sort of "status-by-association" with their important owners, in precisely the same way as experienced by their Roman counterparts. As Gillian Feeley-Harnik says, "Temple slaves in high positions could achieve such eminence that they fell into the category of those to whom the saying was applied 'the King's slave is as the King' (*Sebu.* 47a)" ("Is Historical Anthropology Possible?: The Case of the Runaway Slave," in *Humanizing America's Iconic Book*, ed. Gene M. Tucker and Douglas A. Knight (Chico, California: Scholars Press, 1982), 95-126, at 112. For "status-by-association," see Martin, *Slavery as Salvation*, xxii, 22-26, 47-48.

[47]Arion: Josephus, *Ant.* 12.199-207. An exhaustive study of Josephus's slave terminology demonstrates that everything about Jewish slavery in Josephus fits with Greco-Roman slavery in general. In particular, the authors conclude that Josephus never distinguishes in his terminology between Jewish and non-Jewish slaves. John G. Gibbs and Louis H. Feldman, "Josephus' Vocabulary for Slavery," *Jewish Quarterly Review* 76 (1986): 281-310.

social situation found among slaves in other parts of the Roman East.[48] Also – as was true especially of the large estates in Italy but also some estates in the east – slaves would have been used as field workers in planting and harvesting. This is the situation assumed by the parable recorded in Matthew 13:24-30.[49]

I have elsewhere emphasized the importance of slave managers or business agents. The Gospels portray slaves working in a variety of such roles, collecting rents and produce from tenants on behalf of their masters (Matthew 21:34), functioning as *oikonomoi*, that is, "household managers" who disburse funds and food to other members of the *familia* (Matthew 24:45; cf. Mark 13:34), investing money and conducting independent businesses for the master's ultimate benefit (Matthew 25:14-30). Rabbinic sources also know of such situations: slaves hired out for profit and slaves who work as agents for their owners.[50] Again, the picture that emerges portrays Jewish forms of slavery functioning precisely like the slave structures of the peoples among whom Jews lived.

Of course, there is more that could be said about slaves and the Jewish family. One might point out, for example, that Jewish slaves upon manumission did not automatically gain any kind of citizenship or attain the status of their previous owners; but the same would be true of slaves of any group except the Romans. Furthermore, freedpersons of Jews were not necessarily required to render the same kinds of *operae* to their patrons as were Roman freedpersons (except when some kind of agreement was stipulated in the manumission document, as is the case with the *paramonê* clause of *CPJ* 473); but again, this would be true of other ethnic groups also, excepting the Romans themselves.[51] Finally,

---

[48]For slave families in Greco-Roman households – indeed, maintaining their own households – see Martin, *Slavery as Salvation*, 2-7. For rabbinic references to slave families, see Yu. A. Solodukho, "Slavery in the Hebrew Society of Iraq and Syria in the Second through Fifth Centuries A.D.," in *Soviet Views of Talmudic Judaism* (Leiden: Brill, 1973), 1-9, at 6; Zeitlin, "Slavery during the Second Commonwealth and the Tannaitic Period," 250-251; Ephraim E. Urbach, "The Laws Regarding Slavery as a Source for Social History of the Period of the Second Temple, the Mishnah, and the Talmud," in *Papers of the Institute of Jewish Studies*, Institute of Jewish Studies, vol. 1, ed. J. G. Weiss (Jerusalem: Magnes, 1964), 1-94, at 15-16.

[49]On the debate about the importance of slaves in agriculture in the Roman Empire, see Ramsay MacMullen, "Late Roman Slavery," *Historia* 36 (1987): 359-383.

[50]See Urbach, "Laws," 28; Flesher, *Oxen, Women, or Slaves?*, 38, 127-131. For slave managers in general, see *Slavery as Salvation*, 15-22.

[51]But see Peter Garnsey, "Independent Freedmen and the Economy of Roman Italy," *Klio* 63 (1981): 359-371 for "independent freedmen" even in the Roman system. Flesher points out that according to the Mishnah (unlike Roman law)

one could argue, though I have little confidence in the evidence, that slave labor was not responsible for a great amount of agricultural production in Judea; but it appears the same could be said of other areas of the Mediterranean, except for Italy and the large imperial estates in Asia Minor.[52] In other words, the things that make Jewish slavery look different from Roman slavery have to do with the peculiarities of *Roman* social structures. Slavery among Jews seems to have looked like those slave structures prominent in the time and place of the particular Jews under investigation. In the end, the decisive factors for the structures of slavery were not those of religion or ethnicity but geography and socio-economic position.

---

freedpersons do not remain under the householder's control or continue to owe obligations (such as the Roman *operae* or the Greek *paramonê* duties) to the former owner. Furthermore the freedman's legal status is not linked to the legal status of the former owner; that is, the status of a former owner does not attach to his freedmen (*Oxen, Women, or Slaves*, 38, 140-141). It should be remembered, in the first place, that Flesher is speaking of the textual world of the rabbis and makes no claim about whether or not these structures reflect actual social situations of Jewish slave structures. In the second place, Flesher is speaking of *legal* status, not informal forms of status attribution; it is quite likely that the informal status of an owner "rubbed off" on his or her ex-slaves in social perception regardless of the legal situation. In the third place, it should be remembered that Roman law was rather unusual in the ancient world for so explicitly tying the freedperson's legal status (such as citizenship) to that of the patron. Slaves of Greeks, for example, did not become citizens upon manumission. For other comparisons of Jewish rabbinic codes with Roman legal aspects of slavery see Boaz Cohen, *Jewish and Roman Law: A Comparative Study* (New York: Jewish Theological Seminary, 1966), esp. 122-278; Z. W. Falk, "Jewish Private Law," in *The Jewish People in the First Century*, ed. S. Safrai and M. Stern (Assen: Netherlands: Van Gorcum, 1974), 504-534.

[52]MacMullen, "Late Roman Slavery."

Part Three

RABBINIC LAW

6

Reconsidering the Rabbinic
ketubah Payment[1]

Michael Satlow

In rabbinic literature, the word *ketubah* carries several meanings. It is most often used to designate the Jewish marriage contract, a pecuniary document that specifies the rights and obligations of the spouses. Within this document another *"ketubah"* is specified (whence the document probably derives its name), a marriage settlement or sum of money payable by the husband or his estate to his wife on the dissolution of the marriage. This is distinct from two other payments specified in the document, the dowry (*nedunia*) and the "dowry addition", an overappraisal of the worth of the wife's dowry. All of these monetary stipulations are distinct from the biblical *mohar*, or bride price, a sum paid by the husband or his family to the family (usually father) of the prospective bride. The word *"ketubah"* can, in rabbinic literature, mean any of these payments (see below). This has been a source of confusion of, I will argue, great import.

[1]This project was begun under the guidance of the late Prof. Baruch M. Bokser, to whom this paper is dedicated. I profited greatly from the comments and discussion of the participants of the SBL session at which this paper was read. Professors M.A. Friedman and J. Greenfield offered many useful criticisms of the ideas expressed in this paper. I am especially grateful to Prof. Shaye J.D. Cohen, whose extensive comments improved this paper immeasurably. Much of the work on this paper was conducted with the support from the Lady Davis Fellowship Trust the Hebrew University, Jerusalem.

Most scholars who have studied the history of the *ketubah* as a marriage settlement have based their reconstruction on the evidence of a single tannaitic tradition:

> At first, when the *ketubah* used to be at the home of her father, it would be easy in his eyes to send her away [=divorce her]. Simeon ben Shetah legislated that her *ketubah* should remain with her husband, and he would write for her, "All of my possessions are surety and guaranties for your *ketubah*."[2]

Based on this tradition (and especially its fuller version in the Bavli) and biblical evidence (considered below), scholars have argued that the original Jewish marriage payment was the bride price (*mohar*), a payment made to the father of the bride. Around the time of the first century BCE, because it was easy for the husband to divorce his wife, Simeon ben Shetah changed the primary Jewish marriage payment to a marriage settlement. This marriage settlement, what became known as the rabbinic "*ketubah*", was a sum given from the husband's estate to his wife at the dissolution of the marriage.[3] Other scholars have discussed an intermediate stage of development, hinted at by traditions parallel to the

---

[2]*t. Ketub.* 12:1 (Lieberman 95). The other versions are *y. Ketub.* 8.32b-c and *b. Ketub.* 82b (there are two slightly different versions on this page).
[3]Many of the scholarly reconstructions are based on the other versions of this tradition. The literature on this is vast. Among the more important works are: A. Gulak, *Das Urkundenwesen im Talmud* (Jerusalem: R. Mass, 1935) 53-59; L.M. Epstein, *The Jewish Marriage Contract: A Study in the Status of the Woman in Jewish Law* (New York: Jewish Theological Seminary of America, 1927) 19-24, 193-206, 236-254; M.A. Friedman, "The Minimum *Mohar* Payment as Reflected in the Geniza Documents: Marriage Gift or Endowment Pledge," *PAAJR* 43 (1976) 15-25; Z. Falk, *Introduction to the Jewish Law of the Second Commonwealth* (2 Vols; Leiden: E.J. Brill, 1978) 2.295-304; M.A. Friedman, *Jewish Marriage in Palestine: A Cairo Genizah Study* (2 vols.; New York and Tel Aviv: Jewish Theological Seminary of America, 1980) 1. 239-288, esp. 257-258; M.J. Geller, "New Sources for the Origins of the Rabbinic Ketubah" *HUCA* 49 (1978) 227-245; M.A. Friedman, "Marriage and the Family in the Talmud – From Mohar to Ketubba," *Yad la-Talmud – Selected Chapters* (ed. E.E. Urbach; Jerusalem: Yad la-Talmud, 1983) 29-36, 99-100; J. Hauptman, "An Alternative Solution to the Redundancy Associated with the Phrase *Tanya Nami Hakhi*" *PAAJR* 51 (1984) 86-95; J. Hauptman, *Development of the Talmudic Sugya* (Lanham: University Press of America, 1988) 149-157; M. Elon, *Jewish Law: History, Sources, Principles* (reprinted Jerusalem: Magnes Press, 1988), 1.458-460 (Heb.). Friedman states, "In the final analysis these texts must be seen as containing partial reminiscences of ancient practices which cannot be fully understood without some reading between the lines." ("The Minimum *Mohar* Payment," p. 25). This is the closest that I have seen to an expression of skepticism regarding these historical claims.

one cited above, in which the primary Jewish marriage settlement shifted from *mohar* to dowry.[4]

In this paper I will argue that this methodology is faulty, because (1) it ignores evidence that the marriage settlement was not known in Jewish communities before the rabbinic period; (2) it fails to contend with the possibility that the word "*ketubah*" might mean something other than "marriage settlement"; and (3) it is based on a tradition whose historical validity is at best dubious. After historically reexamining the issue of the Jewish marriage settlement, I will return to tannaitic tradition that led to previous reconstructions, and attempt to show how the tradition might have crystallized and why it is historically misleading.

Sources for the History of Marriage Payments

A. The Bible

Several marriage payments appear in the Hebrew Bible, though the dominant one is the bride price, or *mohar*. This is laid out clearly in the legal texts: "If a man seduces a virgin for whom the bride price has not been paid, and lies with her, he must make her his wife by payment of a bride price," (Exod 22:15).[5] Nonlegal texts assume this institution. Hamor offers Jacob a bride price for his daughter, and Saul demands a bride price of 100 Philistine foreskins from David for his daughter.[6] All of these payments were made by the groom to his bride's father.

In addition to a bride price, there is evidence that a form of indirect dowry is known in the Hebrew Bible. When Eliezer, Abraham's servant, finds Rebekah and brings her back as a wife for Isaac, he gives her several pieces of jewelry.[7] These probably were "returned" to Isaac, being accounted as part of her dowry. It is possible, however, that these gifts were simply part of the courtship ritual and had no role in the marriage payments.

---

[4]The need for such a study was pointed out by S. Baron, *A Social and Religious History of the Jews* (18 vols; 2nd edition; New York: Columbia University Press, 1952) 2.409 n. 5. See E.J. Bickerman, "Two Legal Interpretations of the Septuagint," *Revue internationale des droits de l'antiquité* 3rd series, 3 (1956) 81-104 [reprinted in E.J. Bickerman, *Studies in Jewish and Christian History* (3 vols; Leiden: E.J. Brill, 1976) 1.201-215]. On this article, see B. A. Levine, "Comparative Perspectives on Jewish and Christian History," *JAOS* 99 (1979) 85-86.

[5]See also, Ex. 22:16, 21:32; Deut. 22:28-29.

[6]Gen 34:12; 1 Sam 18:25. See also, Gen 29:15-30. Jacob's work for Laban is most likely to be considered a bride price. On the biblical *mohar* generally, see, S. Lewinstam, "Mohar," *Encyclopaedia Biblica* (1962) 4.702-706 [Heb.].

[7]Gen 24:22, 30, 53.

B. Literature of the Second Temple Period

In this body of literature there are several references to marriage and marriage payments, but not a single reference to anything similar to a *ketubah* payment. A transfer of property accompanies Sarah in her marriage to Tobias in Tobit, 9:21. Although it is not clear whether this is a dowry or a pre-mortem inheritance, there is no sign of payment or pledge from the groom.[8] The Septuagint consistently translates *mohar* with the Greek word for dowry, *pherne*, reflecting the transition from a bride price system (*mohar*) to a dowry based system.[9] The dowry appears repeatedly in Jewish literature of this period.[10] Most references to the dowry in this literature echo the view found in non-Jewish sources from classical Greece to Rome, that a woman's dowry can entice and trap a man.[11] This is pithily stated by Pseudo-Phocylides, living around the turn of the millenia: "Do not bring as a wife into your home a bad and wealthy woman/ for you will be a slave of your wife because of the ruinous dowry."[12]

Philo, too, repeatedly refers to a dowry with no mention of anything resembling a *ketubah*. Thus, Philo talks of the good of amply dowering a bride and of the relationship of the dowry and inheritance.[13] Another passage lends more support to the idea that Philo not only does not mention the *ketubah*, but actually does not know about it. Philo states that the law of double inheritance for the firstborn (Deut 21:15-17) is

---

[8]On this incident in Tobit, see Bickerman, "Two Legal Interpretations," 208.

[9]See, Bickerman, "Two Legal Interpretations," 210-211, and Levine, "Comparative Perspectives". Bickerman uses the rabbinic material to try to understand this shift. This is methodologically problematic. The Septuagint could have used terminology for bride price found already in Homer. That it did not is indicative of an interpretation of the term, but to identify that interpretation with the rabbinic *ketubah* is not necessary. It may well have been that the Egyptian Jews of this period, like their Greek contemporaries, used only dowries for marriage payments.

[10]See, for two Greek examples, *T. Judah* 13:4; *T. Jos.* 18:3. The Jewish origin of these works is debated.

[11]See, Sir 25:21 and B. Cohen, "Dowry in Jewish and Roman Law," *Melanges Isidore Lvy* (1953) 64 [reprinted B. Cohen, *Jewish and Roman Law: A Comparative Study* (2 vols; New York: Jewish Theological Seminary of America, 1922) 1.348-376].

[12]*Pseudo-Phocylides* vv. 199-200 (Charlesworth, 2.581).

[13]See, Philo *Fug.* 29; *Spec. Leg.* 2.125. His use of the term *proix* in this regard might not be consistent. In *Spec. Leg.* 3.70 he apparently uses the word to translate the *mohar* referred to in Exod 22:16-17 and Deut 22:28-29. This, though, should be expected: *proix* is the equivalent at that time for the Septuagint translation of the word, *pherne*. See, C. Vatin, *Recherches sur le mariage et la condition de la femme marié a l'époque hellénistique* (Paris: E. de Boccard, 1970) 180-200 on this linguistic shift.

intended to remedy the case in which after fathering legitimate children a man leaves his family for another woman (Spec. Leg. 2.135-136). Had Philo known about a marriage payment made by the husband on the dissolution of the marriage, that is, the rabbinic *ketubah*, he could have used this as a better example. Even if it is argued that Philo comments expressly in order to explain this strange inheritance law, it is hard to imagine why had he known about it he would not feel compelled to explain the *ketubah*, a law or custom that to his readers would have appeared equally as bizarre.

Almost all of the examples of marriage that Josephus presents deal with royalty. In these, as could be expected, dowries appear, with no reference to a *ketubah* payment. Otherwise, Josephus mentions marriage payments only once: "It [the Law] commands that we marry not being influenced by the dowry," (Ag. Ap. 2.200).

C. Papyri

More important than the silence of the literary evidence is the silence of the documentary evidence. In the fragments of Jewish marriage contracts dating from the early second century CE discovered in the Judaean desert, there appears not a single unambiguous reference to the *ketubah* payment. Here is strong evidence that *ketubah* payments were not known in Judaea even in early rabbinic times. Because of the fragmentary nature of the papyri, and the controversy surrounding them, I will briefly review each of the eight relevant papyri.

1. *P. Mur. 20:*[14] This document is thought, by the editors, to date to 117 CE, and is written in Aramaic. It is quite fragmentary. Lines 4-5 speak of the marriage payment, though only the first few words of each line survive. The editor views these lines as referring to the dowry, although a few scholars, based on parallels from Elephantine and rabbinic sources, prefer to see them as referring to a *ketubah* payment.[15] While any reconstruction of these lines is highly speculative, it seems more likely that these lines refer to a dowry.[16] In any case, it would be

---

[14]DJD 2.109-114. On this document, see also, S.A. Birnbaum, *The Bar Menasheh Marriage Deed: Its Relation with other Jewish Marriage Deeds* (Istanbul: Nederland Historisch-Archaelogisch Instituut in het Nedije Oosten, 1962).

[15]See DJD 2.111, and notes *ad. loc.* 112. Here it is clear that their usage of "*dot*" is unclear, as their notes appeal to parallels that use the word *mohar*. For the view of this contract as referring to a *ketubah*, see especially Birnbaum, *Bar Manasseh Marriage Contract* 19, and L. Archer, *Her Price is Beyond Rubies: The Jewish Woman in Graeco-Roman Palestine* (JSOTSup 60; Sheffield: Sheffield Academic Press, 1990) 291-2.

[16]As Friedman points out, it is striking that this document contains no mention of a dowry, which is known to have been an established institution (*Jewish Marriage*

difficult to see this document as containing a clause referring to the *ketubah* payment.

2. *P. Mur. 21*:[17] This is another fragmentary Aramaic marriage contract, though of uncertain date (probably close to that of P. Mur. 20). This is the first text, to my knowledge, that actually uses the word *ketubah* (lines 10, 13, 16). I believe that "*ketubah*" here simply refers to the dowry. In line 10, *ketubah* serves as the object of the verb, [ך] ואתבנ, "and I will return". The clause is most easily interpreted as referring to money that has already changed hands and is in possession of the groom, namely, the dowry. The other references are vaguer, referring to a sum of money that the husband pledges to give to the wife or her heirs. In these cases, too, *ketubah* can easily be interpreted as dowry. I will return later in this paper to the use of the *ketubah* as meaning dowry.

3. *P. Mur. 115*:[18] This is a Greek marriage contract, in fairly good condition, from 124 CE The sum of the marriage payment is 200 *denars*, and is termed a *proix*. The word simply means "dowry", and there is no reason not to construe it that way in this document. Lines 5-6 make it clear that this marriage payment was made from the bride, or her family, to the groom.[19] This seems to contradict the interpretation that this could be referring to a donation on the part of the groom.

4. *P. Mur. 116*:[20] A very fragmentary Greek marriage contract probably contemporaneous with the other documents. The relevant lines, 5-6, if reconstructed properly, mention a marriage payment as a *pherne*. The document is too fragmentary to identify this as either a *ketubah* or a dowry. Whatever this means, the *pherne* was apparently quite large, if this is the antecedent of the reference to 2,000 *denars* in line 12.[21]

5. *P. Yad. 18*:[22] This is the most complete Jewish marriage document from this period published to date. It was written in Greek in 128 CE. The relevant lines read:

292-293). If the lines in question, though, are taken to refer to a dowry instead of a *ketubah*, this problem vanishes.

[17]DJD 2.114-117. Also published in Archer, *Her Price*, 292-294.

[18]DJD 2.243-254; Archer, *Her Price* 294-296.

[19]The *proix* is mentioned in lines 5, 6, and 12. In all these places, the meaning "dowry" again makes perfect sense.

[20]DJD 2.254-256.

[21]For the problems in reconstructing lines 5-6, see DJD 2.255, note *ad. loc.* If the identification of the *pherne* and the 2,000 *denars* is correct, it would be almost impossible to conceive of this as anything other than a dowry. A sum this large is unparalleled as a *ketubah* payment.

[22]On the Babata archive generally, see, Y. Yadin, "Expedition D- The Cave of the Letters," *IEJ* 12 (1962) 235-248; H.J. Polotsky, "The Greek Papyri from the Cave of

...she bringing to him on account of bridal gift feminine adornment in silver and gold and clothing appraised by mutual agreement...to be worth two hundred denarii of silver, which appraised value the bridegroom Judah called Cimber acknowledged that he has received from her by hand forthwith from Judah her father and that he owes to the said Shelamzion his wife together with another three hundred denarii which he promised to give to her in addition to the sum of her aforesaid bridal gift, all accounted toward her dowry...[23]

In this text, her contribution is termed the *prosphora*, to which the groom adds three hundred *denars*, the resulting sum being called her *proix*. This is the first papyri surveyed here that seems to record any contribution from the groom. Although there is a disagreement as to the exact nature of this contribution, it does appear that it cannot be considered a *ketubah*.[24] It is interesting to note that the combined sum, the *proix*, is translated in the Aramaic subscription as *phern*, a term that primarily denotes dowry, but is vague enough to include other types of marriage payments as well.[25] Here again, though, because *phern* is used to denote the entire sum, bride's family's plus groom's contribution, it does not refer to the *ketubah* payment.

---

the Letters," *IEJ* 12 (1962) 258-262. *P. Yad. 18* was first published, with commentary, as N. Lewis, R. Katzoff, J.C. Greenfield, "*Papyrus Yadin 18*" *IEJ* 37 (1987) 229-250 and is now also found in *The Documents from the Bar Kokhba Period in the Cave of Letters* (ed. N. Lewis, J. Greenfield; 2 vols; Jerusalem: Israel Exploration Society, 1989) 2.76-82.

[23]Lines 8-15. Translation from Lewis, *Documents* 80.

[24]The question hinges on the subject of the phrase (lines 14-15): ἃ ὡμολόγησεν δοῦναι αὐτῆι πρὸς τὰ τῆς προγεγραμμένης προσφορᾶς αὐτῆς. Lewis, *Documents* 82, note *ad. loc.*, seems to be suggesting that this was a sum that she or her father agreed to add to the sum already paid. Katzoff, in his legal commentary, considers this sum to be a dowry addition (Lewis, "Papyrus Yadin 18," 242). In either case, neither scholar here considers this to be a *ketubah*. On Katzoff's view, see, A. Wasserstein, "A Marriage Contract from the Province of Arabia Nova: Notes on Papyrus Yadin 18," *JQR* 80 (1989) 113-115. Wasserstein sees the institution as a dowry addition of the sort common in antiquity. In his broader argument Wasserstein argues for the non-Jewish nature of this document (105-124). Oddly, in his reply to Wasserstein, Katzoff states that *P. Yadin 18* "clearly set out" a *ketubah* payment. See, R. Katzoff, "Papyrus Yadin 18 Again: A Rejoinder," *JQR* 82 (1991) 176. Katzoff himself has offered fine discussions of dowry additions, one of which this appears to be. See, R. Katzoff, "*Donatio ante nuptias* and Jewish Dowry Additions," *Papyrology* (ed. N. Lewis; Yale Classical Studies 28; Cambridge and New York: Cambridge University Press) 231-244; R. Katzoff, "Comment on Gulak's Article," *Shenaton ha-Mishpat ha-Ivri: Annual of the Institute for Research in Jewish Law* 9-10 (1982-83) 15-28, esp. 15-20 [Heb.].

[25]See the note by Greenfield in *Documents* 142-143. See also, D. Sperber, *A Dictionary of Greek and Latin Legal Terms in Rabbinic Literature* (Ramat Gan: Bar Ilan University Press, 1984) 161-163 and the sources cited there.

6. *P. Yad. 37:*[26] A fragmentary Greek marriage contract from 131 CE. Lines 6-7 record the dowry (*proix*) of 96 *denars*. As in the other contracts, the groom acknowledges having received this sum. Once again, there is no sign of a *ketubah* payment.[27]

7. *P. Mur. 19:*[28] This is a divorce document, written in Aramaic c. 111 CE, found at Masada. The part of the line (8) dealing with the financial arrangements, is quite fragmentary. In the editors' reconstruction, this refers to the return of the dowry: "Puis, *[la do]t, je (te la) rends.*"[29] Although there are some problems with this reconstruction and interpretation, it cannot in any case be taken as evidence of a *ketubah* payment.[30]

8. For the sake of completeness, in this survey of papyri I include a marriage contract found in Egypt and written in Aramaic in 417 CE.[31] The contract has a detailed list of the bride's dowry; the groom's donation is made on line 21. Having already been transmitted to the bride and accounted as part of her dowry, this payment is a dowry addition, not a *ketubah*.[32]

---

[26]Lewis, *Documents* 130-133.

[27]The editors of this text make a case for this being a "Jewish" text, though how far this can be stretched is debatable (130). As with *P. Yadin 18*, we might be dealing here with a contract between Jews, combining legal terminology and concepts from a number of different sources.

[28]DJD 2.104-109; Archer, *Her Price* 297-299. On this document, see A.M. Rabello, "Divorce of Jews in the Roman Empire" *The Jewish Law Annual* 4 (1981) 95-97. He is inclined to follow Yaron's dating of 71 CE.

[29]DJD 2.106. Italics are the editors.

30The relevant part of the line reads בדין [ ]קא יהבא. The editors reconstruct the missing word as נמיק or פריק(DJD 2.108, note *ad. loc.*). The problem is that neither is attested as being synonymous with "dowry". Although, as indicated in the note, Krauss, *Griechische und Lateinische Lehnwörter im Talmud, Midrasch und Targum* (reprinted 2 Vols; Georg Olms, 1898) 2.178 translates one meaning of the former as "Morgengabe," and H.L. Strack and P. Billberbeck, *Das Evangelium nach Markus, Lukas und Johannes und die Apostelgeschichte Erläutert aus Talmud und Midrasch* (6 vols; Munich: C.H. Beck'sche, 1924), 2.384 translates נמי as a semantic equivalent to φερνή, it is not clear how they arrive at these meanings. נמי is used only in late texts, and even in those texts is never used to describe a monetary settlement- only a written contract. See M. Jastrow, *A Dictionary of the Targumim, the Talmud Babli and Yerushalmi, and the Midrashic Literature* (2 vols; Lonon: Luzac; New York: G.P. Putnam's, 1903) 1.253 *ad. loc.*; Sperber, *Dictionary* 74-75. Moreover, the verb יהב can mean "to give", but never means "to return". See, M. Sokoloff, *A Dictionary of Jewish Palestinian Aramaic* (Ramat Gan: Bar Ilan University Press, 1990) 235-236. פריק is unattested.

[31]C. Sirat, P. Cuderlier, M. Dukan, M.A. Friedman, *La Ketouba de Cologne* (Opladen: Westdeutscher, 1986).

[32]For the text and translation, see, ibid. 20-22. For discussion of this line, see, 12-13, 54.

None of the extant Jewish marriage contracts from the rabbinic period shows any familiarity with the rabbinic *ketubah* payment. Some of the contracts refer to payments made by the groom, but these are dowry additions, not *ketubah* payments. The word *ketubah* appears several times in these documents, and seems to mean "dowry".[33]

D. Rabbinic Literature

I turn now to the rabbinic evidence on the *ketubah* payment. The only direct evidence in rabbinic literature for the establishment of the *ketubah* payment is the tannaitic tradition, cited at the beginning of this article, and its parallels. Regarding all the parallels as containing a germ of true historical development, Friedman writes:

> In the late tannaitic period there were two traditions which existed, side by side, as the social motivation for the *takkanah*. According to one of these, one was unable to marry a woman unless he paid a *mohar* of 200 *zuz* or a mina [sic], and those who could not afford this would grow old without marrying. According to the second tradition, all men could marry. But since there was no need for any further payment at the time of divorce, there was no deterrent to divorce. The *takkanah* of Simeon b. Shatah solved both problems; it made marriage easier and divorce more difficult.[34]

The evidence clearly supports Friedman's claim that there were two tannaitic traditions about the motivation for Simeon b. Shetah's enactment. Yet to move from the traditions' understanding of history to history itself is a logical leap not justified by the evidence. In fact, there are several reasons to doubt the veracity of these traditions.

a)   Attributions to Simeon b. Shetah: As a number of enactments were attributed to Simeon b. Shetah in his legendary role as a founder of the rabbinic movement, any historical claims in these legends must be carefully examined. Analyzing a tradition that assigns the institution of the *ketubah* and the impurity of metal vessels to Simeon b. Shetah,[35] Goodblatt has shown that at least the latter enactment occurred in the

---

[33]I will return to this use of the word *ketubah*. It should be noted that Yadin, "Expedition D," 244-245, describes the still unpublished marriage contract of Babatha as containing a *ketubah* payment. As I will argue that the *ketubah* payment is probably an early tannaitic innovation, even if the clause does appear it will not invalidate the thesis of this paper. Rather, it would indicate that there were some people following rabbinic advice or legislation in this area.

[34]Friedman, "Marriage and Family," 34.

[35]*b. Sabb.* 14b, 16b; *b. Ketub.* 82b. According to *y. Ketub.* 8.32c: "Simeon ben Shetah legislated three things: that a man does business with the *ketubah* of his wife; and that children should go to school; and he legislated impurity for glass vessels." The first clause refers, apparently, to the ability of a man to use his wife's *ketubah* until the end of the marriage.

tannaitic period, well after Simeon b. Shetah.[36] This throws into doubt the attribution of the rabbinic *ketubah* payment to Simeon b. Shetah.

b) The form of the *takkanah:* The form of these traditions, as well as its association with Simeon b. Shetah, is cause for caution. Often later rabbinic legal institutions were retrojected onto mythological founder figures. Jaffee has noted this tendency especially in the Tosefta: "In the Tosefta, as in the halakhic midrashim...where it is possible to compare recensions of comparable traditions we find compelling reason to conclude that the post-mishnaic taqqanah is a literary trope and little more, a creation of jurisprudence and exegesis rather than a record of the legislative pronouncements of Israelite legal institutions."[37] Although the evidence regarding the *ketubah* is not fit for such an approach, Jaffee's observation does indicate that the historical claims made in these sources should not be accepted uncritically.

c) The meaning of "*ketubah*" in rabbinic literature: As mentioned, the term "*ketubah*" in rabbinic literature can have a number of meanings. If the *ketubah*, that is, a marriage settlement payable on dissolution of the marriage, was enacted by Simeon b. Shetah, we would expect that when the word "*ketubah*" appears in dicta attributed to early rabbinic figures, it would carry this meaning. In fact, the word *ketubah* does appear in these dicta: in each, a meaning of "*dowry*" is possible.[38]

Several traditions ascribed to the Houses of Hillel and Shammai mention the *ketubah*, but the meaning of the term is not clear. For example:

> One waiting levirate marriage...[who] died, what is done with her *ketubah* and with the property which enters and leaves with her? The House of Shammai says: The heirs of the husband divide it with the heirs of the [i.e., her] father. And the House of Hillel says: Property [stays] in their possession! [i.e.,] the *ketubah* is in the possession of the heirs of the husband [so it remains there, and]

---

[36]See, D. Goodblatt, "The Talmudic Sources on the Origins of Organized Jewish Education," *Studies in the History of the Jewish People and the Land of Israel 5* (1980) 86-90 [Heb.]; J. Neusner, *The Rabbinic Traditions about the Pharisees before 70*, (3 vols; Leiden: E.J. Brill, 1971) 1.110-111.

[37]M. Jaffee, "The Taqqanah in Tannaitic Literature: Jurisprudence and the Construction of Rabbinic Memory," *JJS* 41 (1990) 233.

[38]The use of "*ketubah*" for "*dowry*" in rabbinic literature is well known. See, Friedman, *Jewish Marriage* 1.310-311; B. Cohen, "Dowry in Jewish and Roman Law," 62-63, 65-66. This is a distinction that is, strangely enough, ignored by the dictionaries- see *ad. loc., Arukh Completum* (ed. A. Kohut; 8 vols; Berlin: Menorah, 1926),and in the *Additamenta ad librum Aruch Completum* (ed. S. Krauss; Vienna: Alexander Kohut Memoral Foundation, 1937); M. Jastrow, *Dictionary;* J. Levy, *Wörterbuch ber die Talmudim und Midraschim* (4 vols; Berlin and Vienna: Benjamin Harz, 1924) ; Sokoloff, *Dictionary*.

property which enters and leaves with her is in the possession of the heirs of the father [so it remains there].[39]

In this mishnah there is a clear contrast between the *ketubah* and the "property which enters and leaves with her", corresponding to the well-known division of a woman's property into "iron sheep property" – that which constitutes her dowry and is given over to her husband for his use until the dissolution of the marriage, and "plucked property" – her independent property, the usufruct only of which the husband is allowed to enjoy during the marriage. At the very least, the word "*ketubah*" in this passage might refer to the woman's dowry plus the rabbinic *ketubah* payment, but a simple meaning of dowry is the easiest and most fitting. Halivni cites other examples of this usage.[40] The same ambiguity applies also to the other traditions attributed to the Houses that mention the *ketubah*.[41] These are the only traditions regarding the *ketubah* that are attributed to pre-70 CE figures.

The earliest explicit attestation of the *ketubah* payment appears in a statement attributed to R. Eleazer b. Azariah of Yavneh:

A. If she is widowed, or divorced, whether after betrothal or after marriage – she collects all of it [that is, the statutory amount of her marriage settlement plus any additional money pledged to her by her husband].

B. Rabbi Eleazar ben Azariah says: After marriage –she collects all of it; after betrothal – a virgin collects 200 [*denars*], and a widow a *maneh* [=100 *denars*]...[42]

The discussion is over whether a woman collects her entire *ketubah* or just a part of it if she is widowed or divorced in the time between her betrothal and her marriage. Rabbi Eleazar ben Azariah's statement, that she collects only the statutory amount and not any additional money that the husband may have pledged, is predicated on the idea of a rabbinic *ketubah* payment, though he himself does not use that term. At least one

---

[39]*m. Yebam.* 4:3= *m. Ketub.* 8:6. *m. B. Bat.* 9:8-9 are clearly based on this principle, although they are more laconic, and less useful in this context. See, Neusner, *Rabbinic Traditions* 2.237.

[40]D. Halivni, *Sources and Traditions: Nashim* (Tel Aviv: Dvir, 1968) 44 [Heb.]. But see, J.N. Epstein, *Mavo le-Nusah ha-Mishnah* (Jerusalem: Magnes Press, 1964) 1099-1101. Friedman states that it is "unnecessary" to interpret *ketubah* as dowry here, though he does not advance any argument (*Jewish Marriage* 1.311).

[41]See, *m. Yebam.* 15:3; *m. Git.* 4:3; *m. Sot.* 4:2. Both *t. Arak.* 4:5 [Zuck. 547] and *t. Ketub.* 5:6 [Lieberman 73] mention both the Houses and the *ketubah*, but (1) it is not clear in either case what is meant by "*ketubah*", and (2) in neither instance is it clear that the Houses are commenting on the *ketubah* itself and not other issues raised in the pericopes.

[42]*m. Ketub.* 5:1.

other statement ascribed to a Yavnean figure also seems to presume the existence of a *ketubah* payment.[43] Other statements ascribed to other Yavnean sages may refer to *ketubah* payments, but the meaning of the term in those statements is ambiguous.[44]

Post-Yavnean authorities frequently refer to and discuss the *ketubah* payment. Although Rabbis Akiba and Ishmael seem to take no great interest in the institution, those from the following generation do, especially Rabbi Meir and Rabban Simeon ben Gamliel (II).[45] Most of the legal traditions in the Mishnah and Tosefta regarding the *ketubah* are anonymous and perhaps derive from a relatively late date.

Continuity or Innovation

I have demonstrated above that Jewish sources do not mention or presume the existence of the *ketubah* payment before the Yavnean layer in the Mishnah. This fact suggests that the *ketubah* payment may have been a rabbinic innovation, perhaps of the Yavnean rabbis themselves. A potential objection to this suggestion is the fact that other legal systems of the ancient Near East required payments very similar to the *ketubah* payment.

According to Hammurabi's Code, for example:

> 137: If a man sets his face to divorce a lay sister who has borne him sons or a priestess who has provided him with sons, they shall render her dowry to her and shall give her a half-portion of field plantation or chattels and she shall bring up her sons; after she has then brought up her sons, they shall give her a share like (that of) a

---

[43]*m. Ketub.* 2:1.

[44]*m. Yebam.* 15:7, and see the strange interpretation of this source by Rabbi Simeon ben Eleazer in t. Yebam. 14:2 [Lieberman 50–51], and comments by S. Lieberman, *Tosefta Ki-fshutah* (10 vols; New York: Jewish Theological Seminary of America, 1967) 6.169 [Heb.]. While it is almost certain that the *ketubah* referred to here is not a dowry, the next example adduced in this source suggests that this clause, too, should be referring to something which the man received from the woman. See also, *m. Arak.* 6:1, with parallel at *t. Arak.* 4:5 [Zuck. 547].

[45]This, of course, might be a function of source preservation. R. Akiba's few statements on the *ketubah*, though clearly showing familiarity with the rabbinic institution, add very little to the statements on which he is commenting. See the sources cited in I. Konovitz, *Rabbi Akiba* (Jerusalem: Mosad ha-Rav Kook, 1955/56) 325–327 [Heb.]. Rabbi Ishmael's interest in the *ketubah*, aside from the single tradition cited above, is confined to a single, awkward passage, *t. Ketub.* 12:3 [Lieberman 97]. On this, see, G. Porton, *The Traditions of Rabbi Ishmael* (4 vols; Leiden: E.J. Brill, 1976) 1.107–108 and the sources cited there. For a collection of R. Meir's statements concerning the *ketubah*, see, I. Konovitz, *Rabbi Meir* (Jerusalem: Mosad ha-Rav Kook, 1967) 159–162 [Heb.].

> single heir in anything that has been given (to her) for her sons, and a husband after her heart may marry her.

138: If a man wishes to divorce his first [chosen] wife who has not borne him sons, he shall give her money to the value of her bridal gift and shall make good to her dowry which she has brought from her father's house and (so) divorce her.

139: If there is no bridal gift, he shall give her 1 maneh of silver for divorce money.

140: If (he is) a villein, he shall give her 1/3 maneh of silver.[46]

The law clearly penalizes a man who divorces his wife, especially if she has borne him children. These stipulations find many parallels throughout the ancient Near East.[47]

A similar institution is found in the Jewish marriage contracts from Elephantine:

> Tomorrow or (the) next day, should Ananiah stand up in an assembly and say: "I hated my wife Jehoishma; she shall not be my wife," silver of ha[tr]ed is on his head. All that she brought into his house he shall give her – her money and her garments, valued (in) silver (at) seven karsh, [eight] sh[ekels, 4+]1 (=5) [hallurs], and the rest of the goods which are written (above).[48]

In this document the purpose and sum of the "silver of hatred" are not specified. Parallel uses of this term in other marriage contracts from Elephantine indicate that this was a penalty assessed on the initiator of the divorce.[49] The similarity of these clauses to the *ketubah* payment has been long noted, and as a result these contracts have been seen by scholars as one stage of the legal development from *mohar* to *ketubah*.[50]

---

[46]The translation is from G.R. Driver and J.R. Mills, *The Babylonian Laws*, (2 vols; Oxford: Clarendon Press, 1955) 1.55. See also the commentary, (1952) 2.290-306.

[47]For examples, see, R. Yaron, *The Laws of Eshnunna* (reprinted Jerusalem: Magnes Press, 1988) 211-222.

[48]Kraeling 7+15+18/1,3,8,13,18,19,22,26,30 = B. Porten, A. Yardeni, *Textbook of Aramaic Documents from Ancient Egypt* (2 vols; Jerusalem: Hebrew University, Dept. of the History of the Jewish People; Winona Lake, IN, U.S.A.: Distributed by Eisenbrauns, 1989) B3.8 (2.78-83). Translation is from Porten and Yardeni, lines 21-23, p. 82. The text is from 420 BCE.

[49]See, Cowley 15=Sayce-Cowley G= B. Porten, A. Yardeni, *Textbook of Aramaic Documents* B2.6 (2.30-33). The document is from 458 BCE or 445 BCE. See also, Kraeling 2= Porten and Yardeni, B3.3 (2.60-63), from 449 BCE.

[50]See, for examples, H.L. Ginsberg, "The Brooklyn Museum Aramaic Papyri" *JAOS* 74 (1954) 153-162; R. Yaron, "Aramaic Marriage Contracts from Elephantine," *JSS* 3 (1958) 1-39; J. Fitzmyer, "A Re-Study of an Elephantine Aramaic Marriage Contract (AP 15)," *Near Eastern Studies in Honor of William Foxwell Albright*, (ed. H. Goedicke; Baltimore: Johns Hopkins Press, 1971) 137-168; B. Porten, *Archives from Elephantine* (Berkeley: University of California, 1968) 221-231. For excellent examples of harmonizing these documents with rabbinic law,

Demotic marriage documents from Egypt, also have a clause that is nearly identical with the rabbinic *ketubah*. These documents date from approximately the third century BCE.[51]

That there are strong parallels to the rabbinic *ketubah* payment in these three groups of documents is undeniable. Therefore many scholars have suggested that the rabbinic *ketubah* is a continuation of this legal tradition; in this perspective, the *ketubah* is not a rabbinic innovation but an age-old institution that happens, because of our inadequate documentation to be attested securely for the first time only in the Mishnah. But this argument is weak. Parallelism does not prove continuity. Regarding the Elephantine documents, Yaron wrote: "...although there is some relationship between Elephantine and the sources of the Talmudic period – they may, for instance, be following common prototypes – there is no direct line leading from the former to the latter."[52] The same caution applies to the Demotic contracts, and all the more so to the material from the ancient Near East. This evidence then, like the rabbinic traditions and the papyri surveyed above, cannot bear the burden of proving an unbroken legal tradition from *mohar* to *ketubah*.

The ancient Near Eastern documents do prove the antiquity of a monetary penalty for the initiation of divorce. Although some rabbis later saw the purpose of the *ketubah* as discouraging divorce on the part of the man, the *ketubah* payment itself differs in two important respects from these ancient Near Eastern penalties: the *ketubah* payment is made only by the husband (who also, in rabbinic law, is the only spouse who can initiate a divorce) and it is due to the wife in cases of both divorce and death of the husband. It is not surprising that aspects of this idea penalizing the initiator of a divorce, current in the ancient Near East, are also present in rabbinic law and lore. Such a presence, however, proves neither that the rabbinic *ketubah* payment was a codification of an existing practice nor that it was a logical continuation of a pre-existent legal tradition.

The evidence, then, aside from a tradition that seems to date from the third or fourth centuries CE, indicates that the rabbinic *ketubah* payment was a rabbinic innovation of around the late first century CE. Elements for this innovation may have been taken from several legal traditions.

---

see, J.N. Epstein, "Notizen zu den jüdisch-aramäischen Papyri von Assuan," *Jahrbuch der Jüdisch-Literarischen Gesellschaft* 6 (1908) 359-373, esp. 365-372; L. Freund, *Zum semitischen Ehegüterrecht bei Auflösung der Ehe* (Vienna: Alfred Höder, 1917).

[51]See especially, J. Rabinowitz, *Jewish Law: Its Influence on the Development of Legal Institutions*, (New York: Bloch, 1956) 39-47; M.J. Geller, "New Sources".

[52]R. Yaron, *The Laws of the Aramaic Papyri* (Oxford: Clarendon Press, 1961) 128.

Although the legal tradition recorded in the Egyptian contracts appears to have fallen into disuse before the advent of the Roman period, its memory may have somehow been preserved and transmitted to the Rabbis in Palestine years later. Possible models for this transmission are many (for example, preservation in popular consciousness or the transmission of legal documents or codes) but entirely speculative.[53] Using antique, and occasionally contemporaneous, legal concepts and phrases as building blocks, the rabbis constructed an entirely new institution.[54]

An example of how a contemporaneous legal practice might have been reworked by the rabbis is the sum of the minimum *ketubah* payment. As Jewish marriage contracts from the Dead Sea area show, the sum of 200, and sometimes 100, zuz was a standard dowry payment. It is possible that because this sum was used as a standard marriage payment it was adopted, under the guise of biblical justification, as the minimum sum of the rabbinic *ketubah* payment.[55] Although the sum is the same, the use is entirely different: instead of this sum moving from the bride or her family to her husband, it becomes an endowment pledge payable to the wife on dissolution of the marriage. Thus, it is possible that a familiar custom was integrated into the creation of a new legal institution, in the process being radically transformed.[56]

---

[53]Perhaps these legal institutions were transmitted to Palestine via Alexandria. See the story at *y. Ketub.* 4.28d (= *y. Yebam.* 15.14d).

[54]Geller ends his article by saying, "...it is no longer possible to discern the development of Jewish law in the period of the Mishnah without reference to the legal practices of Ptolemaic Egypt," (245). He is not the first to neglect the possibility that a shared corpus of law stands behind many of the ancient Near Eastern law codes, including both the Demotic and rabbinic. This issue was recently raised for the rabbinic law concerning a woman who has two husbands, a case that might be a parallel phenomenon to the development of the *ketubah* in rabbinic law. See, S. Friedman, "The Case of the Woman with Two Husbands in Talmudic and Ancient Near Eastern Law," *Shenaton ha-Mishpat ha-Ivri: Annual of the Institute for Research in Jewish Law* 2 (1975) 360-382 [Heb.].

[55]Rabbinic sources link the sum of the *ketubah* payment to the biblical fine for the seducer (Deut 22:29). See, *Mekhilta d'Rabbi Ishmael* [Horovitz-Rabin 309]; *y. Ketub.* 1.25b.

[56]It might be that 200 zuz conveyed some type of legal "message" in the Near East. See, S. Goitein, *A Mediterranean Society Vol. 3: The Family* (Berkeley and Los Angeles: University of California Press, 1978) 119, 451 n. 7. This might also be the reason behind the phrase ליהבנא ליכי מוהר בתולייכי. On this phrase, dateable to the Gaonic period, see, Friedman, *Jewish Marriage* 1.241-244. The tendency of the rabbis of antiquity to claim continuity for innovative acts is not uncommon. See, B. Bokser, *The Origins of the Seder: The Passover Rite and Early Rabbinic Judaism* (Berkeley: University of California Press, 1984) 89-100.

Nor would this be the first time that the Rabbis innovated family law. S. Cohen has shown that they took on the far more fundamental question of "Who is a Jew," changing *de jure*, in the process, the very definition of what it meant to be a Jew.[57] There would have been far fewer ramifications in legislating a *ketubah* payment than those caused by creation of the "matrimonial principle".

Unlike the matrimonial principle, though, the *ketubah* payment did not succeed in becoming a normative institution. The marriage contracts surveyed above, written contemporaneously with the first attestation of the institution, show no familiarity with it. Even the Jewish marriage contract from fifth-century CE. Egypt does not have a *ketubah* clause! This should not be too surprising. The dowry remained important to both the Greeks and Romans of this period, both as a sign of the legitimacy of the union and of the status of the bride.[58] To some degree, this attitude is also found among the rabbis, and would no doubt be found in the society in which they worked.[59] Because the dowry is a payment from the bride to the groom, and the *ketubah* payment, like the biblical *mohar*, a payment (though delayed) from the husband to the wife,

---

[57]S.J.D. Cohen, "The Origins of the Matrilineal Principle in Rabbinic Law," *AJS Review* 10 (1985) 19-53. Cf., L. Schiffman, *Who Was a Jew: Rabbinic and Halakhic Perspectives on the Jewish Christian Schism* (Hoboken: Ktav, 1985) 9-17.

[58]The Greek orators harped on dowry size as the mark of a legitimate marriage. It was assumed that no respectful man would marry his daughter undowered unless it was as a concubine. See, Demosthenes, "Against Nearera," 113 and Isaeus, III. Though older, these sources were current through the Hellenistic age. See, S. Pomeroy, *Women in Hellenistic Egypt: From Alexander to Cleopatra* (New York: Schocken, 1984) 86-89, 91-93, 136; Vatin, *Recherches* 180-200. For Rome, see, D. Daube, *Roman Law: Linguistic, Social and Philosophical Aspects* (Edinburgh: University Press, 1969) 102-116; P. Corbett, *The Roman Law of Marriage* (Oxford: Clarendon Press, 1930) 147-204.

[59]For rabbinic attitudes regarding the importance of the dowry, see, *t. Ketub.* 6:3 [Lieberman 75]; *y. Ketub.* 4.29a; *b. Ketub.* 52b; *Sipra B'hukotai* 5:3 [Weiss 111d]. *t. Ketub.* 6:4 [Lieberman 75] hints at the importance of honor as a consideration in dowry size. *m. Ketub.* 6:5 is less subtle. Anthropological studies predict the same: Goody has argued that stratified societies with advanced agricultural systems tend toward a dotal system. See, J. Goody, *Production and Reproduction: A Comparative Study of the Domestic Domain* (Cambridge and New York: Cambridge University Press, 1976) 20. Cf., J. Comaroff, "Introduction," *The Meaning of Marriage Payments* (ed. J. Comaroff; London and New York: Academic Press, 1980) 9-11; D. Rheubottom, "Dowry and Wedding Celebrations in Yugoslav Macedonia," in Comaroff, 221-249; S. Harrell and S. Dickey, "Dowry Systems in Complex Societies," *Ethnology* 24 (1985) 105-120. Palestine was apparently agriculturally rich and quite stratified. See, D. Sperber, *Roman Palestine 200-400: The Land* (Ramat-Gan: Bar Ilan University Press, 1978) 33-34. Josephus attributes the Great Revolt to (among other things) the highly stratified nature of Judea (*J.W.* 7. 260-261).

the two payments are somewhat in tension. Hence, in a society that traditionally valued the dowry, the *ketubah* payment would have difficulty finding acceptance. In Babylonia the *ketubah* was made into little more than a legal formality, and in the Palestinian tradition preserved in the Genizah it resembled the *mahr* (or *mohar*) of their Islamic neighbors.[60] This will set the stage for the way in which the elements of the system of Jewish marriage payments are played out throughout history: in environments in which a bride price (usually Arab countries) is emphasized, the *ketubah* (that is, a payment from the husband to the wife) is emphasized, but in those emphasizing dowries the practical force of the *ketubah* becomes negligible.[61]

The Literary Question

If, as I have argued, the *ketubah* payment is a rabbinic legal innovation of around the first century CE, the rabbinic tradition ascribing its innovation to Simeon ben Shetah remains to be explained. On the one hand, the rabbinic tendency toward "creative historiography" has long been noted.[62] By attributing an innovative practice to a founder figure and tracing its historical development from the Bible, the framers of this tradition may have hoped to give the institution a legitimacy felt to be lacking.

On the other hand, there may also be a historical "kernel" in this tradition. I suggest that if there is a "kernel", it is the legislation of the clause in the Jewish marriage contract that holds all of the husband's property as surety for the return of the wife's *ketubah*. This is a clause found in nearly all of the Jewish marriage documents surveyed above, and is frequently attested in contemporaneous Greek and Demotic marriage contracts.[63] Perhaps the rabbis received a tradition that

---

[60]See, *Encyclopaedia of Islam*, s.v. mahr, 3.137-8; Goitein, *Family* 120, 451 n. 10; Friedman, *Jewish Marriage* 1.283-285. It is worth noting that although the minimum *ketubah* payment of 200 *zuz* would have been a healthy but not insurmountable amount of money at the end of the second century, perhaps by the third and certainly by the fourth century this sum would have been insignificant.

[61]To my knowledge, no one has yet studied the interaction of Jewish law relating to marriage payments and its application with its environment.

[62]See, I. Heineman, *Darke ha-Aggadah* (Jerusalem: Masada, 1954) 7-13, and the bibliographical note in R. Kalmin, "Saints or Sinners, Scholars or Ignoramuses? Stories about the Rabbis as Evidence for the Composite Nature of the Babylonian Talmud," *AJS Review* 15 (1990) 203-205.

[63]For the non-Jewish parallels in Greek and Demotic marriage documents, see, A. Gulak, *Das Urkundenwesen* 57-58; R. Taubenschlag, *The Law of Greco-Roman Egypt in the Light of the Papyri 332 BC-640 AD* (New York: Herald Square, 1944) 94; J.J. Rabinowitz, *Jewish Law* 43; Geller, "New Sources," p. 243.

identified Simeon ben Shetah with the introduction of this clause into the Jewish marriage documents.[64] *But, as is clear from comparing this clause to those found in the Greek and Demotic documents, in its original meaning in this clause ketubah stood for nothing more than "dowry".* Later, against the background of the shift of meaning of "*ketubah*" from dowry to delayed endowment payment, the received tradition associating Simeon ben Shetah with this clause was read as the first reference to the rabbinic *ketubah*. From this misunderstanding the clause "Simeon ben Shetah legislated that her *ketubah* should remain with her husband" (t. *Ketub.* 12:1) flowed easily, as with the other explanations offered in the traditions that survive in the talmudim. All of these traditions, then, must be considered as rabbinic historiography rather than as reliable reports of historical reality.

Summary and Conclusions

In this article, I have argued that the *ketubah* payment is a rabbinic innovation datable to around the late first century CE. No pre-rabbinic documents either mention or refer to the *ketubah*; other legal systems of the ancient Near East are familiar with legal stipulations paralleling the *ketubah*, but there is no evidence that the rabbinic *ketubah* derives from pre-rabbinic times or is continuous with the practices of previous generations. The rabbinic traditions that ascribe the *ketubah* to pre-rabbinic times are historiographical compositions in which a received tradition might have been interpreted anachronistically to yield a coherent historical explanation for a rabbinic legal institution.

A serious methodological issue, that of continuity vs. innovation in rabbinic law, has been raised. As work continues (as it hopefully will) exploring the relationship of rabbinic to other ancient Near Eastern law codes, we must always be sensitive to the possibility that the rabbis used legal ideas and phrases, and popular practices, in a very selective fashion. The presence of parallels does not prove that there was continuity.

I have left unexplored the question of motivation for this innovation. A proper study of this issue, which involves an analysis of both the rabbinic law and evidence concerning all marriage payments and the rabbinic perception of divorce, goes beyond the scope of this paper.[65]

---

[64]M. Friedman thinks that "it may be assumed that the pledging of one's goods was already used in promissory notes" in Palestine in the time of Simeon ben Shetah ("Marriage and the Family," 34). Geller thinks that the introduction of this clause into Jewish legal documents might have originated with Simeon ben Shetah ("New Sources" 235).

[65]I will return to this issue in future work.

Ultimately, it will be in the exploration of this issue, in light of the conclusions reached in this paper, that will help us to begin exploring marriage and divorce among Jews during the rabbinic period.

Part Four

BY WAY OF COMPARISON:
SOME GREEK FAMILIES

7

Some Greek Families:
Production and Reproduction

Sarah B. Pomeroy

The English word "family" has no exact ancient Greek equivalent.[1] The Greek word *oikos* may be translated as "family," or "household," or "estate." The oikos was a larger entity than what we think of as a family, for it embraced the members of the family, and movable and immovable property including slaves, animals, the house itself, land, and all that was produced, consumed and disbursed by its members. This definition of oikos which emphasizes property, and ignores affective relationships, makes clear the great difference between the Greek concept of family and the modern western version.

In this paper I will look at some Greek families in the Classical and Hellenistic period, and use these examples as the basis of some general remarks about the economic foundation of the family, the relationship between generations, congruences and conflicts between family law and

---

[1]The text of this paper is presented here, with minor changes, as delivered at the 1991 annual meeting of the American Academy of Religion and Society for the Study of Biblical Literature. For extensive discussion of the *oikos* with fuller documentation see Sarah B. Pomeroy, *A Social and Historical Commentary on Xenophon's Oeconomicus* (Oxford, 1994). For the Greek family see *eadem, The Family in Classical and Hellenistic Greece* (Oxford, to be published).

With a few obvious exceptions, journal titles are abbreviated according to the form in *L'Année philologique.* Accepted abbreviations will be used for standard works. Lists of such abbreviations may be found in reference books such as the *Oxford Classical Dictionary*, 2nd edn., and in the major Greek and Latin dictionaries.

family history, demographic and onomastic issues, and matrilineal and patrilineal structures in a patriarchal society.

All the known lawcodes of Greek states in the Archaic period included regulations governing family relationships. The polis did not hesitate to intrude in some areas that many contemporary societies consider private. Solon's laws were the first in Athens to regulate families. One of his laws was that a father must teach his son a trade, or give him some means of support so that, in return, the son could look after his parents when they became old (Plut., *Sol.* 22, Galen, *Protrept.* 8, D.L. 1.55, Aesch. 1.28, cf. Aelian, *Hist. An.* 9.1). Otherwise, a son was not obliged to maintain his parents. Like so many of Solon's laws, this one codified what must have been normal behavior, not only in Athens, but throughout the Greek world – at least under the pressure of peers, or as a result of common sense.

How this system works among families whose economy is based on agriculture is obvious. For the details about the family farm and the domestic economy we can read Xenophon's *Oeconomicus,* a "Treatise on the Skills of Estate Management."[2] Consistent with Solon's law and Greek custom, Xenophon mentions that children will be the support and allies of their aged parents (*Oec.* 7.12). Furthermore, as Xenophon states, farming requires no special knowledge. All a man needed to do was look around and see how his father and neighbors did it (*Oec.* 6.9, 15.4,10, 16.3).

In the present brief survey we will look at some Greek families whose economic foundation was not agriculture, but rather skilled labor, where children inherited from their parents the materials and tools of the trade, their reputation, their long-time customers, and perhaps their native talent. In the Greek world, these practitioners of the liberal arts and skilled professions were not at the bottom of the social and economic scale, nor slaves (as some of them were at Rome), but they were not usually members of the top class.[3] Landowners were the highest class socially and economically. However, most of the families we will examine were wealthy and important enough to have left monuments bearing their names and to have gotten into the historical records.

Families of physicians are probably the most obvious example. They are well attested in the Greek world, many in Cos, the birthplace of

---

[2]See Sarah B. Pomeroy, *Xenophon's Oeconomicus: A Social and Historical Commentary,* Chapter 5.

[3]Pheidias, for example, was a friend of Pericles. In contrast to the Greek world artists and sculptors who worked in Rome were not regarded highly. See R.R.R. Smith, "Greeks, Foreigners, and Roman Republican Portraits," *JRS,* 71 (1981), 24-38.

Hippocrates and a center of medicine. The Hipppocratic oath enjoins the physician to transmit his knowledge to his sons.[4] A pupil who was not a blood relative of his teacher swore to treat his teacher as though he were his father, to maintain him and share his life, and to teach the art of medicine to his teacher's sons, if they so wished. But this prescription was not necessary. The oath is more likely to have described the ordinary situation. A physician's son was his father's natural apprentice.[5] The Greeks had no compunctions about putting young children to work. *The Canon and Decorum* contain some suggestions that training in medicine should begin in childhood. Moreover, the profession was attractive, for it was both prestigious and lucrative, so much so that inscriptions from Cos include physicians in lists of public benefactors.[6]

Biographical traditions about Hippocrates himself allude to a family of doctors that endured for at least seven generations. There are several versions of the biography of Hippocrates, with most of the variations occurring among the earliest generations. According to the *Suda*, the famous Hippocrates, the second one by this name, was the son of a physician, the grandson of the first Hippocrates, who was a physician, and was descended from a certain Chrysus ("The Golden One") and Elaphus ("The Ivory One") who were also physicians. The family tree as reported by the *Suda* is given in Figure 1.[7]

---

[4]For the text and commentary see Ludwig Edelstein, *The Hippocratic Oath* (Supplements to the Bulletin of the History of Medicine, 1; Baltimore, 1943).

[5]Plato, *Laws* 4.720B, *Protagoras* 311B, Galen 2.1 p. 280 (K.).

[6]See note 11 on Hippocrates III below.

[7]*The Suda* (Adler) s.v. Hippocrates, paras. 564-69.

Figure 1:

Chrysus
/
Elaphus
/
Gnosidicus
/
Hippocrates I
/
Heracleides
/
Hippocrates II
/
Thessalus   Draco
/   /
Hippocrates III   Hippocrates IV

Thymbraeus
/
Hippocrates V   Hippocrates VI

Praxianax
/
Hippocrates VII

Two sons of Hippocrates, Thessalus and Draco, became physicians, and their sons, in turn, both named Hippocrates were physicians. The *Suda* mentions three more physicians named Hippocrates who were members of the same family. Other ancient biographical sources provide a few additional details.[8]

Most ancient biographies are a blend of fact and fiction. Modern scholars may summarily reject the gods, "the Golden One," and "the Ivory One," although the biographers and their audience probably

---

[8]For example, Soranus, *Life of Hippocrates* in J. Ilberg, *CMG*, 4, pp. 175-78, gives an abbreviated genealogy, but he does name the father, mother (Phaenarete), and sons of Hippocrates II, and adds that Hippocrates traced his ancestry back to Heracles and Asclepius. See also Littré 9.314 = Wesley D. Smith, *Hippocrates. Pseudepigraphic Writings* (Leiden, 1990), pp. 48-50, number 2: Paitus to Artaxerxes; the pseud-epigraphic "Embassy," attributed to Thessalus, son of Hippocrates: Littré 9.405 = Smith, *Hippocrates. Pseudepigraphic Writings*, p. 110, 27.1; Arist., HA 3.512b; Galen, CMG 5.9.1, pp. 7-8; and Hipp.: Littré 9.420.

would have placed credence in them as they did in the mythical ancestors of heroes. It is less easy to dismiss or to corroborate the existence of the human ancestors whom the biographers name, but this is not the proper place to discuss the notorious scholarly crux of the biographical tradition of Hippocrates.⁹ However, the general picture the *Suda* and other sources give of men in each generation of a family practicing medicine is credible. Epigraphical evidence for such families begins to appear in the Hellenistic period.¹⁰ Hippocrates III, son of Thessalus, is attested in two inscriptions. ¹¹

Striking examples of career continuity through as many as five or six generations appear among the families of tragic and comic poets including Aeschylus, Sophocles, and Euripides.¹² Dyads of father and son who were actors are common. The work was highly specialized. There was no crossing over between genres: some families worked exclusively in tragedy, others in comedy. The longest sequence appears in the family of Aeschylus. These kinsmen are shown in Figure 2.

---

⁹For source criticism see now Jody Rubin Pinnault, *Hippocratic Lives and Legends* (Leiden, 1992). See also Wesley D. Smith, "Notes on ancient medical historiography," *Bulletin of the History of Medicine*, 63 (1989), pp. 73-109. Smith (pp. 105-06) does not totally reject the traditions about the genealogy of the family of Hippocrates, but suggests that the biographies contain "the remains of a genuine insular succession." Because of ambiguities in the text of the *Suda*, Smith's genealogical table differs slightly from my own. For a critical view of the biographical tradition, especially as it concerns the attribution of authorship of parts of the Hippocratic corpus to members of Hippocrates' family, see Wesley D. Smith, *Hippocrates. Pseudepigraphic Writings*, and *The Hippocratic Tradition* (Ithaca and London, 1979), esp. pp. 221-22.

¹⁰For a family of physicians in Cos, see, e.g. Jost Benedum, "Inscriptions grecques de Cos relatives à des médecins hippocratiques et Cos Astypalaia," in *Hippocratica. Actes du colloque hippocratique de Paris (4-9 septembre 1978)* ed. M.D. Grmek (Paris, 1980), pp. 35-43, esp. pp. 36-37.

¹¹A man named Hippocrates lent money to Calymnus in the middle of the fourth century. I. *Cos* 10a, line 51 (end of third century B.C.E.) records that a Hippocrates, son of Thessalus contributed money around 200 B.C.E. Louis Cohn-Haft, *The Public Physicians of Ancient Greece* (Northampton, Mass., 1956), p. 20, n. 58, no. 5, identifies him as a physician and a descendant of Hippocrates II. Jost Benedum, "Griechische Arztinschriften aus Kos," *ZPE*, 25 (1977), 264-76, esp. pp. 272-73, confirms Cohn-Haft's identification and gives the text of an inscription recording honors awarded to a physician named Hippocrates, son of Thessalus around 200 B.C.E. See also Susan Sherwin-White, *Ancient Cos* (Hypomnemata 51, Göttingen, 1978), p. 262, note 33, p. 265, n. 51, and p. 271 n. 83a.

¹²See Dana Ferrin Sutton, "The Theatrical Families of Athens," *AJP*, 108 (1987), pp. 9-26.

Figure 2:[13]

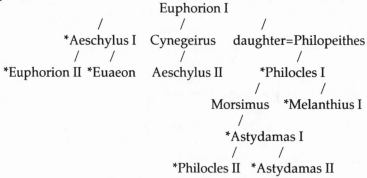

Euphorion I
/   /   /
*Aeschylus I   Cynegeirus   daughter=Philopeithes
/   /   /   /
*Euphorion II *Euaeon   Aeschylus II   *Philocles I
/   /
Morsimus   *Melanthius I
/
*Astydamas I
/   /
*Philocles II   *Astydamas II

*Aeschylus III(?)   *Astydamas III(?)

In this family continuity is achieved through the descendants of Aeschylus' sister among whom appear Melanthius I, who also wrote tragedy, and Aeschylus III, who was a tragic actor. Legally, children belonged to the oikos of their father, but this stemma illustrates that contact with the maternal family was often retained – especially when such a family had some property or renown, or a child available to adopt or to receive an inheritance.[14] Matrilineal succession is found also among philosophers. In the family of Plato we start perhaps with his mother Perictione who was reputed to have studied with Pythagoras, and note with more certainty that inasmuch as Plato did not have children the leadership of the Academy passed to Speusippus who was a son of Plato's sister. Aristippus, grandson of Socrates' associate Aristippus and founder of the Cyrenaic school, was called "Mother's Disciple."[15] Intellectual and vocational capital, as it were, was sometimes transmitted through women, and matrilineal naming advertised connections to the mother's family, but such traditions were not sustained for as many generations as when they were transmitted through men.

For respectable women in Classical Athens the only desirable profession was that of priestess. The position of priestess of Athena Polias was hereditary. When a new priestess was required, the office

---

[13]Adapted from Sutton, "The Theatrical Families of Athens," p. 108. The names of the men who were involved in the tragic theater are preceded by an asterisk.

[14]There are many others, for example the tradition about Polybus, son-in-law of Hippocrates II, mentioned just above.

[15]See further Sarah B. Pomeroy, "Technikai kai Mousikai: The Education of Women in the Fourth Century and in the Hellenistic Period," *AJAH*, 2 (1977), pp. 51-68.

passed to the eldest daughter of the eldest male. The tenure of the office by Theodote Polyeuktou II between 200 and 150 indicates that sometime between 255/254 and her inauguration into the priesteshood there were no descendants in the male line and the office passed directly to the eldest female. Names of some of the women who held the post over a period of seven centuries, starting in the fifth century B.C.E. are known. The genealogy of some of the priestesses is shown in Figure 3.

Figure 3.[16]

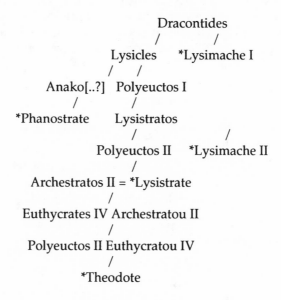

Not very many women could become priestesses. In the Classical period, far more women followed the lucrative career of prostitution. From a speech attributed to Demosthenes (59.18-19, 50, 67) we learn that the skills necessary for working as an expensive hetaira were transmitted through three generations beginning with an adoptive mother Nicarete who raised and trained seven girls. She referred to the young prostitutes whom she owned as "daughters" so that she could charge higher fees for them. One of these girls was the infamous Neaera who, in turn, allegedly exploited her own daughter Phano as a prostitute. In a society

---

[16]Adapted from Judy Ann Turner, *Hiereiai: Acquisition of Feminine Priesthoods in Ancient Greece* (Ph.D. Diss. University of California, Santa Barbara, 1983), p. 250, to show only the family members effective in the transmission of the priesteshood. The names of the women who held the priesteshood are preceded by an asterisk.

lacking social mobility, it was extremely difficult for the daughter of a prostitute to ascend to a higher status than her mother.[17]

No women sculptors are known by name. But sculptures endure, especially the bases on which the artists' signatures appear. Thus it is among sculptors that we can trace the largest number of generations in a single family practicing the same profession. The names of members of the family of Praxiteles, son of Cephisodotus, and the artistic works they produced over a period of five centuries are known. These appear in Figure 4. Pliny seems to have credited the success of some of the descendants to inherited talent, rather than instruction. Praxiteles had three sons, but Pliny comments that his son Cephisodotus was the heir of his father's art (*NH* 36.24).

Figure 4.[18]

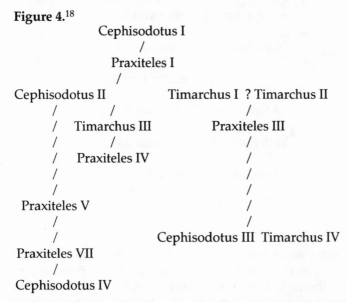

There are many examples of the continuity of the family even where the principal source of income is not immovables. The family that is economically successful reproduces itself in each generation: the same names and the same economic activities occur. This repetition can make the primary sources difficult to interpret: it is not always possible to

----

[17]But in the Hellenistic period we have some respectable female professionals, including some artists. Pliny names pairs of fathers and daughters whose paintings were famous (*NH* 35.147). See further Sarah B. Pomeroy, "Technikai kai Mousikai."

[18]Adapted from J.K. Davies, *Athenian Propertied Families* (Oxford, 1971), p. 289, to show the recurrence and relative chronology of the sculptors' names: Cephisodotus, Praxiteles, and Timarchus.

determine to which Praxiteles, son of Cephisodotos, a particular sculpture should be attributed. Some people deliberately created a fictitious genealogy. Although they were not related to the famous bearers of the name, they assumed it or bestowed it upon their children, expecting to enjoy the fame and fortune of the earlier homonymous practitioner. A name might be chosen for a baby in anticipation of the job that child was destined to perform. So, for example, Athenian parents who expected their daughter to serve as a priestess named her Theano, after a priestess of Athena in *Iliad* 6.300.[19]

Scattered bits of information indicate that even among less exalted families, the same economic dynamic appears. Thus, for example, Patrocles, a sculptor, named his son Daedalus (Paus. 6.3.4-5). Socrates inherited his trade as stonemason from his father. His abandonment of his trade in favor of philosophy probably precipitated his fall into poverty.[20] Hellenistic mercenaries bequeathed their horses and armor to their sons.[21] Sometimes the state itself obliged sons of soldiers to assume military responsibilities.[22] It is clear that few children in such families would face the risks and pleasures ours do in selecting a career. A society composed of such families would be characterized by conservatism, and little change over time, despite political changes in the larger society.

---

[19]Priestesses named Theano are mentioned in Plut., *Alc.* 22; IG II^2 1514.36; 1515.30; 1516.14; 1517B,II.142; 1524B,II 22; 153; 5164, 3634, and see further Blaise Nagy, "The Naming of Athenian Girls: A Case in Point," *CJ* 74 (1979): 60-64.

[20]D.L. 2.18-19; Libanius, *Apol.* 17-18. By the time the second version of Aristophanes' *Clouds* was produced, he was poor. (ca. 420-417 B.C.E.: see *Clouds* 103, 175, 362.)

[21]Willy Clarysse, *The Petrie Papyri*, 2nd ed., 1: *The Wills* (Collectanea Hellenistica, 2, Brussels, 1991), *passim*, and Dryton's will (*P. Grenfell* I. 21, ll. 3-4 = *Select Papyri* I.83).

[22]On the inheritance of *stathmoi* and *kleroi* (houses and land allotted to soldiers) in Ptolemaic Egypt see Clarysse, *The Petrie Papyri*, 2nd ed., 1, pp. 37-39.

Index

Abraham, 42, 63, 83-84, 90, 92, 135

Aeschylus, 159

Alexandria, 3, 40, 49, 61-64, 76, 85-86, 105, 127, 147

Antioch, 111

archives, 1, 15, 99, 101, 138, 145

Asia Minor, 32, 34, 112, 118, 124-125, 129

Augustus, 17

Babatha, 15, 99-101, 104, 141

children (see also sons, daughters), 2-4, 11, 13-14, 17-20, 28, 31-32, 37, 39, 41-54, 56-59, 61-88, 91-93, 95-99, 102-109, 111, 119-120, 124, 137, 141, 145, 156-157, 160, 163

Christianity, 17, 20, 34, 62, 69, 94, 102, 111-112, 113-114, 118-121, 135, 148

circumcision, 42, 87, 123

daughters, 1, 3, 14, 16, 18, 21-23, 31, 42, 46, 61, 65, 73, 77, 82, 86-87, 89-112, 119, 123, 135, 148, 160-163

diaspora, 1, 41, 49, 105, 117

divorce, 4, 11, 13, 26, 57, 102-104, 108-111, 134, 140-141, 144-146, 150-151

dowry, 4, 72-73, 87, 100-101, 133, 135-145, 147-150

Egypt, 13, 32, 40, 58, 63-64, 76, 96, 98-99, 112, 118-120, 123, 140, 145-149, 163

epitaphs, 1, 95-96, 114, 120

family, 1-5, 9-36, 39, 41, 46-49, 53, 56-59, 61-64, 66, 72-73, 76-77, 79, 81-88, 89, 92, 94, 98, 101-110, 113, 118, 122-124, 126-128, 133-134, 137-139, 141, 147-150, 153, 155-163

father (see also parents), 14, 17-18, 31-32, 39-40, 42-56, 58, 65-70, 72-77, 79-87, 90-95, 100, 103, 105, 107, 125, 133-135, 139, 142-143, 145, 156-160, 162-163

freedmen, 17, 106, 113-114, 118-128

Galilee, 2, 9, 15-17, 28-31, 33-34, 117-118

(Aulus) Gellius, 54-55

Greece, 81, 86, 105, 118, 123, 136, 155, 159, 161

Hierocles, 50, 53

Brown Judaic Studies

140001	*Approaches to Ancient Judaism I*	William S. Green
140002	*The Traditions of Eleazar Ben Azariah*	Tzvee Zahavy
140003	*Persons and Institutions in Early Rabbinic Judaism*	William S. Green
140004	*Claude Goldsmid Montefiore on the Ancient Rabbis*	Joshua B. Stein
140005	*The Ecumenical Perspective and the Modernization of Jewish Religion*	S. Daniel Breslauer
140006	*The Sabbath-Law of Rabbi Meir*	Robert Goldenberg
140007	*Rabbi Tarfon*	Joel Gereboff
140008	*Rabban Gamaliel II*	Shamai Kanter
140009	*Approaches to Ancient Judaism II*	William S. Green
140010	*Method and Meaning in Ancient Judaism I*	Jacob Neusner
140011	*Approaches to Ancient Judaism III*	William S. Green
140012	*Turning Point: Zionism and Reform Judaism*	Howard R. Greenstein
140013	*Buber on God and the Perfect Man*	Pamela Vermes
140014	*Scholastic Rabbinism*	Anthony J. Saldarini
140015	*Method and Meaning in Ancient Judaism II*	Jacob Neusner
140016	*Method and Meaning in Ancient Judaism III*	Jacob Neusner
140017	*Post Mishnaic Judaism in Transition*	Baruch M. Bokser
140018	*A History of the Mishnaic Law of Agriculture: Tractate Maaser Sheni*	Peter J. Haas
140019	*Mishnah's Theology of Tithing*	Martin S. Jaffee
140020	*The Priestly Gift in Mishnah: A Study of Tractate Terumot*	Alan. J. Peck
140021	*History of Judaism: The Next Ten Years*	Baruch M. Bokser
140022	*Ancient Synagogues*	Joseph Gutmann
140023	*Warrant for Genocide*	Norman Cohn
140024	*The Creation of the World According to Gersonides*	Jacob J. Staub
140025	*Two Treatises of Philo of Alexandria: A Commentary on De Gigantibus and Quod Deus Sit Immutabilis*	Winston/Dillon
140026	*A History of the Mishnaic Law of Agriculture: Kilayim*	Irving Mandelbaum
140027	*Approaches to Ancient Judaism IV*	William S. Green
140028	*Judaism in the American Humanities I*	Jacob Neusner
140029	*Handbook of Synagogue Architecture*	Marilyn Chiat
140030	*The Book of Mirrors*	Daniel C. Matt
140031	*Ideas in Fiction: The Works of Hayim Hazaz*	Warren Bargad
140032	*Approaches to Ancient Judaism V*	William S. Green
140033	*Sectarian Law in the Dead Sea Scrolls: Courts, Testimony and the Penal Code*	Lawrence H. Schiffman
140034	*A History of the United Jewish Appeal: 1939-1982*	Marc L. Raphael
140035	*The Academic Study of Judaism*	Jacob Neusner
140036	*Woman Leaders in the Ancient Synagogue*	Bernadette Brooten
140037	*Formative Judaism I: Religious, Historical, and Literary Studies*	Jacob Neusner
140038	*Ben Sira's View of Women: A Literary Analysis*	Warren C. Trenchard
140039	*Barukh Kurzweil and Modern Hebrew Literature*	James S. Diamond
140040	*Israeli Childhood Stories of the Sixties: Yizhar, Aloni, Shahar, Kahana-Carmon*	Gideon Telpaz
140041	*Formative Judaism II: Religious, Historical, and Literary Studies*	Jacob Neusner
140042	*Judaism in the American Humanities II: Jewish Learning and the New Humanities*	Jacob Neusner

Brown Studies on Jews and Their Societies

Brown Studies in Religion